A Short Story Writer's Companion

A Short Story Writer's Companion

TOM BAILEY
Susquehanna University

New York & Oxford
OXFORD UNIVERSITY PRESS
2001

Oxford University Press

Oxford   New York
Athens   Auckland   Bangkok   Bogotá   Buenos Aires   Calcutta
Cape Town   Chennai   Dar es Salaam   Delhi   Florence   Hong Kong   Istanbul
Karachi   Kuala Lumpur   Madrid   Melbourne   Mexico City   Mumbai
Nairobi   Paris   São Paulo   Shanghai   Singapore   Taipei   Tokyo   Toronto   Warsaw

and associated companies in
Berlin   Ibadan

Published by Oxford University Press, Inc.
198 Madison Avenue, New York, New York 10016
http://www.oup-usa.org

Oxford is a registered trademark of Oxford University Press

Library of Congress Cataloging-in-Publication Data

Bailey, Tom, 1961–
   A short story writer's companion / by Tom Bailey.
      p. cm.
   Includes bibliographical references.
   ISBN 978-0-19-513555-8
      1. Fiction—Technique. 2. Short story. I. Title.

PN3373 .B14 2000
808.3′1—dc21

00-033652

9 8

Printed in the United States of America
on acid-free paper

In memory of Richard Marius

For my students

Contents

Preface

> To the great artist, anything whatever is possible. Invention, the spontaneous generation of new rules, is central to art. And since one does not learn to be a literary artist by studying first how to be something different from a literary artist, it follows that for the young writer, as for the great writer he hopes to become, there can be no firm rules, no limits, no restrictions. Whatever works is good. He must develop an eye for what—by his own carefully informed standards—works.
>
> —*John Gardner, The Art of Fiction*

Some years ago, when I was a graduate student at The University of Iowa's Writers' Workshop, I took a class from the fiction writer and critic Doris Grumbach. It was a memorable writing workshop in many ways, but I remember one class meeting in particular. A student was commenting on a short story that was "up" for workshop. "It just doesn't work," she said, shaking her head. Some of us nodded. Doris Grumbach looked around at our nodding—our agreement with this seemingly obvious statement. Then she turned and directly addressed the young woman: "What do you mean by 'work?'" she asked. The young woman sat still. A long, uncomfortable buzzing from the overhead fluorescence grew to rule the room. Nobody answered. But I think we all got it; we all understood what Doris Grumbach meant. What, *exactly,* did we mean when we dared to say a story "worked" or didn't?

Certainly we had examples enough to go by. As readers—for it is the basic tenet of being a writer that one must be a reader first—each of us held in mind short stories that we *knew* worked. And although I'm sure insisting on unanimous agreement of what those stories were would have provoked rioting up and down the halls of EPB, the English-Philosophy Building where the weekly workshops were then held, a poll of the class probably would have yielded a consensus about a selection of such successful short stories.

Perhaps numbered among these might have been Maupassant's "The Necklace" or Tolstoy's "The Death of Ivan Ilych," Chekhov's "Lady with a

Pet Dog"; possibly Conrad's "Heart of Darkness," Joyce's "Araby" or "The Dead," or maybe Isaac Babel's "Crossing into Poland," Jorge Luis Borges's "The Garden of Forking Paths," Gabriel Garcia Marquez's "A Very Old Man with Enormous Wings." Some of us might have raised our hands for Melville's "Bartleby, the Scrivener" or Flannery O'Connor's "A Good Man Is Hard to Find," James Baldwin's "Sonny's Blues" or William Gass's "In the Heart of the Heart of the Country," Milan Kundera's "The Hitchhiking Game," Cynthia Ozick's "The Shawl," Tillie Olson's "I Stand Here Ironing," Kafka's "The Metamorphosis"; Toni Cade Bambara's "The Lesson"; John Updike's "A & P," Raymond Carver's "What We Talk About When We Talk About Love." I would have been the first to shoot up my hand for James Alan McPherson's "Gold Coast."

As readers, we all knew, or thought we knew through these examples of short stories we'd read, what "worked" meant, but we couldn't say exactly why the story before us didn't work. Doris Grumbach was trying to teach us what we, as aspiring writers, needed to be able to say—what we writers had to know and be able to put into words. "And thus," as Joseph Conrad says in his "Preface to *The Nigger of the 'Narcissus'*," "we talk a little about the aim—the aim of art, which, like life itself, is inspiring, difficult—obscured by mists. It is not the clear logic of a triumphant conclusion; it is not in the unveiling of one of those heartless secrets which are called the Laws of Nature. It is not less great, but only more difficult."

In other words: no rules. That would be too easy! "Whatever works is good," John Gardner assures us. But "since one does not learn to be a literary artist by studying first how to be something different from a literary artist. . . . [we] must develop an eye for what—by (our) own carefully informed standards—works."

A Short Story Writer's Companion is a *companionable* introduction to the *workings* of fiction—a guide to help young writers understand and better employ its myriad elements in creating working short stories of their own. It is not a rulebook. Rather, it hopes through examples and close readings of a variety of short stories that illustrate craft to help the young short story writer decide for himself or herself what works and what doesn't and why.

For best results in the classroom, I would suggest that this book be used in conjunction with an anthology or collection(s) of short stories so that the works examined here to example particular elements of fiction—such as "Chrysanthemums" by John Steinbeck for setting as motive or "The Lesson" by Toni Cade Bambara for dialogue—can be read in their entirety. One reason the stories represented here were chosen was because of their easy accessibility, but I trust the instructor or young writer who uses this book will employ stories of his or her own choosing to put the practices of craft to the test.

Admittedly, *A Short Story Writer's Companion* does not attempt to speak directly to the special interests of such genres as science fiction, fantasy, werewolf and vampire stories, or screen plays, though any student interested in these specific genres would benefit from familiarizing themselves with the concerns of craft promulgated here, no matter what other conventions they believe they must uphold. The book has been written with the young writer in mind who aspires to write literary fiction. This is the sort of fiction most of us would-be writers grew up reading in literature classes, the sort of fiction that still appears weekly, monthly or quarterly in the contemporary magazines that still publish such work—*The New Yorker, Harper's, The Atlantic Monthly, Esquire, Double Take,* and any of a good host of other fine journals and magazines like *Ploughshares* and (until recently) *Story, The Greensboro Review, Tri-Quarterly, Epoch, Other Voices.* (For a complete listing of "Magazines, Journals, and Quarterlies Publishing Short Stories" check the appendix of *On Writing Short Stories.*) *The Short Story Writer's Companion* is very much concerned with fiction written by both men and women, heterosexuals and homosexuals, people of every color and possible creed. Fiction is about feeling, which is to say that short stories are about *all* of *us.*

I will state here as well that though the book takes note of "alternative" types of fiction—meta-fiction, deconstruction, formal experimentation, and anti-epiphanic writing—it assumes that the "great tradition" of essentially realistic fiction is the ideal place to begin to try to teach young writers how to write, and offers a forum for the young writer to hear, perhaps for the very first time, the voices of writers and critics from Aristotle to Maupassant and Poe, the two O'Connors, Frank and Flannery, John Gardner, Raymond Carver, and contemporary voices like Margaret Atwood and Richard Bausch. A mentor of mine, Barry Targan, put it this way: "You learn the piano in the tradition of diatonic scale—THEN Schoenberg. You learn to understand what Rembrandt and Caravaggio were doing—THEN de Kooning." Just so with learning to write short stories. Another great truth Barry told me, which I've tried to keep in mind throughout the writing of this book, is that "you have to teach a lot of introductory fiction writing to realize just how fundamental you need to be. . . . You *can't be* too introductory for a beginner writer."

The *aim* of *A Short Story Writer's Companion* is to start the young writer out on the odyssey of the transmuting event that is the writing of any short story. The concerns contained herein are signposts to be read to guide the young writer on that journey. Like road signs, they help to mark the way; but the writer himself or herself will have to choose his or her own route. Indeed, they're encouraged to be masters of their own destinations as artists, as they gain mastery of the craft of writing short stories.

A Short Story Writer's Companion is divided into three parts. By initiating the idea of Fictional Truth and Significant Detail in Part One, it hopes to make sense of the creative writing maxim: SHOW, DON'T TELL! Showing is the basic precept in any introductory class in the writing of fiction. Too often students think they understand. They are trying to be specific. *He went to the store,* they write. And the creative writing teacher nods. On the board he or she writes, "Bob Mueller sauntered down Apple Street, past Big Sally's place with the clay potted geraniums on the stoop out front, and creaked open the screen door of Burke's Fruit and Produce." We understand the first student sentence—it takes us to the store—but in the second we begin to *believe* in the concrete truth of the world the specifics create. Showing or what I've termed "significant detail" helps us on our way.

Part Two, Elements of the Short Story and Advice on Technique, breaks down the fictional machine into its separate working parts or elements—character, points of view, plot, setting and time, metaphor, and voice—using specific examples from working stories to help us better see how each component functions as a part of the whole. The elements of fiction, of course, do not exist or work alone in a story. *Character* is nothing without *plot,* worse than nothing (in my estimation) without *meaning.* It is a basic tenet of this book that the elements—separated out here for a pedagogical purpose—must work in concert together to make a true story. But it can be useful for the young writer to see all the ways in which setting, for example, may inform a story, or to be alerted to the seemingly infinite complexities of shifting points of view. Creating an entire story from scratch can be intimidating. In my many years of teaching fiction writing, I've found that young writers are almost always more adept—and confident!—practicing these separate aspects of craft. The writing exercises included help beginning writers take their first steps toward writing a complete story.

Part Three, Notes on the Fiction-writing Process, investigates how writers put all the elements we've worked to separate together in, as Coleridge says, "a single, coherent gesture." Process makes all the separate things we've come to understand about fiction operate as an entity, complete and inscrutable, a story inseparable from its separate parts and practices: *seamless.* It is process—the writer's right (*obligation*) to revise again and again until he or she gets each word just so that makes us believe the lie that is at the heart of the truth of the short story—that allows the writer to produce a fiction that, at last, we may say "works."

Acknowledgments

A Short Story Writer's Companion was born out of my desire to build significantly on the essay on "Character, Plot, Setting and Time, Metaphor, and Voice" that I wrote for *On Writing Short Stories,* and as such I'd first like to acknowledge my deep gratitude to D. Anthony English, Senior Editor at Oxford University Press, for his continued support of my work. My lasting thanks and appreciation also go out to two of my mentors whose writing I admire and whose teaching I respect and both of whom I think upon with tremendous fondness: John Vernon, who read, approved, and further encouraged the initial proposal for this second book, and to Barry Targan whose invaluable words of wisdom and advice I've taken to heart and incorporated throughout its pages, as well as during my career as a fiction writer and as a teacher of fiction writing. To Charlene Steele, proprietor of the White House in Magnolia, Massachusetts (978–525–3642!), a pleasantly-perfect place to write and relax close to the rocky coast of the Atlantic Ocean on Cape Ann, where I began this book and finished it, I'd like to express my warm gratitude for the "rooms with a view," which she provided for me and my rambunctious young family. Several books were instrumental in my being able to write *A Short Story Writer's Companion,* among them Ann Charters's fine anthology, the Fourth Edition of *The Story and Its Writer,* and John Gardner's great book *The Art of Fiction,* as well as Richard Marius's *A Writer's Companion.* Richard "hired" me at Harvard, or so he liked to say, and he remained an important figure in my development as a teacher of writing in my years in The Expository Writing Program until his death, which happened to coincide with our accepting a professorship at Susquehanna University and leaving Cambridge. This book has been written and titled in the memory of Richard and his fine work. Several individuals played key roles in the production and/or creation of this book, and I'd like to voice my appreciation for them here: To Anne Surrette, recently graduated from Susquehanna University, who in countless hours of work-study labored to amass the Works Consulted included in the appendix at the end of the book; to Kathy Dalton, the reference librarian at Susquehanna, who though she may *scram* when she sees me coming "again" has always been a great "resource" in helping me with any research; to Crystal Vanhorn, the English Department's secretary, for her assistance in copying and sending out the manuscript; to Benjamin Clark, my production editor at Oxford, who bumped up the schedule for publication and managed, somehow, to keep us on it, and to Regina Knox for her good work copyediting the manuscript. Much thanks must also go to Susquehanna University for granting me the Winifred and Gustave Weber Chair in the Humanities that I held during the writing of this book, the funds from which allowed me to spend the winter break and summer steadily at work on it. I very much would like to thank Gary Fincke, my counterpart at the Writers' Institute at Susquehanna University, for the many Friday afternoon "strategy sessions" at BJ's discussing vital aspects of this book. Working closely with Gary is one of the great pleasures I find in teaching creative writing at Susquehanna. And, finally, I want yet again to thank Sarah LeWine, my wife and partner, without whom though such projects as *A Short Story Writer's Companion* might well be possible, much of the joy in completing them would be lost.

A Short Story Writer's Companion

Art is long and life is short, and success is very far off. And thus, doubtful of strength to travel so far, we talk a little about the aim—the aim of art, which, like life itself, is inspiring, difficult—obscured by mists. It is not the clear logic of a triumphant conclusion; it is not in the unveiling of one of those heartless secrets which are called the Laws of Nature. It is not less great, but only more difficult.

To arrest, for the space of a breath, the hands busy about the work of the earth, and compel men entranced by the sight of distant goals to glance for a moment at the surrounding vision of form and color, of sunshine and shadows; to make them pause for a look, for a sigh, for a smile—such is the aim, difficult and evanescent, and reserved only for a very few to achieve. But sometimes, by the deserving and the fortunate, even that task is accomplished. And when it is accomplished—behold!—all the truth of life is there: a moment of vision, a sigh, a smile—and the return to an eternal rest.

—Joseph Conrad, preface to
"The Nigger of the 'Narcissus'"

Fictional Truth and Significant Detail

"Fiction is a lie," Eudora Welty reveals to us in her essay "Place in Fiction," and we're forced to admit it's true. As Edward Hoagland reminds us in his "Introduction" to *The Best American Essays 1999,* it was Picasso who said, "Art is not truth. Art is a lie that makes us realize truth." (It is worth noting here that though this idea that fiction is a lie is a much-used and generally accepted notion we don't mean lie in terms of a deception, usually with bad intent. A mentor of mine, Professor Barry Targan at The State University of New York at Binghamton, where I earned a Ph.D., believed strongly in fiction as a construction that attempts to reveal the truth of humanness. Of course, there is fiction that *does* lie—as Barry pointed out—"fiction which disguises and distorts the nature of human experience"—Judith Krantz, Sidney Sheldon, Danielle Steel *ad infinitum,* alas! But, as Barry said, "fiction that lies is not the same as fiction being a lie.")

And yet, beginning writers often insist on the truth of a story they've written simply because it happened to them, or to someone they know.

"But it's *true,*" a student explains to me during a one-on-one conference in my office when I raise questions about some unlikely event in a short story he's written. This student is a composite of the many students I've taught over the years. He is, I realize, *me* as a student myself, an undergraduate at Marshall University sitting across from my creative writing teacher, Richard Spilman. "I mean it *really* happened this way. I *swear.*" The student—let's call him Jack—holds up the flat of his hand to testify to what *really* happened to him no matter what I can see for myself happens on the page. "I mean, I just told that guy at The Buffet Royale I quit. I mean I'd had enough of that place. Hush puppies. Ugh!"

And I say, "But, Jack, this character—the one in your short story—he just quits. He simply stomps out. He's standing by the bus boy cart and then he unties his apron, tosses it on the counter next to the Pepsi machine, and leaves. *Why* does this character quit? What *makes* him go at that moment?"

"I told you," Jack says, "I just told the manager: 'I quit.' I'd had enough. I couldn't take it anymore. I hate that place. All those folks slopping on the gravy! I walked out. I was gone. So long, I said. That place isn't for me."

The student grins. He sits up straight in his chair and crosses his arms over his chest between us. He shrugs. The truth is obvious to him. How could I—or the other members of our fiction writing workshop—dare to question the believability of his story? It happened.

I spin around in my chair and take John Updike's *Pigeon Feathers and Other Stories* down off the shelf. I flip straight to the spine-break in the book that marks the short story "A & P." I hold the flattened book out to him (the text I'd like for him to lay both hands on now.)

"Read this," I say. "Then come back on Tuesday, and we'll talk more."

FICTIONAL TRUTH

In "Reading Blind," Margaret Atwood says: "Expressing yourself is not nearly enough. You must express the story":

> A writer with nothing but a formal sense will produce dead work, but so will one whose only excuse for what is on the page is that it really happened. Anyone who has been trapped in a bus beside a nonstop talker graced with no narrative skill or sense of timing can testify to that. . . .

The truth is, life *is* stranger than fiction. Events in our lives often do occur at random; they may well be unexplainable. The days roll on nonstop, lacking apparent sense or meaning. On our way to the most important interview of our lives, our car overheats and spews to a stop, sending up a smoke signal of distress on the berm of the interstate, or we inherit three hundred thousand dollars from long-lost Uncle Herbie—so long lost, in fact, that we never even knew our mother had an older brother! Yes, in life anything can happen, and very often does. But not in fiction—not at random, not unexplainably. Though the car trouble and the inheritance are both events that might launch us into interesting short stories, or add significantly to the development of a story, in and of themselves they remain merely anecdotal.

In the daily paper we might very well flap open the front page of the newspaper one morning to see the headlined account of a plane crash in which all two hundred and fifty-eight people aboard were killed, and we may well gasp at the awfulness of the event. People gather at water fountains at work, shaking their heads. It's *tragic,* we say, trying to explain the way we feel. But, even if we walk around all day feeling strangely otherworldly, we don't sink into the same depths of grief we would have if a cherished friend or loved relative of ours had happened to be aboard that flight. Fiction offers us a heartfelt understanding of terms like *tragedy.* Fiction, it seems, affords us a more humane understanding of events. In a talk with students before a recent reading he gave at Susquehanna University, the novelist and short story writer Richard Bausch said it this way: "Fiction deepens feeling; if it doesn't do that, it isn't fiction."

In fiction, feeling is created; readers are *made* to feel. The writer introduces us to certain characters, choosing to reveal them participating in particular scenes and highlights certain details for us to take note of, leaving others out entirely, all in an effort to produce an intended emotion in the reader. As a result of the arrangement of words on the page, the reader actually experiences a story, feeling with the character. We *empathize.* An intellectual understanding can be gained from reading newspapers or watching the news on TV—we *understand* the calamity that is the loss of life—but the connection I'm talking about goes deeper. Flannery O'Connor calls the emotional identification we may feel when we are finished reading a short story the "experience of meaning" that stories are capable of offering us.

Take, for instance, the newspaper piece about a downed airplane. We've all read one at some point or another. Now consider a short story like Bharati Mukherjee's "The Management of Grief."

This particular short story opens in a curious moment of calm before the storm of grief. The narrator, Mrs. Bhave, finds herself surrounded by women she doesn't know "boiling tea the Indian way in [her] kitchen." They are waiting to hear the "official word" on the plane that has crashed carrying her husband and children as well as many other members of the "Indo-Canada Society" back to India: "it could be an accident or a terrorist bomb." Dr. Sharma is there to take charge. He answers the phone when it rings. "'We're with her,' he keeps saying. 'Yes, yes, the doctor has given calming pills. Yes, yes, pills are having necessary effect.'"

And all Mrs. Bhave can do is "wonder if the pills alone can explain this calm. Not peace, just a deadening of quiet." "I was always controlled," she tells us, "but never repressed. Sound can reach me, but my body is tensed, ready to scream. I hear their voices all around me. I hear my boys and Vikram cry, 'Mommy, Shaila!' and their screams insulate me, like headphones."

Indeed, Mrs. Bhave is well insulated. The crash—the situation of Mrs. Bhave "managing her grief"—begins to reveal *her.* Mrs. Bhave is a traditional Indian wife who "never told [her husband] [she] loved him. [She] was too much the well-brought up woman. [She] was so well brought up [she] never felt comfortable calling [her] husband by his first name."

The group suffers together, though, because of her seeming calmness, Mrs. Bhave is considered a "pillar." They are flown to Ireland where rescue teams are recovering the bodies. Some are "lucky":

> The lucky ones flew here, identified in multiplicate their loved ones, then will fly to India with the bodies for proper ceremonies. Satish is one of the few males who surfaced. The photos of faces we saw on the walls in an office at Heathrow and here in the hospital are mostly of women. "Women have more body fat," a nun said to me matter-of-factly. "They float better."

It is the dramatization of Mrs. Bhave's specific situation that allows us to feel her grief. When Mrs. Bhave is faced with the photos for the purpose of identifying the bodies that have been found, she recognizes "a boy very much like [her son] Vinod; the same intelligent eyes, the same thick brows dipping into a V. But this boy's features, even his cheeks, are puffier, wider, mushier."

"No," she says. Then her "gaze is pulled by other pictures. There are five other boys who look like Vinod."

Such particular moments bridge the distance between factual newspaper accounts of tragedy and our own lives.

If we had simply been told the story of a woman who lost her husband and two sons in an airplane crash, the feeling of it would be unimaginable. We would say it was tragic, but we wouldn't, we couldn't, have experienced her sense of loss. But now we know her. Our connection with Mrs. Bhave and her loss is an intimate one. The details that shaped her character have brought her to life for us. She and her husband and sons are no longer statistics, no longer faceless, or without personalities. We *care* about them.

Having read "The Management of Grief," the grief we find welling up in us may seem *un*manageable. And yet Mrs. Bhave does *manage* it. She copes. One afternoon some months later as she stands at a crossroad of paths "looking north to Queen's Park and west to the university," she hears, "*Go, be brave,*" the "voices of [her] family." And though "she [does] not know where this voyage [she has] begun will end. . . . [or] what direction [she] will take. . . . [she drops] the package on a park bench and [starts] walking."

Mrs. Bhave steps beyond herself. In effect, she too dies as a traditional Indian woman, as a wife and as a mother, and is reborn. She sheds her old life and assumes a new one. She lives. In this, we manage to feel *hope*.

Much of what I've said here echoes what seminal thinkers from Aristotle to well-known writers of the short story, among them Edgar Allan Poe, Flannery O'Connor, Eudora Welty, Margaret Atwood, Raymond Carver, and Richard Bausch, have had to tell us about the ways in which fiction works. All writers draw from other writers, whether or not they like to admit it, or even know they're borrowing. We don't write in a vacuum. It's important for beginning writers to read widely whether, at the time, they can affix a name or term to the craft they see materialized on the page. Richard Bausch said that every time he met a writer who he felt was "better" than him he found out that that writer was also better read. He advised my students to read all the great works and not to worry about understanding everything as they read, simply "to take as much from it as you can at the time as you go along."

In this excerpt from the preface to Guy de Maupassant's novel *Pierre and Jean* written in 1888, the great French short story writer exposits his theory of how realism works in fiction. The great point that he makes is that "the writer would find it impossible to describe everything in life, because he would need at least a volume a day to list the multitude of unimportant incidents filling up our hours." From this observation, Maupassant brings us to the conclusion that "[the author] should know how to eliminate, among the minute and innumerable daily occurrences, all those which are useless to him," while *emphasizing* those that add to the story the writer is trying to tell. Maupassant writes:

> Life can leave everything the same as it was. Or it can speed up some events and drag out others. Literature, on the other hand, presents cleverly orchestrated events and concealed transitions, essential incidents highlighted by the writer's skill alone. In giving every detail its exact degree of shading in accordance with its importance, the author produces the profound impression of the particular truth he wishes to point out.
>
> To make things seem real on the page consists in giving the complete *illusion* of reality, following the logical order of facts, and not servilely transcribing the pell-mell succession of chronological events in life.
>
> I conclude from this analysis that writers who call themselves realists should more accurately call themselves illusionists.

From what Maupassant says, we gather that, when Jack returns to my office on Tuesday well-equipped now for our conversation after reading "A

& P," I may safely tell him that his written-down and sworn-upon account of quitting and walking out of The Buffet Royale needs to be less real and more *illusory.*

"What did you think of the story?" I ask.

Jack shrugs. "I guess it was good," he says. "I didn't think that kid was going to quit."

"Do you believe it?"

"Yeah, I believe it."

"Okay," I say. "Why do you believe he quit when you didn't think he would?"

He sits down and we set the story on the desk before us. "In walks three girls in nothing but bathing suits," I read out loud. I stop. "Why do you think the story begins there?"

"Because he's bored to death, man! I mean Sammy's just nineteen and all he ever sees in the A & P are those rouged-up fifty-year-old cash-register-witches, and the house-slaves with all those blue veins mapping their legs pushing their screaming kids up and down those green and white checker-board tiles of those one-way aisles, or his buddy Stoksie, who's only like two years older than him, with his two kids chalked up on the fuselage and his greatest aspiration in life is to be manager some, what did he say?—some sunny day in 1990 when it's called the Great Alexandrov and Petrooski Tea Company, which I don't get at all, I was only like ten years old. But can you imagine all those Hi-Ho crackers and Diet Delight peaches and the pineapple juice those bums buy that he has to check through? And it doesn't seem like this is a summer job. He never mentions going to school in the fall. And there's that little song he plays on the cash register, "Hello (*bing*) there, you (*gung*) hap-py *pee*-pul (*splat!*) to keep from going crazy from the monotony of it all, you know: the cat-and-dog-food-breakfast-cereal-macaroni-rice-raisins-seasonings-spreads-spaghetti-soft-drinks-crackers-and-cookies aisle, and his dreary boss Lengel haggling over a truckload of cabbages as if it were the most important thing in the world. I mean can you imagine what he feels like? I can! That's exactly how it was at The Buffet Royale. Sammy's just living to die in that tiny town where people haven't seen the ocean in twenty years even though they're only five miles from the beach, and he owes something to his parents, you know, because they seem to rely on him or something. I mean his mother irons his shirts for Chris' sakes."

"Right," I say. "So, he walks out to impress the girls. It's obvious."

Our student stares down at the pages spread before us, the story unfolding before him; then he wolfs a grin. "It wouldn't hurt. I mean the way he describes them in the beginning: the seams on Queenie's bathing suit top with the straps down around her arms, and the chunky one with the pale belly, even Big Tall Goony-Goony, who he guesses other girls call 'striking' because they know they don't have to compete with her. He even says something like he's their 'unsuspected hero.' But, no. I don't think Sammy walks out because of them. They're gone, right? He says that after he quits—he looks for them, but 'they're gone, of course'—and anyway if he'd wanted to he could have gone back into the store and put his apron and bow tie back on. He doesn't want to. There's that line in the middle of the story, remember: 'Now here comes the sad part of the story, at least my family says it's sad, but I don't think it's so sad myself.' I think when he says it 'seems to him that once you begin a gesture it's fatal not to go through with it' that he knows. This is his chance. Maybe that's why he tells the whole thing the way he does. "In walk these three girls in nothing but bathing suits. . . ." It's immediate, you know. I can see him going home to his folks and telling them he *had* to do it. Lengel treated these girls so shabbily. It really wasn't *right*. He embarrassed them. For sure he can't tell his parents that he doesn't want to work at a grocery store any more because he wants something else out of his life. I don't think they'd understand that."

"Perhaps," I say, quoting Maupassant for Jack, "we might conclude from this analysis that writers who call themselves realists should more accurately call themselves illusionists."

"That's me: I'm an *illusionist*," Jack nods. "I get it now."

SIGNIFICANT DETAIL

John Gardner was almost as famous as a teacher of creative writing as he was for his own works, so attests the blurb on the back of *The Art of Fiction*. Gardner, who was killed in a motorcycle accident in September 1982 at age forty-nine, managed in his short lifetime to publish twenty-eight books. He produced novels, short stories, poetry, tales for children, volumes of criticism on Chaucer and Sir Gawain and the Green Knight, and two extremely important guides to the writing of fiction—*The Art of Fiction* as well as *On Becoming a Novelist.*

In *The Art of Fiction,* Gardner vitalizes the use of showing our stories through the use of significant detail in the writing of fiction. "If we carefully inspect our experience as we read," he writes,

> we discover that the importance of physical detail is that it creates for us a kind of dream, a rich and vivid play in the mind. We read a few words at the beginning of a book or the particular story, and suddenly we find ourselves seeing not words on a page but a train moving through Russia, an old Italian crying, or a farmhouse battered by rain. We read on—dream on—not passively but actively, worrying

about the choices the characters have to make, listening in panic for some sound behind the fictional door, exulting in characters' successes, bemoaning their failures. In great fiction, the dream engages us heart and soul; we not only respond to the imaginary things—sights, sounds, smells—as though they were real, we respond to fictional problems as though they were real: We sympathize, think, and judge. We act out, vicariously, the trials of characters and learn from the failures and successes of particular modes of action, particular attitudes, opinions, assertions, and beliefs exactly as we learn from life. . . .

Whatever the genre may be, fiction does its work by creating a dream in the reader's mind. We may observe, first, that if the effect of the dream is to be powerful, the dream must probably be vivid and continuous—*vivid* because if we are not quite clear about what it is that we're dreaming, who and where the characters are, what it is that they're doing or trying to do, and why, our emotions and judgments must be confused, dissipated, or blocked; and *continuous* because a repeatedly interrupted flow of action must necessarily have less force than an action directly carried through from its beginning to its conclusion. There may be exceptions to this general rule . . . but insofar as the general rule is persuasive it suggests that one of the chief mistakes a writer can make is to allow or force the reader's mind to be distracted, even momentarily, from the fictional dream.

The value of significant detail in establishing a "vivid and continuous dream" cannot be overstated. Fiction writers—and teachers of fiction writing courses—state it over and over, in their own words, in every conceivable way, coming at the same fundamental idea from every possible angle in an effort to get the point across.

In its most popular incantation, the importance of the use of such significant details in creating a vivid and continuous dream that we believe in as fiction is the mantra of introductory creative writing workshops everywhere:

SHOW, DON'T TELL!

Show, don't tell! Your English teacher used to say this all the time. Perhaps you remember her scrawling the maxim in big letters across the blackboard. Maybe you've even gone so far as to write *SHOW, DON'T TELL!* for yourself in caps on the cover of a journal, emphatically slashing and dotting the exclamation mark and then underlining it for good measure, not once but *twice.* (I know I did.)

Edgar Allen Poe, who was one of the first short story writers to talk theoretically about the form in which he wrote, stressed the use of showing through the use of significant detail in creating a "certain unique or single *effect* to be wrought out." Poe believed that "if [the writer's] very initial sentence tends not to the outbringing of this effect, then he has failed in his first step. In the whole composition there should be no word written, of which the tendency, direct or indirect, is not to the one pre-established design."

As I've already noted, Flannery O'Connor felt:

> The meaning of a story has to be embodied in it, has to be made concrete in it. A story is a way to say something that can't be said any other way, and it takes every word in the story to say what the meaning is. You tell a story because a statement would be inadequate. When anybody asks what a story is about the only proper thing is to tell him to read the story. The meaning of fiction is not abstract meaning but experienced meaning. . . . ("Writing Short Stories")

Raymond Carver adds:

> It's possible, in a poem or a short story, to write about commonplace things and objects using commonplace but precise language, and to endow those things—a chair, a window curtain, a fork, a stone, a woman's earring—with immense, even startling power. It is possible to write a line of seemingly innocuous dialogue and have it send a chill along the reader's spine—the source of artistic delight, as Nabokov would have it. That's the kind of writing that interests me. I hate sloppy or haphazard writing, whether it flies under the banner of experimentation or else is just clumsily rendered realism. . . .
>
> That's all we have, finally, the words, and they had better be the right ones, with the punctuation in the right places so that they can best say what they are meant to say. If the words are heavy with the writer's own unbridled emotions, or if they are imprecise and inaccurate for some other reason—if the words are in any way blurred—the reader's eyes will slide right over them and nothing will be achieved. The reader's own artistic sense will simply not be engaged. Henry James called this sort of hapless writing "weak specification." ("On Writing" in *Fires*)

The use of significant detail is not a particularly difficult concept, and I don't mean to make it sound more mysterious than it needs to be by invoking these resounding voices in support of a relatively simple theory. However, in all my years of teaching I still find it the most difficult principle of fiction to get across. Perhaps this is because when we write—*He was a good man* or *Jeanie felt happy*—we feel as if we are *showing*. But what is a good man? How could we portray him so that we can see his goodness for ourselves? And if Jeanie felt happy, what does she do? Maybe *Jeanie smiled*. Or perhaps *Jeanie laughed and clapped her hands*. We could go even further to show how *Jeanie jumped up and down, screaming, "Wahooo!"*

You know exactly what I mean if I write:

> She went to the store.

The sentence works in conveying action. But the sentence, as is, remains a telling. We are simply told where she went; we are not shown. The sentence can be greatly improved by simply making the words more concrete.

Martha walked to the grocery store.

Better, right? Now we have a person, *Martha*. Simply by naming her we have breathed new life into our sentence.

We find that the verb *walked* helps, too, because it gives our subject, Martha, a specific action to perform. *Grocery store* improves the sentence also. There are many kinds of stores. The sentence would be better still if we knew the store she walking to was called Produce-n-Pies. This gives us some idea as to why Martha is walking there. But the sentence could still be much more vivid and interesting (and a lot more fun):

> Martha skipped and hopped, jumped and twirled, singing *Lalalalala!* all the way down Beale Street, past Amy Shaughnasee's house (last year's soon-to-be V-A-N-Q-U-I-S-H-E-D champ), to Market Street, where she curtsied to the bag boy, Frank, who was also in her fourth grade class at Elmwood Elementary but who, poor boy, hadn't even made it to the second round (though it was none of her B-U-S-<u>Y</u>-N-E-S-S), and sauntered, chin up, head held high, brown eyes flashing left and then right, into Mr. Nagel's Produce-n-Pies in search of the Sunkist oranges that she'd read in an advertisement in her mother's most recent issue of *Parenting* magazine were chock-full of Vitamin C: Martha's ticket for an ever-quickening A-N-A-M-N-E-S-I-S—her classmates didn't stand a chance against her this year!

I'm just trying to have a little fun. Still, a lot is revealed in the names of Martha's friends, the street names she skips, hops, and twirls down, the specific way she thinks about both Amy and Frank, the words she spells, the fact that she's been reading her mother's *Parenting* magazine, and wants to win the fourth-grade spelling bee badly enough to make a special trip to the Produce-n-Pies to stock up on brain-booming Vitamin C. But other than having a little fun trying to use as many significant details in writing such a long sentence for yourself, another experiment you might try on your own is to check out a collection of short stories from your library by one of the writers mentioned or to take one down from your own bookshelf.

The essentiality of showing through significant detail will reveal itself in nearly any paragraph you happen to choose. I take down an anthology of short stories entitled *Matters of Life and Death: New American Stories* edited by Tobias Wolff. Below follows the opening paragraph of the first story in the collection, Ann Beattie's "The Burning House" (Also found in *The Burning House: Short Stories:*)

> Freddy Fox is in the kitchen with me. He has just washed and dried an avocado seed I don't want, and he is leaning against the wall, rolling a joint. In five minutes, I will not be able to count on him. However: he started late in the day, and he has

already brought in wood for the fire, gone to the store down the road for matches, and set the table. "You mean you'd know this stuff was Limoges even if you didn't turn the plate over?" he called from the dining room. He pretended to be about to throw one of the plates in the kitchen, like a Frisbee. Sam, the dog, believed him and shot up, kicking the rug out behind him and skidding forward before he realized his error; it was like the Road Runner tricking Wile E. Coyote into going over the cliff for the millionth time. His jowls sank in disappointment. . . .

Beattie has chosen details (which the narrator portrays for us in her first person narration) that prove significant in establishing the characters and their situation. The plates aren't just any old plates, but "Limoges," and valuable, we suspect, even if we ourselves do not recognize the brand. The make reveals to us something important about the narrator's taste. The dog's name is "Sam." Simply by naming him, Beattie summons up for us an actual dog. By naming the dog "Sam," we imagine a much different sort of dog (the owner a different sort of owner) than we might if its name were "Socrates" or "Man Eater" or "Coco." A history exists between the two characters. In "five minutes," the narrator tells us, she "will not be able to count on Freddy Fox" (Freddy Fox!), who is busy at the moment "rolling a joint."

The vivid and continuous dream significant details conjure for our readers sparks certain feelings, garners specific reactions, and creates expectations. The choices the writer makes send particular signals, and so they had better be the right signals. Consider it the other way: insignificant details may unintentionally *mislead* the reader.

But wait, we might protest, Beattie's "The Burning House" is a realistic story (even if perfectly illusory). It makes sense that she would have to use specific details. She's writing about a world in which there are Frisbees and Road Runner cartoons. But what about another kind of story entirely? What about the type of fiction called *magic realism* or *fantasy?* Significant details are equally important in such other types of fiction. Read Gabriel Garcia Marquez's much-anthologized short story "A Very Old Man with Enormous Wings" (also found in his collection *Leaf Storm and Other Stories*), in which an angel crashes to earth on a mission to take a dying child from his parents.

The angel that appears before us here in the short story is no flight of fancy, no white-robed, bold-trumpeting, haloed-fantastic Gabriel; he is much more authentic than that, bearing his "unbearable smell" and crawly "parasites." Certainly, this ragged old man with his wind-failed wings does not portray an angel most of us would care to idolize. The townspeople in the story have become all too familiar with him; they don't believe in him as an angel precisely because he is no longer imaginary. His fantasticality has become too real to entertain. But we believe, don't we? We believe simply because his wings, his snaggle-toothness, his off-odor, his itchy infestations, his rough sailor's tongue make him excruciatingly real; such authenticity transforms the old man, turning him fantastic again!

In Flannery O'Connor's essay, "Writing Short Stories," she makes sense of how Gabriel Garcia Marquez is able to persuade us to believe in the realness of this smelly angel:

> Fiction is an art that calls for the strictest attention to the real—whether the writer is writing a naturalistic story or a fantasy. I mean that we always begin with what is or with what has an eminent possibility of truth about it. Even when one writes fantasy, reality is the proper basis of it. A thing is fantastic because it is so real, so real that it is fantastic . . .
>
> I would go so far as to say that the person writing a fantasy has to be even more strictly attentive to the concrete detail than someone writing in a naturalistic vein—because the greater the story's strain on credulity, the more convincing the properties in it have to be.

A thing is fantastic because it is so real, so real that it is fantastic.

O'Connor cites the short story "The Metamorphosis" by Franz Kafka to example the point. "This is a story," she goes on to tell us,

> about a man who wakes up one morning to find that he has turned into a cockroach overnight, while not discarding his human nature. The rest of the story concerns his life and feelings and eventual death as an insect with human nature, and this situation is accepted by the reader because the concrete detail of the story is absolutely convincing. The fact is that this story describes the dual nature of man in such a realistic fashion that it is almost unbearable. The truth is not distorted here, but rather, a certain distortion is used to get at the truth. If we admit, as we must, that appearance is not the same thing as reality, then we must give the artist the liberty to make certain rearrangements of nature if these will lead to greater depths of vision. The artist himself always has to remember that what he is rearranging *is* nature, and that he has to know it and be able to describe it accurately in order to have the authority to rearrange it at all. ("Writing Short Stories")

Significant detail works as well, if not better, for the writer of magic realism or fantasy than it does for the writer concerned with creating the illusion of reality.

The Abstract Versus the Concrete

The power of significant detail in creating a vivid and continuous dream seems clear. The trouble is that young writers often seem to feel that abstractions and generalizations work better than specifics. Two reasons exist for

this. The first, as we've explored, is simply that we don't realize what showing is. The second is that beginning writers wish to make their writing universal in the same way that they think the literature they've read in school
has been made universal. In high school, literature is often taught by theme,
and theme abstracts the experience of meaning given by short stories. Also,
when we write about short stories, there's no sense in simply saying again
what the story has said best. To do that we would have to copy the story word
for word! Instead, we discuss the ideas a story raises, or we analyze aspects
of fiction, setting, or motif.

My student, Jack, returns to my office bearing the next draft of his story
about walking out of The Buffet Royale. We find the draft much improved:
Jack has begun to take responsibility for the significant details in his prose.
But he's named his character Everyman.

"Oh, oh," I say.

"What now!"

"This fellow is named 'Everyman.'"

"So?" Jack says. "I told you it was me and Sammy, Sammy and me. I
wanted to get at the idea that this isn't just about me. I mean I felt what
Sammy went through in "A & P" too. We've all been through this. Themati-
cally, this is a story about our growing up. It's a sort of fall from innocence
story. It has its roots in that apple tree in the garden of Eden. Eve biting the
apple and Adam taking a crunch on it too. And trying to cover up with fig
leaves!"

"But his name is Adam. Hers is Eve. And what about Odysseus? Gulliver?
What about Madame Bovary? How about Captain Ahab? And then you've
got Bartleby? And Celie from Alice Walker's *The Color Purple*. And. . . ."

It is a seemingly paradoxical concept that it is through individual experience that we actually connect to the universal, but, as we've seen, this is our
fictional truth. Tell us about Mrs. Bhave managing her grief, and we will feel
the universality of "grief" the writer wishes us to understand.

Student Example

The importance of significant detail was taught to me by my first creative
writing teacher, Jane Wells. One of the characters in the first story I ever
wrote had a shovel in his hand. In our conference about the story, Mrs. Wells
looked from where her pen had stopped on the page on her desk to me, and
then back at the page again: "What kind of shovel is it?" she asked.

I remember looking back at her, completely mystified. "It's a shovel," I
said, thinking to myself. *Who cares!*

Mrs. Wells did!

She sent me to Brady Hardware. There, my education as a writer began. Shovels! I had no knowledge of such a variety of shovels. Until you have been to the hardware store shovel shopping, you cannot imagine. You cannot know. I remember well the lesson I learned that day, but to refresh my memory, I walked down to Cole Hardware here in Selinsgrove to get a handle on shovel technology.

"Anatomy of the World's Best Shovel" I read. "Up to 60% stronger than quality ash handles. Up to 40% stronger than other fiberglass handles," the advertisement said. The STRUCTRON FIBERGLASS ROUND POINT LONG HANDLE SHOVEL seemed a shovel of dreams.

1. Rolled step for smoothed edges

2. Steel power collar

3. Steel connector

4. Safety yellow reinforced fiberglass handle

5. Solid fiberglass core

6. High-density SGS foam grip

7. High-density polyethylene end cap

8. D-handle grip

And all for $26.99! How could there be another shovel? Why would there be a need for other shovels? The Structron, obviously, is no mere shovel, but a dream machine. Other choices, though, adorned the wall of Cole Hardware. In fact, there were about thirty or so other choices. And thank goodness I wasn't looking at rakes!

The research I did was painless. With no digging at all, I found you could get a long-handled shovel or a short-handled shovel, that there were straight shafts and D-handle grips; some shovels, I discovered, were called spades, and you could get a spade in all the above flavors of handles and/or grips. Shovels come in round point, like the dream machine mentioned earlier; shovels also come in squares, scoops and spades, and general purpose wide-mouth straights. The "faces" of shovels may be made of steel, aluminum, even plastic. Shovels come produced ready for use by companies like the above-mentioned Structron Union Tools, and Razor Back.

You may buy a special Lady Gardner from Union Tools, model LH Floral with a pretty, stippled ash handle and a petite round-point steel face for $16.99. For $11.99, Razor Back makes a stumpy, tough-looking Little Hog about two and half feet long for concrete form work, track clearing, or tight spaces. You got your #10 Scoop Aluminum Western for $31.99; your #12

Scoop Aluminum Western for $34.99; your basic Scoop #6 Eastern in steel for $39.99; and your Scoop Grain in Plastic for 19.99. The Roof Ripper looks like a shovel but is not. Its prying edge jags up and down like Bart Simpson's haircut. A Drain Spade D Handle is thin and sleek, gunmetal blue on top and silvery sharp underneath, needle-nosed like the shark.

I discovered for myself that a LHSP Dura Torque Steel shovel with a long straight handle is "Better for transferring and distributing heavy soils," while a DHRP Dura Torque shovel with a short D-handle and round point is "better for digging in rocky and drier soils." Do not use any old shovel for any old job—even if it is the dream machine Structron—that's what I learned! (I dare not mention SNOW SHOVELS, of which there are more than many.

Of course, the question that was pertinent to me was which of these shovels would my character use? The cheapest shovel I could find was the Union Tools long, straight handle, round point, a mere $17.99. The character I was writing about was *not* spending his money, what money he had, on shovels. A Structron was out of his sphere. That was for someone who actually gave a damn about digging. My character did not; he was just plain hot. "We keep digging. Me and Halsey, mindless with these Unions." It made a difference, sure. It made *all* the difference.

The opening paragraph below comes from a draft of a short story by one of the students—I'll change her name to Sally—in my Introduction to Fiction class at Susquehanna University this past semester. In her self-critique letter that I have my students turn in as a preface to their final portfolio, Sally wrote that "The most important thing that was drilled into me throughout the semester was significant detail. Now every time I write something I go back to make sure that it's not just a generic issue, but that it really has feeling and shape to it. I found myself trying to be very precise with my writing, which was always a problem before. . . ."

Sally's story begins:

"So what does this mean for us?"
   Steve turned his back to me. He couldn't face me—to tell the truth. I was glad. Looking into his dark eyes I always lost complete control. I had never met a man with such fascinating eyes. The kind of eyes that could draw you in and never let you go. He sat down on the couch. He took out his wallet, looked inside. I looked away. Steve found it when he was 13, three years after his dad's death. It was the only thing of his father's he ever owned. He cherished it.

My students know that by better learning to critique each other's fiction that we become better writers ourselves. And by looking closely at Sally's opening we aren't picking on her. We can all improve our writing.

In helping Sally and ourselves we might speak first about what she's done well in the opening. Certainly she has created a certain air of mystery about Steve. We wonder about his magnetic eyes, and we're curious to find out about his father. The opening question is also intriguing: "So what does this mean for us?" We imagine, with such a leading question, that perhaps their relationship is at stake. We can't help feel that the wallet and the father play some part—their details are significant enough for Sally to call our attention to them.

I can tell you about the rest of the story—that in the wallet is a picture of Lisa, whom Steve dated for "three years. Actually, three years, five months, and sixteen days." Our narrator is jealous that Steve opens his wallet "no less than twenty times a day." "At first I didn't mind," the narrator says, "then it drove me crazy. There was no reason for it. Or. That's what he told me. It wasn't even the constant checking of the wallet; it was the fact that he still had her picture in it. I just couldn't understand why he needed that picture. It made me question myself." This obsession on both their parts is the primary tension of Sally's story.

Now, knowing these things, what can we say about the use of significant detail in Sally's opening?

Though the question the story opens with is somewhat alluring we might wonder why the conflict isn't more specifically drawn for us. We are intrigued, in this line, not because of a conflict, but because of the hook of not knowing what in the world the narrator is really asking. Yes, the mystery of it works in hooking us (perhaps!), but Sally seems to be missing an opportunity to involve us specifically in this story, their conflict!

The question really is: "Why are you still carrying around that picture of Lisa in your wallet?" or "If you look at your ex-girlfriend's picture twenty times a day, how can I believe you when you say you care for me?"

I doubt we'd want to start our story this way. To be sure, it isn't a very elegant beginning, but at least we would know from the outset exactly what's at stake between our two characters.

The next few sentences work at trying to reveal for us the significant details of their relationship. Specifically, we know the boyfriend's name is "Steve." We're told that Steve has "fascinating eyes." We know Steve found the wallet "when he was 13, three years after his father's death" and that he "cherish[es] it."

It seems that the idea Sally is trying to get at here is that Steve is obsessed with the photo in the wallet while the narrator is obsessed with Steve, in particular, his eyes. This is important—given the concerns/tensions of the story—otherwise how could we possibly believe that the narrator would put up with such behavior?

And yet the details revealed to us here are not significant enough to make us feel the power of Steve's eyes. We're merely told that his "were the kind of eyes that could draw you in and never let you go," and that "looking into his dark eyes I always lost complete control." The narrator," we're told, "had never met a man with such fascinating eyes."

But, in fact, Steve's eyes aren't "fascinating" at all; at best, they are CVS generic-brand eyes. We know intellectually what the writer is driving at, but we can't possibly feel it. Sally is relying on our having had such an experience. She is being general in the hope that we "know what she means;" she's counting on us to be able to imagine the magnetic power of such eyes for ourselves. "You know, the kind of eyes that. . . ." We know what she means, but we can't feel it. And we doubt that the writer sees these eyes clearly either. It's as if they're being described through someone else's writing or understanding of such "fascinating eyes." The narrator doesn't see them, so we can't see either. The power of Steve's eyes is being "told" away. And, no, it isn't up to the imagination of the reader!

What is in someone's eyes—*Steve's* eyes!—that would "draw" us in and "never let us go?" Are there flecks of green in the brown that the narrator must lean forward, close-close, to really see? Do those flecks change, like some sort of passion ring? Or, are they so black, so shiny, impenetrable, that when the narrator looks into his eyes she sees the image of herself, peering in, and so she peers closer, attempting to see herself in his eyes?

What other men has she known? How were their eyes different? "John's eyes had been a plain blue, but Steve's. . . ." Sally has the right idea that a contrast to the eyes of other men she's known would make Steve's eyes more unique, but the contrast is dulled—nullified really—by the fact that a specific difference hasn't been made.

The other concern of this paragraph is the wallet. It seems vital, doesn't it? We would imagine from the weight given to the wallet in this paragraph—the significance of the wallet that is hinted at—that the wallet, and the fact we're alerted to the fact that it is the father's wallet, will play a major role in the story. But it doesn't! Neither the father nor his death are mentioned again in the story. The wallet, it turns out, is only significant in that it holds the picture of Steve's ex-girlfriend.

In the second paragraph we are given concrete details—he was thirteen when his father died, and he found the wallet "three years" after his death— that aren't important to the story at all. In fact, these details misdirect our expectations for the story. By noting them, the writer points at their significance, but they aren't vital. Such details raise more questions than they answer. "It was the only thing of his fathers he ever owned." Wow, we say, the *only* thing? Subconsciously we wonder how he grew up, where his mother is, how his father died, what happened to all of his other things, and what importance did his father's death have on Steve's life. . . .

What we have on our hands is a paragraph written willy-nilly without regard for the story. Sally's paragraph is completely "made up!"; as is, it isn't creating believable fiction.

I find the lack of significant detail fascinating. Sally talked about her "problem" with significant detail before she wrote this draft, and so I know she is striving to be exact. She herself believes she's showing! She pictures for us Steve turning his back and she has him "[sit] down on the couch" and pull out his wallet . . . and "look inside." Sally is directing us, but she's missed opportunity after opportunity to significantly detail events. We become trapped in the narrator's head—we're told that "he couldn't face [her]" and that she's "glad," etc, and miss the possibilities for a more revealing [shown] interaction between them.

Of course, it's not our job to rewrite Sally's story. The purpose of our critique is simply to make her aware of such things. The work to be done sentence to sentence, and on the focus of the story as a whole, is entirely up to her. Sally might even go so far as to start the story somewhere else, or even reconsider the point of view—I would advise her to remain alive to every possibility.

To be fair to Sally, I should show you the opening paragraph of the story she's writing for me in independent study this semester. Our focus, from our first meeting, has been significant detail. The title as of now is "Shades of White":

> Abby never realized there were so many shades of white. Lady Whitley's Bridal Boutique had them all, everything from blinding bright white to soft ivory. *To ensure your dreams come true,* that was Lady Whitley's motto. It was painted with cream and gold paint, in crisp calligraphy, over the top of the entryway door, and almost everywhere else. There was even an antique gold framed sign tacked to the inside of the rose-colored toilet stall—hand embroidered on a piece of pale pink muslin. The entire store was wallpapered in pink foil with a paisley print. The window frames were painted white and gauzy. White curtains billowed down to the plush sea foam carpeted floor.
>
> She browsed through a rack of "just arrived" dresses. All of them were modern designs, slim cuts and smooth fabrics. She studied an ivory satin A-line dress. It had the tiniest amount of pearl beadwork along the scoop neck and little cap sleeves. *Simply elegant,* its tag read: *Six hundred and eighty dollars.*
>
> Abby walked over to the three-angled mirror and stepped up onto a small oak pedestal. She held the dress up and slipped the hanger behind her neck. She twisted her long chestnut corkscrew curls up onto the top of her head. She stared at her reflection.

In the left mirror, her mother, Ruth, stood visible, looking through some dresses on a round rack. Kitty, Lady Whitley's niece, searched next to her. Kitty's graying hair was dyed blonde, too blonde. It was hennaed the color of a banana peel. She wore it pulled tightly back into a bun at the nape of her neck like a school marm, a few frizzy curls sprouted from behind her ears. Her fuschia painted lips were cracked from faking smiles. Gold-plated cubic zirconia rings flashed on her fingers. She wore no engagement ring, no wedding band. Her job was simply to help make everyone else's dream come true. Ruth and she were up to their necks in tulle and lace.

Abby smoothed her hands down sides of the fabric, fitting the dress to her. "What do you think of this one, Mom?" she asked, turning. The fabric swooshed as it settled about her. Her mom emerged from a cloud of taffeta and walked over. She pinched the soft fabric between her thumb and forefinger.

"What's wrong?" Abby asked.

"It's cute," her mom replied.

"No, really," Abby said. "What do you think?"

"It seems flimsy, Abigail. It won't last. It could never hold up."

"Well, I only need it for the one day."

Her mother stretched her lips. "Yes, dear, but you should have it for a lifetime. It's got to last. . . ."

Fun! Sally's got the hang of it now. The happy truth we learn to uncover about the short story is that they are all lies! As writers, we can learn to add significant details to make them feel true.

Working element by element through the necessary parts of fiction, [the writer] should make the essential techniques second nature, so that he can use them with increasing dexterity and subtlety, until at last, as if effortlessly, he can construct imaginary worlds—huge thoughts made up of concrete details—so rich and complex, and so awesomely simple, that we are astounded, as we're always astounded by great art. This means, of course, that he must learn to see fiction's elements as only a writer does, or an occasional great critic: as the fundamental units of an ancient but still valid kind of thought.

—John Gardner, *The Art of Fiction*

The Elements of the Short Story and Advice on Technique

As we've said, there are no rules in the writing of fiction, but it would seem equally as true that the serious writer "must learn to see fiction's elements as only a writer does" if he or she aspires to great art.

But what are the essential elements or "necessary parts of fiction," and how can an aspiring writer "make the essential techniques second nature, so that [we] can use them with increasing dexterity and subtlety, until at last, as if effortlessly, [we] can construct imaginary worlds—huge thoughts made up of concrete details—so rich and complex, and so awesomely simple, that we are astounded?"

We must learn to read and to recognize the elements of fiction and strive to understand them in all of their webbed connections, complexities, and subtleties. Most of all, the aspiring writer must act to employ the elements in the practice of his or her own writing of fiction so that the elements all but disappear and become, *as if miraculously* (if not quite effortlessly), this thing we call a short story.

In the following pages I will suggest an understanding of the fundamental elements of fiction—character, point of view, plot, setting, time, metaphor, and voice—and offer advice on how to use them.

"WE ARE OUR DESIRES": CHARACTER

From some good authority somewhere I once heard it said that there are only a dozen plots available to the writer: basic Cain and Abel conflicts of brother against brother, or King Lear-like tragedies of betrayal, tales of revenge such as Hamlet's righting his father's "foul and most unnatural murther," seminally sharp, bittersweet bites of the apple—the loss of innocence Adam and Eve suffer in the Garden of Eden—Ahab's maniacal hunt for the great white whale, love stories in which boy or girl meets girl or boy, and one of them or both loses the other, the action or reaction of requited or unrequited love as in James Joyce's "The Dead." But when we walk into any mall's Barnes and Noble or The Harvard Bookstore on Massachusetts Avenue in Cambridge or Prairie Lights in Iowa City, we come face to face not with a mere eleven titles, or even a generous baker's twelve, but with perhaps as many as twelve thousand! *Where did all these plots come from?* we ask. Didn't I hear from some authority somewhere that there are only a dozen plots available to the writer? Then how can there possibly be so many books? So many different stories?

Then we recall the many characters we've met in our reading. No two seem the same. No matter how similar the basic story line of Shakespeare's *King Lear* and Jane Smiley's novel *A Thousand Acres*—where an aged patriarch puts his daughters' love to the test—or Homer's *The Odyssey* and *Cold Mountain* by Charles Frazier—where a warrior journeys home from war—the characters remain distinctly different. We may find them in similar situations, they may even meet similarly tragic fates, but the characters who people each story remain separate for us because they're full-up with their own desires—sharply drawn by the defining lines of their own motives, wishes, wants, needs, likes and dislikes, prejudices, the sum of where they grew up and how they were raised, the histories of their parents and grandparents, their great-grandparents, their cultures, colors, and creeds, their talent for playing Chopin or lowering their helmets and blindly busting a football up the two hole, their failings at their accounting job or success at a second marriage, IQ or other kinds of "smartness" such as the ability to feel, *intuit*—in short, their very *who-ness*. As we read, we get to know such things about our characters, these myriad concerns shape and power them and so simply knowing the story before we begin doesn't give the characters away.

Character in literature is the always shifting and changing element that makes each story different no matter how similar the plot (an element we'll discuss on its own terms later). Character, in fiction in general and in the short story in particular, acts as the *x* variable in what would otherwise be a too-obvious and easily enumerated, fixed equation. Character pumps as the heart of fiction. It is character—and the "love and honor and pity and pride and compassion and sacrifice" in our character's life, to quote the "old verities of the heart" that William Faulkner named in his Nobel Prize acceptance speech—that, as Raymond Carver says in "On Writing," carr[ies] news from their world to ours."

Round Versus Flat Characters

But what is character? Or, rather, *who?* And, as writers, how do we make people stand up and take shape on the bright white flatness of the page?

The central problem in creating a believable character has to do with the first truth of this book: *Fiction is a lie.* Characters in fiction aren't any more real than the story that my student Jack told me actually happened to him at the Buffet Royale. Even if we modeled a character after our eccentric Uncle Herbie who left us that dump truck load of money, we would still be making him up. We would still have to choose which significant details about Uncle Herbie to include—his pink-striped, Egyptian cotton pajamas (which he never took off), his everyday lunch of sardines and peanut butter, the practice he had of pinning the stock page to the wall and throwing darts at it to decide what to trade, a strategy that has made him rich beyond anyone's wildest dreams—red darts = SELL!; blue darts = BUY!)

Human beings are awfully complex. Characters defined in short stories are held to certain limitations that real people aren't, such as page length— let's say twenty or so pages in an average short story—and, at best, can only be sounded in part. This, of course, is the argument that Maupassant makes. Character, in fiction, is illusory more than real—once again we must consider the significance of significant detail. A physical description, for instance, might be exact in that the writer tells us that Charles Melton Thayer III has brown hair and wide-spaced brown eyes, that he wears white button-down Oxford shirts and Gap khakis (36 waist, 30 length), and brown, size 10 Bass Wejun loafers, DD. We might even know that he has a mole, the size of a water drip, in the middle of his back. And, knowing these things, we know a lot about the way Charles Melton Thayer looks, but there is a lot, certainly, that we still don't know about him—what are his hands like, does he chew his nails? How does he wear his brown hair, in a neat side-part or does it hang down boyishly in a chop? Is he, in fact, balding? (Though he wears a 30 length trouser, he has a long trunk. We would be surprise to find he is six foot one!) How much does Charles Melton Thayer weigh? And so on. . . .

While fiction, even if it strives to capture a person exactly, is—as we've discussed—an imitation bound by certain limitations, we could also argue that it is through this focused limiting of a character in fiction that makes the fictional being more knowable than another human being—a wife or husband, brother, a father or mother, our best friend—who will always remain something of a mystery to us, no matter how well we think we know them. Certainly, a character on the page becomes his or her own person by the focus of characteristics that the writer chooses to reveal about them to the reader. The created illusion of a real person as part of the fictional dream conveyed to the reader through significant detail is an attempt to fathom that character's "particular truth." So, a character in a short story can be built to offer us as much—if not more!—of himself or herself than of a person we believe we *really* know.

As Flannery O'Connor says in another of her essays, "The Element of Suspense in 'A Good Man Is Hard to Find'" (Charters's *The Story and its Writer*), the action at end of a story must be both "in character and beyond character" to make the story "work":

> I often ask myself what makes a story work, and what makes it hold up as a story, and I have decided that it is probably some action, some gesture of a character that is unlike any other in the story, one which indicates where the real heart of the story lies. This would have to be an action or gesture which was both totally right and totally unexpected; it would have to be one that was both in character and beyond character; it would have to suggest both the world and eternity.

Fiction has the wonderful ability to draw out apparently complete characters for us so that we can experience their desires and drives in our own lives. A wife's tears may well remain a mystery to her husband; but in Richard Bausch's "The Fireman's Wife" (*The Fireman's Wife and Other Stories*) we live with Jane's tears, and thereby grow to know her completely through the seemingly contradictory aspects of her character.

Outwardly, we see that Jane doesn't fit in with the group of friends with whom her husband, Martin, who is a fireman, spends most of his time—Teddy Lynch and Milly and Wally Harmon. They play Risk late into the night. They drink and smoke dope, and when Jane declines to join them, they think her a spoilsport. Milly, who is pregnant, follows Jane into her bedroom, where she says, "Listen . . . I know we can all be overbearing sometimes. Martin doesn't realize some of his responsibilities yet. Wally was the same way."

But Jane doesn't have anything she wishes to "confide": "I just have this headache," she says.

Inwardly, of course, Jane lives a different story. The next evening after Martin has left for his four-day shift at the station, Jane is sitting with Eveline, her friend from the car dealership where they both work and where "she sits behind a window with a circular hole in the glass, where the people line up to pay for whatever the dealer sells or provides," when she" sees the person she is now, with Martin, somewhere years away, happy, with children, and with different worries. It's a vivid daydream. She sits there fabricating it, feeling it for what it is and feeling, too, that nothing will change: the Martin she sees in the daydream is nothing like the man she lives with. She thinks of Milly Harmon, pregnant and talking about waiting to be surprised by love.

"'I think I'd like to have a baby,' she says. She hadn't known she would say it." To which Eveline replies, "'Yuck,' blowing smoke."

Jane no longer feels herself connected to her husband. She doesn't quite know why. He has grown to be something of a stranger to her. Martin flies model airplanes with "the boys," as Milly Harmon calls them; Jane can't understand this part of him. Worse, Jane feels lost as to the meaning of her own life; she doesn't know herself and is uncertain about her future. She begins to believe she has fallen out of love with Martin.

Jane is going to leave Martin; she doesn't quite know why. That night when she returns home the night after Martin has departed for his four-day shift at the station, Jane begins to pack her things. She "[loses] herself in the practical matter of getting packed." "She is hurrying, stuffing everything into the bag, and when the bag is almost full she stops, feeling spent and out of breath." Then she decides this is the sort of thing she should do "in the light of day, not now, at night."

The next morning Jane "wakes to the sound of voices." Two other fireman bring Martin home to her—there's been a bad fire, "'the Van Pickel Lumberyard went up. The warehouse,'" and Wally Harmon is dead. Martin's hands have been badly burned. "He's lying on his side on the couch, both hands bandaged, a bruise on the side of his face as if something had spilled there." When the firemen leave, Martin sees Jane's clothes laid out on the bed. He looks at her. "'Jesus, Jane, are you'—He stops, shakes his head. 'Jesus.'"

"Martin," Jane tells him, "this is not the time to talk about anything."

Martin needs her, and Jane takes care of him. "She has to help with everything." She puts him to bed and the next morning she has to take off his clothes; she feeds him, bathes him. Both of his hands are bandaged, and he can't use the bathroom by himself. Jane takes down his pants, "helps him. The two of them stand over the bowl."

What happens at the end of the story is both exactly what we expect from Jane, given who we've discovered she is, and a complete "surprise" in revealing the full complexity of her character to us—in fact, the moment of both the realization of her love for Martin and the fact that she's going to leave is as much of a shock to her as it is to us. "In their bedroom she helps him out of his jeans and shirt, and she actually tucks him into the bed. Again he thanks her . . . "

> At last he's asleep. When she's certain of this, she lifts herself from the bed and carefully, quietly withdraws. As she closes the door, something in the flow of her own mind appalls her, and she stops, stands in the dim hallway, frozen in a kind of wonder: she had been thinking in an abstract way, almost idly, as though it had nothing at all to do with her, about how people will go to such lengths leaving a room—wishing not to disturb, not to awaken, a loved one.

It is, then, the contradictory aspects of Jane's character, which have been made believable to us through the dramatization of her as a person in the story, that make her final "gesture" both "in character and beyond character." There would seem to be a choice for her at this crucial point in the story because of the possibility of choice created by her character—she could stay with Martin—but now she has no alternative. Given who she is, given what's happened to her and to Martin to bring them to this crossroads in their lives, there is only one way for her to act at end, one "choice" for her to make, even if she is "surprised" by her love for him. This "action or gesture," her tiptoeing realization of her love for Martin, is the other side to the argument of Jane's relationship; it makes Jane whole. It makes her lifelike, even if it doesn't solve the problems in her life. (What could be more real than that!) Such characters who possess the possibility to act both as we would expect them to and yet who still possess enough contradictory properties of self (what Aristotle called "consistent inconsistencies" of character) to be able to go believably beyond our expectations to surprise not only us, but even to leave them the opportunity to make discoveries about themselves, have been termed *round characters*.

E. M. Forster introduced the idea of "round" and "flat" characters in his book *Aspects of the Novel*. Flat characters are flat because they exist in one dimension. Flat characters are stand-ins for ideas, simply evil or merely good; they are caricatures of people, cartoons: Snidely Whiplash types or Snow Whites. They do not exhibit the *x* variable of *who-ness* mentioned before. These possibilities shape round characters.

This is not to say that flat characters aren't necessary, even vital to a short story; they are, they are! Round characters, however, are usually built to carry the brunt of meaning in a story (an idea we'll come back to later) and so—at least in a traditional short story such as "The Fireman's Wife"—must necessarily be complex enough, that is, reveal enough "consistent inconsistencies" to hold the possibility for change or discovery. We necessarily have both round and flat characters and to help us to distinguish between the two we might designate them as *primary* and *secondary characters.*

Such a character, like Jane in "The Fireman's Wife," is a *primary character;* it is Jane who is round enough to act both in character and beyond character. A flat character, or *secondary character,* might necessarily be less developed—Martin is a secondary character as are Milly Harmon and Eveline, Jane's friend from work. They act as Jane's supporting cast. Each of these characters is necessary—Martin obviously vitally so—but their perceptions (at least insofar as we're aware) do not change in the story; they are not invested with the possibility for change as is Jane, our narrator, with whom we spend the entire story getting to know.

By making these distinctions, I don't mean to imply that a secondary (in importance) character can't also be round. Certainly they can—read Dickens! *Hard Times* is an especially good example of the use of round/flat characters. But for our purposes here, I think it's useful to at least note such a differentiation.

Tobias Wolff's short story "Bullet in the Brain," which can be found in his collection *The Night in Question: Stories,* is primarily about Anders, a world-weary critic whose withering cynicism gets him shot in the head when he "burst[s] out laughing" in the face of a third-rate secondary character, a cliched, pistol-toting bank robber, who pokes his weapon under Anders's chin as he stands in line and warns him, "Fuck with me again, you're history. *Capiche?*"

The story, which is only six pages long, rounds out what appears at first to be the flat, one-dimensional cynicism that Anders's character exhibits from the moment he enters the bank. When the long line Anders is in is closed, the woman standing in front of Anders says, "Oh, that's nice" and "[turns] to Anders . . . confident of his accord, 'One of those little human touches that keep us coming back for more.'"

And even though "Anders had conceived his own towering hatred of the teller . . . he immediately turn(s) on the presumptuous crybaby in front of him. 'Damned unfair,' he [says]. 'Tragic, really. If they're not chopping off the wrong leg, or bombing your ancestral village, they're closing their positions.'"

But the woman "stands her ground. 'I didn't say it was tragic,' she [says]. 'I just think it's a pretty lousy way to treat your customers.'"

"'Unforgivable,' Anders [says]. 'Heaven will take note.'"

As a "book critic known for the weary, elegant savagery with which he dispatched almost everything he reviewed," Anders has become bored to death by everything he has read or is tiredly reading now. We don't know exactly when "he began to regard the heap of books on his desk with boredom and dread, or when he grew angry at writers for writing them . . . when everything began to remind him of something else," we only see him as he is here, in this moment before he is shot as he stands in line critiquing the way the robbers' speak: "Oh, bravo . . . *Dead meat* . . . Great script, eh? The stern, brass-knuckled poetry of the dangerous classes."

But it is in this here and now of Anders's moment of reckoning in the bank that we are given the hint of who he was before, or, under different circumstances, who he might have become. It is the *possibility* of another side to Anders's character, our understanding in considering the things he does *not* remember in the final "microsecond" of his life after the robber shoots him for laughing in his face, that there was a time when he wasn't bored to death, a time when "his eyes had burned" at hearing a professor of his recite *Aeschylus* in Greek, or the "respect he had felt" after reading a novel by a college classmate, a time when Anders actually experienced "the pleasure of giving respect," that makes him complete.

The story slows the moment for us, shifting the last tock of Anders's life into "brain time" as the bullet, "scattering shards of bone into cerebral cortex, the corpus callosum, back toward the basal ganglia, and down into the thalamus," sets off "a crackling chain of ion transports and neurotransmissions"—in short, sparking a single flashbulb pop of memory in stark relief against all that Anders does not recall about his life, a single rememberance that makes Anders whole: "This is what he remembered. Heat. A baseball field. Yellow grass, the whir of insects, himself leaning against a tree as the boys of the neighborhood gather for a pickup game . . . Coyle and a cousin of his from Mississippi" who, when asked what position he'd like to play, says, "Shortstop. Short's the best position they is." It is this "They is" that Anders hears, words at which he remembers being "strangely roused, elated, by . . . their pure unexpectedness and their music."

Of course, Anders will soon be dead, "that can't be helped," but as the bullet "leave[s] the troubled skull behind, dragging its comet's tail of memory and hope and talent and love into the marble hall of commerce" we find Anders wholly defined. *"They is, they is, they is"* is the "soft chant" we're left with, the call for us to completely understand the tragic life story of who Anders really, roundly, is, now that he's as good as dead, how he became who he was, the acerbic critic standing in line late at the bank. This moment is our realization that Anders is more than just a critic; he is a human being. In his appreciation for and awe at this simple phrase, we can view him in 3D, so to speak. And though we may be surprised at our discovery, we are not shocked. The fact is that Anders had it in him all along, whether we knew we knew it or not.

Considering this example of a round character, it would seem that the writer's job at least when constructing primary characters in traditional short stories, is to offer us such seemingly contradictory possibilities. But how can we actually go about doing this? After all, the page *is* flat even if our primary characters can't be.

Characterization

By characterization we simply mean to make note of the ways in which characters are created on the page. There are two basic modes of characterization, *indirect* and *direct.*

As we have seen in "The Fireman's Wife" and "Bullet in the Brain," perhaps the best possible characterizations simply show who characters are by having them act as themselves. Remember Anders's exchange with the woman in the bank or Jane's answer to Milly's question if she "feels trapped": "I just have a headache." (We'll return to this discussion in the following segment on "Dialogue.") What these characters say or do—Anders's guffaw in the face of the robber who's threatening his life with the pistol or Jane's sneaking quietly out of Martin's room—draw a perfect portrait for us. *How* they are and *what* they do is part and parcel of *who* they are. This is *indirect characterization* at work. In nearly every story you read you will see writers working hard to employ this method of characterization: Show, don't tell! One action is worth a thousand words—simply imagine the reams we could write about Jane's gesture of love in quietly leaving Martin's room.

Showing works best at indirectly characterizing any character for us, but undoubtedly there are times when the writer relies on *direct characterization* to shape our understanding of a character, whether primary or secondary.

In Andre Dubus's "A Father's Story" (*Selected Stories*), the primary character tells us this about himself:

> My name is Luke Ripley, and here is what I call my life: I own a stable of thirty horses, and I have young people who teach riding, and we board some horses too. This is in northeastern Massachusetts. I have a barn with an indoor ring, and outside I've got two fenced-in rings and a pasture that ends at a woods with trails. I call it my life because it looks like it is, and people I know call it that, but it's a

> life I can get away from when I hunt and fish, and some nights after dinner when I sit in the dark in the front room and listen to opera. The room faces the lawn and the road, a two-lane country road. When cars come around the curve northwest of the house, they light up the lawn for an instant, the leaves of the maple out by the road and the hemlock closer to the window. Then I'm alone again, or I'd appear to be if someone crept up to the house and looked through a window: a big-gutted grey-haired guy, drinking tea and smoking cigarettes, staring out at the dark woods across the road, listening to a grieving soprano. . . .

Luke Ripley not only describes his own physical appearance—a big-gutted grey-haired guy—but tells us other interesting, even contradictory things about himself: he has an outward life of horses and (we find out in the next paragraph) a "real life . . . nobody talks about anymore. . . ."; and he sits in the dark and listens to opera; he drinks "tea." He himself has given us these clues to let us know he, Luke Ripley, is not who he seems to be.

In "Saint Marie" collected in Louise Erdrich's *Love Medicine,* Marie Lazarre directly reveals herself and her desires:

> So when I get there, I knew the dark fish must rise. Plumes of radiance had soldered on me. No reservation girl had ever prayed so hard. There was no use in trying to ignore me any longer. I was going up there on the hill with the black robe women. There were not any lighter than me. I was going up there to pray as good as they could. Because I don't have that much Indian blood. And they never thought they'd have a girl from this reservation as a saint they'd have to kneel to. But they'd have me. And I'd be carved in pure gold. With ruby lips. And my toenails would be little pink ocean shells, which they would have to stoop down off their horse to kiss.
>
> I was ignorant. I was near age fourteen. The length of the sky is just about the size of my ignorance. Pure and wide. And it was just at—the pure and wideness of my ignorance—that got me up the hill to Sacred Heart Convent and brought me back down alive. For maybe Jesus did not take my bait, but them Sisters tried to cram me right down whole . . .
>
> I had the mail-order Catholic soul you get in a girl raised out in the bush, whose only thought is getting into town. . . .

Much of what Marie Lazarre tells us about herself in these first few paragraphs is bolstered by her unique voice. (For a more concrete understanding of the possibilities of using such a voice, read "First Person" in the section on "Point of View.") Her beginning her story by saying, "so when I get there, I knew the dark fish must rise" strikes us in its oddness and beauty. The language she uses—her words, "dark fish," "rise"—the syntax and immediateness of her sentence, all help indirectly characterize Marie Lazarre—even as she tells us directly that she is a "reservation girl" that "don't have that much

Indian blood" and that she's "fourteen," painting a picture of herself "the black robe women" would have to "kneel to" as she "would be" "as a saint": "carved in pure gold" with "ruby lips" and "toenails" of "pink ocean shells."

Primary characters don't only use direct characterization to tell us about themselves. Here is nineteen-year-old Sammy, the primary character of John Updike's "A & P" (*Pigeon Feathers and Other Stories*), from his vantage point at his checkout slot as he directly describes the three girls who have just walked into the store in "nothing but bathing suits":

> They didn't even have shoes on. There was this chunky one, with the two-piece— it was bright green and the seams on the bra were still sharp and her belly was still pretty pale so I guessed she just got it [the suit]—there was this one, with one of those chubby berry-faces, the lips all bunched together under her nose, this one, and a tall one, with black hair that hadn't quite frizzed right, and one of those sunburns right across under the eyes, and a chin that was too long—you know, the kind of girl other girls think is very "striking" and "attractive" but never quite makes it, as they very well know, which is why they like her so much—and then the third one, that wasn't quite so tall. She was the queen. She kind of led them, the other two peeking around and making their shoulders round. She didn't look around, not this queen, she just walked straight on slowly, on these long white prima-donna legs. She came down a little hard on her heels, as if she didn't walk in her bare feet that much, putting down her heels and then letting the weight move along to her toes as if she was testing the floor with every step, putting a little deliberate extra action into it.

Sammy has perfectly drawn the girls for us; he has animated them and even offered insights into their relationships to each other, all from the picture he presents of them walking near-naked through the A & P. But, now that we're aware of his direct characterization, we can't help but be clued to the fact that Sammy's noticing them—the words he uses to describe them, and the inferences he draws about them, say as much—if not more—about him as about the girls. His directly characterizing them, indirectly characterizes him.

I've always gotten a kick out of this paragraph in which a primary character directly characterizes another character from Ron Hansen's novel *Desperadoes:*

> Eugenia Moore was her alias; she was baptized Florence Quick. She was five-feet-nine inches tall and twenty-five years old and wore her blond hair in a bun. She was brown-eyed and pretty, if somewhat boyish, with teeth so white it looked like she'd never drunk tea. She had a sultry voice and a sturdy, broad-shouldered body and breasts that were not large; her hands were strong and branch-scratched and calloused; she chewed her fingernails down so close to the quick they looked

like cuticle. When she wasn't in boots she was barefoot, but that evening she was wearing a white calico dress with ties on the sleeves and looked more like a lady than she was. She'd been to Holden College and she taught school for two years and there was a lot of that in her speech; when she didn't hear what was said completely, she'd say, "I beg your pardon?" She had blond bangs that she kept brushing with a finger as she talked. She said meeting us was a pleasure and glided away to sit at a smaller table by the burlap-curtained front windows. Her face was brown from the sun

We can't help but have as much fun as Hansen's character is having in describing Eugenia Moore, and from this specifically detailed description we come to know her about as well as we can from a single paragraph. Far beyond the fact that she's "pretty" we understand her attractiveness for ourselves.

Another way of directly characterizing characters is to have them tell us about themselves. The first two-thirds of Andre Dubus's "A Father's Story" are a veritable expository accounting—Luke Ripley explaining to us who he is: "My name is Luke Ripley and here is what I call my life. . . ." This telling—or *re*telling—of who he is, this explication of his two lives, his outward life as an owner of horses and his hinting at the depth of his inner life (we'll soon discover that Luke Ripley is a devout Catholic who has been divorced by his wife and therefore can't marry again), is vitally important in building a firm foundation of understanding of Luke's motive in the story. When the action begins, when his daughter knocks on his door late one night with the news that she's hit someone with the car, we don't balk in the recounting of what happens from that moment on to find out why Luke Ripley does what he does. Luke Ripley's actions may surprise us, given what he's gone on to relate to us is most important to him, his relationship with the Lord, but they don't shock us. We've spent the entire story finding out why he is who he is from what he's told us is most true about himself. Given who he is, Luke Ripley—at heart "the father of a girl"—can do nothing else: he hides the fact of his daughter's involvement, vowing "they won't get Jennifer," and proceeds to the scene of the accident without first calling the authorities, in effect taking the sin of the boy's death, still faintly alive when he finds him, on his own head. He thereby sacrifices the comfort of his "real life," his relationship with God, for his love of his daughter, just as he says God sacrificed his Son for us.

Dialogue

Of course one of the best ways of having characters describe themselves or others—gaining the immediate benefits of both indirect and direct characterization—is through their own words. What we say and how we say it helps us see (hear!) for ourselves so much more than reams of exposition who people are—and this is true whether they are telling us the truth about themselves or not, perhaps more true if they aren't! Dialogue, which in fiction is simply the written version of the way people seem to speak, is another form of dramatization, of letting the character show themselves.

Once again, there are any number of short stories that we could use as an example of effective dialogue. Below is an excerpt that utilizes dialogue from Grace Paley's short story "Goodbye and Goodluck" collected in *The Little Disturbances of Man:*

> Nowadays you could find me any time in a hotel, uptown or downtown. Who needs an apartment to live like a maid with a dustrag in the hand, sneezing? I'm in very good with the bus boys, it's more interesting than home, all kinds of people, everybody with a reason. . . .
>
> And my reason, Lillie, is a long time ago I said to the forelady, "Missus, if I can't sit by the window, I can't sit." "If you can't sit, girlie," she says, politely, "go stand on the street corner." And that's how I got unemployed in novelty wear.
>
> For my next job I answered an ad which said: "Refined young lady, medium salary, cultural organization." I went directly by trolley to the address, the Russian Art Theater of Second Avenue, where they played the best Yiddish plays. They needed a ticket seller, someone like me, who likes the public but is very sharp on crooks. The man who interviewed me was the manager, a certain type.
>
> Immediately he said: "Rosie Lieber, you surely got a build on you!"
>
> "It takes all kinds, Mr. Krimberg."
>
> "Don't misunderstand me, little girl," he said. "I appreciate, I appreciate. A young lady lacking fore and aft, her blood is busy warming the toes and the finger tips, it don't have time to circulate where it's most required."
>
> Everybody likes kindness. I said to him: "Only don't be fresh, Mr. Krimberg, and we'll make a good bargain."
>
> We did: Nine dollars a week, a glass of tea every night, a free ticket once a week for Mama, and I could go watch rehearsals any time I want.

What fun! I could go on, and I encourage you to find Paley's collection and read all of her stories for yourself. But the point I'm trying to make using this brief excerpt from a twenty plus-page story is about how dialogue works on the page. The words written here don't waste away like the sorts of "Hello-how-are-you-I'm-fine-and-you?" conversations we find ourselves participating in every day. The words "spoken" here actually cog the plot. Dialogue is deftly used to snug up the tension, actually taking the place of certain actions or gestures, which we can see perfectly anyway from what has been said. And, most obviously perhaps, dialogue well characterizes

Rosie Lieber and Mr. Krimberg, indirectly and directly. From this short exchange we come to know them—their ages and backgrounds, their physical appearance and desires—better than we would have if Grace Paley had written twenty pages simply telling us about them, their date of birth, political affiliations, the kind of pastries they like.

This may be the most difficult aspect of writing dialogue for the young writer to understand, but it's really no different from any other use of significant detail that creates the believability of fictional truth. Dialogue is not real speech, and it can't course along as real conversations are apt to do. Dialogue in fiction is directed, aimed, used. It adds—in one of the many ways we've spoken about—to the complete effect of the work.

Hemingway, a writer often touted for the "realistic" dialogue he wrote, doesn't copy real talk at all. Where, in a story like "Hills Like White Elephants" (*Men Without Women*) composed almost completely as a conversation between a couple waiting at a railroad station for the train which will take them on to Barcelona, are all the "wells . . . " and "ohs" and "you knows" that litter daily speech, even, I'm sure, the speech of the 1920s? These sorts of naturalistic touches are edited in favor of lines of dialogue that directly advance the character's concerns and tensions in the story, in the case of "Hills" the question of whether or not the young woman is going to have an abortion. (We will return to this same example again in our section on "Point of View").

The young woman, Jig, begins, and the man with her, the American, answers:

"And you really want to?"

"I think it's the best thing to do. But I don't want you to do it if you don't really want to."

"And if I do it you'll be happy and things will be like they were and you'll love me?"

"I love you now. You know I love you."

"I know. But if I do it, then it will be nice again if I say things are like white elephants, and you'll like it?"

"I'll love it. I love it now but I just can't think about it. You know how I get when I worry."

"If I do it you won't ever worry?"

"I won't worry about that because it's perfectly simple."

"Then I'll do it. Because I don't care about me."

"What do you mean?"

"I don't care about me."

"Well, I care about you."

"Oh, yes. But I don't care about me. And I'll do it and then everything will be fine."

In Toni Cade Bambara's "The Lesson" (*Gorilla, My Love*), Sylvia, the irrepressible narrator, speaks up for herself in speaking to us:

> Back in the days when everyone was old and stupid or young and foolish and me and Sugar were the only ones just right, this lady moved on our block with nappy hair and proper speech and no makeup. And quite naturally we laughed at her, laughed the way we did at the junk man who went about his business like he was some big-time president and his sorry-ass horse his secretary. And we kinda hated her too, hated the way we did the winos who cluttered up our parks and pissed on our handball walls and stank up our hallways and stairs so you couldn't halfway play hide-and-seek without a goddamn gas mask. Miss Moore was her name. The only woman on the block with no first name. And she was black as hell, cept for her feet, which were fish-white and spooky. And she was always planning these boring-ass things for us to do, us being my cousin, mostly, who lived on the block cause we all moved North the same time and to the same apartment then spread out gradual to breathe.

While not actually dialogue, we can note several interesting things about Syvia's "speaking" voice before examining her conversations in the story. First of all, her voice sounds much more naturalistic in the way we've noted earlier. Bambara uses phonetic spellings cush as "cept" for *except* and "kinda" for *kind of*. The misspellings work well here; they don't get in the way of our understanding what Sylvia is trying to communicate, and they add greatly to our understanding of Sylvia's character. Bambara has used such spellings to capture the semblence of Syliva's speech without distracting us unnecessarily. But look carefully at how else, besides phonetic spellings, that Bambara has accomplished this feat. Note the repitition of the words "hated" and "laughed" in rolling the rhythms of Sylvia's speech, and the curious way Bambara has Sylvia drop the expected "hated her" for "hated the. . . ." And note the words, the language, Sylvia chooses: "laughed the way we did at the junk man who *went about his business* like he was some *big-time* president and his *sorry-ass* horse his secretary" (italics mine).

In capturing the conversation—the dialogue—between the children who go with Miss Moore to be taught the lesson of the disparity of wealth between Harlem, where Sylvia lives, and fifth Avenue, where they go to visit FAO Schwarz, Bambara exercises the same techniques:

> "This is the place," Miss Moore say, presenting it to us in the voice she uses at the museum. "Let's look in the windows before we go in."
> "Can we steal?" Sugar asks very serious like she's getting the ground rules squared away before she plays. "I beg your pardon," say Miss Moore, and we fall out. So she leads us around the windows of the toy store and me and Sugar

screamin, "This is mine, that's mine, I gotta have that, that was made for me, I
was born for that," till Big Butt drowns us out.
"Hey, I'm going to buy that there."
"That there? You don't even know what it is, stupid."
"I do so," he say punchin Rosie Giraffe. "It's a microscope."
"Whatcha gonna do with a microscope fool?"
"Look at things."
"Like what, Ronald?" ask Miss Moore.

The first thing we're apt to notice here is how well the dialogue characterizes each speaker. We clearly imagine slow, pudgy Big Butt and upright, uptight Miss Moore. "Like what, Ronald?" Each character naturally gives voice to himself or herself and his or her predicament in this place: "Can we steal?"

As writers, we might also notice the way Bambara uses tags to keep us abreast of who's speaking when she needs to—"Miss Moore say" and "Sugar asks"—but also be aware of how quickly she drops such tag lines when whoever is speaking is obvious or the voice is meant to pop out of the group (though we suspect it's Sylvia): "Watcha gonna do with a microscope fool?" Beginning a new paragraph to indicate a change in speakers is another good technical device to keep who's saying what straight.

What else can we learn from the above passage? Bambara punctuates her dialogue with gestures from her characters—"I do so," he say *punchin* on Rosie Giraffe"—to emphasize how something was said. A pet peeve I have is when writers overload lines of attribution with unnecessary adverbs: *"Wahoo!" Frank shouted loudly.* Most of the time, if the dialogue is doing its job, there's no need to explain how something was said. "He said" or "she asked"—though they may seem boring, repetitive, or uninspired, don't flag unnecessary attention to themselves. Such simple tags do their job of keeping us oriented as to who is speaking, while becoming all but invisible in our prose. Lastly, we learn, once again, that the writer hasn't wasted one line. Everything the characters say, and the way they say it, in some way advances the story.

So, dialogue is a good and useful way of characterization, among a lot else. But dialogue can be tough to write. The writer has to be a good mimic; but what if you have a tin ear? Although it works well for Bambara here, substituting "goin" for "going" is not the only way to capture the way a character speaks.

To think about techniques to use in capturing believable dialogue on the page, read any of the stories I've excerpted thus far. Reading short stories offers young writers some of the best advice on technique they'll ever get for themselves. Besides phonetic spellings, be aware of the hard work writers do to capture syntax of speech—the ordering of words in a sentence—and strive to choose the exact word the character would use. There is a world of difference in Miss Moore's straight ahead: "You sound angry, Sylvia. Are you mad about something?" and Sylvia's, "Miss Moore lines us up in front of the mailbox where we started from, seem like years ago, and I got a headache for thinkin so hard."

I read everything I write onto tape. This allows me to listen to the words I've written, and I find I can hear a gap in tension in a story more readily than I can see it on the page. These gaps, for me, are often overly long passages of exposition, of telling that interrupts the more natural flow of actual events. But listening back to the recording of what I've written helps me hear my characters' voices more clearly too. It forces me to say what they would say, and to put the pertinence of what they're saying to the test in the context of the concerns of the story as a whole. Reading your written dialogue out loud is a helpful and good habit to get into. Also, try keeping a journal in which you record actual conversations you've overheard on the bus while standing in the aisle swaying over a mother and daughter on their way back from shopping for discount wedding dresses at Filene's Basement. Or you might write up a rehearsal of a conversation by two characters, keeping at heart some central concern (as Sally did in Part One), such as the issue of which wedding dress to buy, while the crux of the discussion is really the husband the bride-to-be has chosen. In other respects, writing dialogue is just like the other aspects of crafting our prose. It means writing it, and then writing it again and again until it *works*.

These designations of character and the techniques of characterization of which I've been speaking—round and flat, primary and secondary, indirect and direct—don't hold fast, nor are they necessarily meant to. Certainly the terms I've offered aren't the final word. Any number of books on writing fiction will have called them what they will as they see fit. The terms I've catalogued are simply one way to talk about the element of character and the fictional technique of characterization we find working on the page of a short story or novel. No doubt these designations can be—and should be—coupled endlessly to create all sorts of variations on the basic theme.

It's obviously true, too, that a character does not operate alone in a story. Even if, as in traditional realistic fiction, the story is *about* them, characters aren't the whole story. No matter how brilliantly done, a paragraph that describes the appearance of a character does just that: describes the appearance of a character. What does our character need to become a story? "Desire," Aristotle, for one, has said. In *The Poetics,* Aristotle says, "We are our desires." For our purposes, we'll term this desire a character's *motivation.* Motivation *animates* character.

In bringing any character to life, motivation casts that character, and, in effect, shapes the form of the short story as a whole—an idea we'll return to when we discuss the element of *plot.* For now, let's hold fast to the beginnings of all we've learned about character and characterization, keeping in mind for the time being this idea of the importance of motivation in driving a character into developing a short story and turn the focus of our discussion to another essentially related element, *point of view.*

Writing Exercises

Below I've offered several writing exercises that emphasize the different aspects of character on which this section has focused. Work on each as you see fit and try not to put too much pressure on yourself. They are, after all, exercises. *Trying* is what they're all about.

1. Getting started. If character is the single most important aspect of fiction, then why not begin by imagining a character? I've found this exercise works best if you bring to mind people you know or have seen—a kind of Mr. or Mrs. Potato Head mix of people. Say, your cousin, Jimbo, or your Great-Aunt Smyrna. List as many specific details as you can about a character, from his or her name, to shoe size (9 1/2 EEE), to the kind of ice cream they like to eat (Ben and Jerry's Double Fudge Chunk).

2. Once you've made a list, try putting your character into motion by giving them a motivation. It's lunchtime and your character is ravenous. She is walking past Angelo's, a dark, deliciously-aromaed pizza joint on Broadway, but she only happens to have fifty cents. Or, driving to make a long-awaited secret assignation with a lover, your character has engine trouble on a windy mountain road at night. In a page or so, try to entertain as many of the possible details you've listed about your character that are *significant* given the situation.

3. To practice characterization, have the character you've created indirectly characterize himself or herself, utilizing the words, judgments, or comparisons he or she would choose in describing someone or something else, a cousin from Mississippi who's come to visit for the summer, or a sunrise at a resort by the sea.

4. Have another character directly characterize your character.

5. Directly characterize your character or have the character directly characterize himself or herself by some convenient means, seeing an old photo in a high school yearbook or looking up to catch themselves looking straight back in some unlikely reflection, the distortion in the chrome bumper of a car or a funhouse mirror.

6. Use an exchange of dialogue to characterize two characters as completely as you can.

7. Write down a conversation you hear. What, at heart, is the central concern of what was said? Write a new conversation taking on this central concern. Try interspersing the dialogue with gestures and action. You might also try writing the dialogue without using "he said" or "she said," working to keep who's speaking clear and to make each voice distinct. If you have a tape recorder, read and then listen back to what you've written. Having listened, what changes would you make? Make them, re-read the passage, and then listen back to it again.

THE EYE OF THE STORY: POINT OF VIEW

In any discussion of how writers create round characters, point of view (or POV) is of vital concern. At its most basic, POV can simply be thought of as the teller of the story, our narrator, or the point from which the narration of the story arises.

Most stories are told from one of three possible points of view: first person (I, We); second person (You); or third person (He, She, It). Each choice of POV has its advantages and disadvantages, its freedoms and limitations. First person may offer the freedom of slinging around a strong voice, to once again invoke Marie Lazarre in Louise Erdrich's "Saint Marie": "So when I went there, I knew the dark fish must rise. Plumes of radiance had soldered on me. No reservation girl had ever prayed so hard. . . ." Such a mesmerizing voice casts a strong spell over the reader, but it can also be confining. Though I believe Marie Lazarre's voice works here, any first person narration runs the risk of confining the use of language to that particular character's level of diction and overall knowledge. (Of course, that can work in the writer's favor as well, as it does in "Saint Marie." We know from the beginning that she's only fourteen, and so recognize things about her of which she can't possibly be aware.) In "A & P," Sammy shows himself to be awfully perceptive, terribly sharp in his description of the girls, but he would never use the word *lascivious* in describing the way the butcher, McMahon, "siz[es] up their joints." Such a word denotes another character, calling for another POV.

In choosing POV we not only consider the person in which the story is told—first person, second person, third person—but whether the narration will be *subjective* or *objective*. In "Bullet in the Brain," the first half of the story is told in *third person subjective*, "Anders had conceived *his* own towering hatred for the teller, but *he* immediately turned it on the presumptuous crybaby in front of him" (italics mine). The second half, beginning at the point at which Anders is shot and so no longer has the ability to narrate, is told from the distanced perspective of *third person objective*, "The bullet smashed Anders's skull and ploughed through his brain and exited behind his right ear. . . ."

All this might seem a bit confusing at first, but it's really as simple as who tells the story and the distance employed by the writer between the teller and the tale that is told.

First Person

There are many, many fine examples of short stories told in the first person subjective POV. In previous parts and sections of this book we've recognized a few contemporary American examples: Bharati Mukherjee's "The Management of Grief"; Ann Beattie's "The Burning House"; Louise Erdrich's "Saint Marie"; John Updike's "A & P"; and Andre Dubus's "A Father's Story." Read through any two of these stories—or a few first person narratives that you've read—to compare. You will quickly see that they each share several things in common as first person narratives.

Right away you may notice that first person is by its very nature subjective. That is, the speaker is the subject, even if the story is about someone or something else. In Tillie Olsen's "I Stand Here Ironing," to add another fine story to our list, the narrator is concerned about the call she's received from the guidance counselor from school who has phoned to talk about the narrator's daughter, Emily: "I wish you would manage the time to come in and talk with me about your daughter. I'm sure you can help me understand her. She's a youngster who needs help and whom I'm deeply interested in helping." And though the story is *about* her daughter's troubles, it is the narrator's own guilt, shame, understanding, and, finally, "wisdom" that the counselor's call causes to "move . . . tormented back and forth with the iron": "Even if I came, what good would it do? You think because I am her mother I have a key, or that in some way you could use me as a key?"

Another common denominator of stories told in first person is the unique voice of the narrator. Listen to "Bub," the narrator of Raymond Carver's story "Cathedral" (*Cathedral and Other Stories*), as he describes the blind man, his wife's friend, who has come to visit them for the weekend:

I've never met, or personally know, anyone who was blind. This blind man was late forties, a heavy-set, balding man with stooped shoulders, as if he carried a great weight there. He wore brown slacks, brown shoes, a light-brown shirt, a tie, a sports coat. Spiffy. He also had this full beard. But he didn't use a cane and he didn't wear dark glasses. I'd always thought dark glasses were a must for the blind. Fact was, I wished I had a pair. At first glance, his eyes looked like anyone else's eyes. But if you looked close, there was something different about them. Too much white in the iris, for one thing, and the pupils seemed to move around in the sockets without his knowing it or being able to stop it. Creepy. As I stared at his face, I saw the left pupil turn in toward his nose while the other made an effort to keep in one place. But it was only an effort, for that eye was on the roam without his knowing it or wanting it to be.

Or Sandra Cisneros's "Never Marry a Mexican" (*Woman Hollering Creek and Other Stories*):

Drew, remember when you used to call me Malinalli? It was a joke, a private game between us, because you looked like a Cortez with that beard of yours. My skin dark against yours. Beautiful, you said. You said I was beautiful, and when you said it, Drew, I was.

My Malinalli, Malinche, my cortesan, you said, and yanked my head back by the braid. Calling me that name in between little gulps of breath and the raw kisses you gave, laughing from that black beard of yours.

Before daybreak, you'd be gone, same as always, before I even knew it. And it was as if I'd imagined you, only the teeth marks on my belly and nipples proving me wrong.

Your skin pale, but your hair blacker than a pirate's. Malinalli, you called me, remember? *Mi doradita.* I liked when you spoke to me in my language. I could love myself and think myself worth loving.

Or the teller of James Alan McPherson's "A Solo Song: For Doc" (*Hue and Cry*):

So you want to know this business, youngblood? So you want to be a Waiter's Waiter? The Commissary gives you a book with all the rules and tells you to learn them. And you do, and think that is all there is to it. A big, black book. Poor youngblood.

Look at me. *I* am a Waiter's Waiter. I know all the moves, all the pretty, fine moves that big book will never teach you. *I* built this railroad with my moves; and so did Sheik Beasley and Uncle T. Boone and Danny Jackson, and so did Doc Craft. That book they made you learn came from our moves and from our heads. There was a time when six of us, big men, danced at the same time in that little Pantry without touching and shouted orders to the sweating paddies in the kitchen. There was a time when they *had* to respect us because our sweat and our moves supported them. We knew the service and the paddies, even the green dishwasher, knew that we did and didn't give us the crap they pull on you.

Do you know how to sneak a Blackplate to a nasty cracker? Do you know how to rub asses with five other men in the Pantry getting their orders together and still know that you are a man, just like them? Do you know how to bullshit while you work and keep the paddies in their places with your bullshit? Do you know how to breathe down the back of an old lady's dress to hustle a bigger tip.

No. You are summer stuff, youngblood. . . .

I can't resist one more. This is from David Foster Wallace's "Girl with Curious Hair" (*Girl with Curious Hair*).

Gimlet dreamed that if she did not see a concert last night she would become a type of liquid, therefore my friends Mr. Wonderful, Big, Gimlet and I went to see Keith Jarrett play a piano concert at the Irvine Concert Hall in Irvine last night. It was such a good concert! Keith Jarrett is a Negro who plays the piano. I very much enjoy seeing Negroes perform in all areas of the performing arts. I feel they are a talented and delightful race of performers, who are often very entertaining. I especially enjoy watching Negroes perform from a distance, for close up they frequently smell unpleasant. Mr. Wonderful unfortunately also smells unpleasant, but he is a good fellow and a sport and he laughs when I state that I dislike his odor, and is careful to remain at a distance from me or else position himself downwind. I wear English Leather which keeps me smelling attractive at all times. English Leather is the men's cologne with the television commercial in which a very beautiful and sexy woman who can play billiards better than a professional makes the assertion that all her men wear English Leather or they wear nothing at all. I find this woman very alluring and sexually exciting. I have the English Leather Cologne commercial taped on my new Toshiba VCR and I enjoy reclining in my horsehair recliner and masturbating while the commercial plays repeatedly on my VCR. Gimlet has observed me masturbating while I watch the English Leather Cologne commercial and she agrees that the woman is very alluring and states that she would like to lick the woman's vagina for her. Gimlet is a bisexual who is keen as anything on oral sex.

Each of these narrators has a particular (perhaps peculiar) manner of speaking, a distinctive way of voicing their world. What they say—and how they say it—is who they are. They are drawn for us not so much from physical descriptions as from what they choose to tell us and the words they use to describe what they see. (Bub: "Creepy"; the Spanish sprinkled through

"Never Marry a Mexican Man"; the use of "youngblood" in McPherson's "Solo Song: For Doc" as opposed to the use of "Negro" by the narrator of Wallace's "Girl with Curious Hair.") The specifics of the words they choose to express themselves, even the syntax of their sentences—the way the words are grouped, "Mr. Wonderful unfortunately also smells unpleasant, but he is a good fellow and a sport and he laughs when I state that I dislike his odor, and is careful to remain at a distance from me or else position himself downwind."—tell us much about them, a hint of their race, social class, sensibilities, age, education, and tastes.

We can guess a lot from the way people talk, and when we choose to tell a story from the first person point of view, it is our job as writers to be as true to the person speaking as possible. It really isn't about us, no matter how much of us is in the story or how true to life the story may be. And no matter how interested we might be in what Carver, as a writer, may have to say about "Cathedral," he can't simply interject his own commentary—not if he wishes to remain true to the narrator of the story, not if his goal is to create a believable fictional truth that casts the spell of "a vivid and continuos dream." "Cathedral" is Bub's story. And when the narrator wonders aloud to his wife if he might take the blind man who is coming to visit them bowling, we are being shown who our narrator is, complete with all his limitations, contradictions, bigotry, and ignorance.

At a reading I once heard Andre Dubus give at the Cambridge Public Library, a man from the audience asked Dubus how he created his characters. Dubus had been sipping water from a plastic Dixie cup. It was empty, and he picked it up and set it down, picked it up and set it down again. He pointed at the cup and, in reference to a female character he was then trying to write about in the first person POV, said (and later wrote in an essay "The Habit of Writing" included in *On Writing Short Stories*), "You must know what a glass of beer feels like in her hand; you must know everything." Some days, in three or four hours at his desk, he said, he could only manage three or four sentences that were *hers*.

Yet such attention to character certainly isn't the rule. It is possible, certainly, as some writers of metafiction do, to purposely disrupt the first person narration, to burst the bubble of the dream—whether by breaking out of character or by alerting the reader to the fact that the narrator *is* a character. The story can still work in creating an effect, even if we are aware that an effect is being created. In part, the difference is simply a matter of taste. But there is a trade-off, and the young writer ought to be aware, at least, of the value of the exchange: Fiction is about *life*, metafiction is about fiction.

In the following excerpt from William Gass's story "In the Heart of the Heart of the Country" (*The Heart of the Heart of the Country and other Stories*) we are never allowed to fully enter the dream:

A Place

O I have sailed the seas and come . . .

to B . . .

a small town fastened to a field in Indiana. Twice there have been twelve hundred people here to answer to the census. The town is outstandingly neat and shady, and always puts its best side to the highway. On one lawn there's even a wood or plastic iron deer.

You can reach us by crossing a creek. In the spring the lawns are green, the forsythia is singing, and even the railroad that guts the town has straight bright rails which hum when the train is coming, and the train itself has a welcome horning sound.

Down the back streets the asphalt crumbles into gravel. There's Westbrook's, with the geraniums, Horsefall's, Mott's. The sidewal shatters. Gravel dust rises like breath behind the wagons. And I am in retirement from love.

Weather

In the Midwest, around the lower Lakes, the sky in winter is heavy and close, and it is a rare day, a day to remark on, when the sky lifts and allows the heart up. I am keeping count, and as I write this page, it is eleven days since I have seen the sun.

My House

There's a row of headless maples behind my house, cut to free the passage of electric wires. . . .

Of course, this story is captivating in its own way, its own right, and the first person voice is still unique and engaging—a character "writing to us" is emerging—but there's no doubt we're aware of the writing. The "weather" is separated for us, as is his "house." We are just beginning to be lulled into the setting, say, when we're nudged alert. The narrator defies the sorts of expectations the other first person narratives I've offered readily provide.

In a debate on fiction versus metafiction between William Gass and John Gardner held in Cincinnati in 1978 (Thomas LeClair moderator, found in *Conversations with John Gardner* edited by Allan Chavkin), Gass says that "In fiction, I am interested in transforming language, in disarming the almost insistent communicability of language." What he "wants" is to plant some object in the world. Now it happens to be made of signs, which may lead people to think, because it's made of signs, that it's pointing somewhere. But actually I've gone down the road and collected all sorts of highway signs and made a piece of sculpture out of these things that say Chicago, 35,000 miles. What I hope, of course, is that people will come along, gather in front of the sculpture, and just look at it—consequently forgetting Chicago. I want to add something to the world which the world can then ponder the same way it ponders the world.

Gardner, on the other hand, believes that his "activity [as a fiction writer] leads to a feeling state, whereas the philosopher has only cold clarity." He adds:

the ultimate apparition, the ultimate dream of the novel, is a continuous one. When you decide as a writer that the novel is just a house you're trying to get somebody to go through in various ways, you have broken faith with the reader because you are now a manipulator, as opposed to an empathizer. If the novelist follows his plot, which is the characters and the action, if he honestly and continuously proceeds from here to here because he wants to understand some particular question, the reader is going to go with him because he wants to know the same answers. On the other hand, if the writer makes the reader do things, then I think he puts the reader in a subservient position which I don't like.

Of course, for our purposes here, neither William Gass nor John Gardner has to be "right." The important thing for the young writer to understand is that there is such a debate going on, and that it's been going on for quite some time now.

Our final example of a first person POV is the consideration of the possibility of a "we" narration, or first person plural POV. A good story to use here is William Faulkner's "A Rose for Emily" (*Collected Stories*). The narrator remains undisclosed. We are never told whether it is a woman or a man, but much is revealed by the fact that this narrator speaks for the town:

So the next day we all said, "she will kill herself"; and we said it would be the best thing. When she had first begun to be seen with Homer Barron, we had said, "She will marry him." Then we said, "She will persuade him yet," because Homer himself had remarked—he liked men, and it was known that he drank with the younger men in the Elks' Club—that he was not a marrying man. Later we said, "Poor Emily" behind the jalousies as they passed on Sunday afternoon in the glittering buggy, Miss Emily with her head high and Homer Barron with his hat cocked and a cigar in his teeth, reins and whip in a yellow glove.

The voice is aged, gray-haired itself, a bit stagey-grand, certainly gossipy; complicity is understood. This is *our* town, *our* story. Miss Emily is *our* concern and what happens to her is about *us*.

Second Person

Second person as a narrative technique has the curious effect of both putting distance between the narrator and the reader—"You" is somehow more abstract and obviously fictional than either the first persons I/We or the third persons He/She/Them—while at the same time including the reader in a more subjective, universal narrative. *You* points at us and can make us feel as if we were there.

In Susan Minot's short story "Lust" (*Lust and Other Stories*) the narrator begins her story in the first person, but as the list of the boys she's "fucked"—Leo, Roger, Bruce, Tim, Philip, Johnny, Eben, Simon, Mack, Paul, Oliver—grows out of control she distances herself from the act in which she has become merely a "body waiting on the rug." Her "I" "disappears" from her own narration and is replaced by a more objective, less personal (perhaps less painful) way of telling us what she knows full well she's doing to herself:

> After sex, you curl up like a shrimp, something deep inside you ruined, slammed in a place that sickens at slamming, and slowly you fill up with an overwhelming sadness, an elusive gaping worry. You don't try to explain it, filled with the knowledge that it's nothing after all, everything filling up finally and absolutely with death. After the briskness of loving, loving stops. And you roll over with death stretched out alongside you like a feather boa, or a snake, light as air, and you . . . you don't even ask for anything or try to say something to him because it's obviously your own damn fault. You haven't been able to—to what? To open your heart. You open your legs but can't, or don't dare anymore, to open your heart.

Yet, again, strangely enough, at the same time she is distancing herself she is including us in this feeling you get "after sex."

Hemingway is a writer who often used the second person narrative to good effect. In "Chapter XII," one of the short-short stories spaced between the full-length pieces of his first short story collection, *In Our Time,* he uses the second person to make us feel as if we, too, are at the bullfights. The effect achieved is of a brilliant, active moment in which we are immediately involved. *If it happened right down close in front of you,* he begins,

> you could see Villalta snarl at the bull and curse him, and when the bull charged he swung back firmly like an oak when the wind hits it, his legs tight together, the

muleta trailing and sword following the curve behind. Then he cursed the bull, flopped the muleta at him, and swung back from the charge his feet firm, the muleta curving and at each swing the crowd roaring. . . .

In this passage, the you acts as a universal sort of invitation for us to take a seat "ringside" and view the fights, up close and personal.

Second person can be a powerful, fresh and inclusive, universalized POV, able to create a felt empathetic effect. But it does carry the flag of caution we've noted above in the debate between Gass and Gardner of calling attention to itself as a *technique*. We are somehow more aware that we're in second person than first or third, which have the curious ability to "disappear", leaving us more completely—more believably—inside the dream of the narrative. Second person is also filled with presumption. "You would go to the store and buy a six pack of Red, White and Blue beer for $1.98," I might write. But you might already be shaking your head. *You* would, you say, not *me*.

Third Person

After a reading given to introduce his collection of short stories, Bear and His Daughter, Robert Stone was asked why he never wrote in the first person POV. The woman asking the question, an older woman wearing a big, drooping hat with a blue plastic flower attached, wondered if, perhaps, first person wasn't, well, a little "tacky," which got a laugh. Stone laughed, too, but then he rubbed his chin, considering it. He wagged his head; with his full beard and glasses he looked like a kind of Walt Whitman up there. No, he said, it wasn't that first person was "tacky," but, as a writer, he did feel its "limits." In third person he felt *stronger.* He could still gain the effect of first person—still get that close subjective POV—but he wasn't as confined. I took him to mean that he felt that he could simply *do more* in third.

Third person POV can allow the writer to put a little distance between himself or herself and the character who is the subject. It can offer the writer a view beyond what the character can see. Third person may also give the writer more freedom in the use of language. Vocabulary is not determined solely—though of course it must be a consideration—by the word choice of the character.

For the purpose of discussion, third person can be separated into three perspectives: subjective, objective, and omniscient. These points of view do not necessarily exist separately. Rather, they are like primary colors that the writer, like the painter, may use boldly as blue or mix with yellow to gain green. Part of the beauty of third person—the strength of which Stone spoke—is its versatility, the seemingly unlimited effects and shadings of color, with which such a perspective affords the writer to explore his or her subject.

THIRD PERSON SUBJECTIVE

Anton Chekhov's "The Lady with the Pet Dog" (translated from the Russian by Avrahm Yarmolinsky, *The Portable Chekhov*) is about as complete an example of the full use of a third person subjective POV as we could hope to find. The general perspective is established from the outset:

> A new person, it was said, had appeared on the esplanade: a lady with a pet dog. Dmitry Dmitrich Gurov, who had spent a fortnight at Yalta and had got used to the place, had also begun to take an interest in new arrivals. As he sat in Vernet's confectionary shop, he saw, walking on the esplanade, a fair-haired young woman of medium height, wearing a beret; a white Pomeranian was trotting behind her. . . .
>
> "If she is here alone without husband or friends," Gurov reflected, "it wouldn't be a bad thing to make her acquaintance."

One of the beautiful things about this opening is the fluidity with which Chekhov, utilizing every nuance of the third person subjective POV, moves us from the interest at the general "appearance" of the lady with the pet dog to the understanding that we have of Gurov's apparently offhand interest in "making her acquaintance." It is understood that if is she is "alone" then he would like to manage an affair with her.

It is worth our while to take note of the artistry being displayed. From the first line of the story, Gurov's sensibilities and his desire have been quietly invoked. By the fourth paragraph, Chekhov has already maneuvered to set the wheels of the story into motion and has found a moment to still the forward momentum and begin to build the foundation of Gurov's motivation, the history of the reason behind his wish to go to bed with the lady with the pet dog, whom he will soon come to know as Anna Sergeyevna.

In third person subjective POV we are intimately tied to Gurov's perceptions throughout the story; the narrative seems subjective in much the same way a first person POV would be subjective. We "hear" what Gurov hears "was said," and we see what he sees, that she's "alone" in the "public garden and in the square," we "reflect" with him as he thinks to himself "it wouldn't be a bad thing to make her acquaintance." And yet the third person subjective POV distances the perspective just enough to allow us to take a step back in the fourth paragraph to note *about* him, that Gurov was

> under forty, but he already had a daughter twelve years old, and two sons at school. They had found a wife for him when he was very young, a student in his

second year, and by now she seemed half as old again as he. She was a tall, erect woman with dark eyebrows, stately and dignified and, as she said of herself, intellectual. She read a great deal, used simplified spelling in her letters, called her husband, not Dmitry, but Dimitry, while he privately considered her of limited intelligence, narrow-minded, dowdy, was afraid of her, and did not like to be at home. He had begun being unfaithful to her long ago—had been unfaithful to her often and, probably for that reason, almost always spoke ill of women, and when they were talked of in his presence used to call them "the inferior race."

And we haven't blinked! Chekhov has used third person subjective to move without a hitch from what Gurov sees, to his reflections, to a long outside view of his life. The POV has allowed the writer to intrude without being intrusive.

I love to read Chekhov; it's as if he isn't there! But it is Chekhov's apparent absence, of course, when we stop to consider the seamless effects his flawless third person has wrought, that makes us note how powerfully present he really is.

During a trip to Oreanda, as Gurov and Anna sit silently together on a bench "look[ing] down at the sea," we are introduced to a furthering of the third person POV perspective. Thus far we have "heard" with Gurov; "seen" with Gurov; "reflected" with him; stepped back with him to take a long view of his history; but in this scene we are taken completely into his consciousness. We are nearly as close as we can get; we enter a reverie with him:

Yalta was barely visible through the morning mist; white clouds rested motionlessly on the mountaintops. The leaves did not stir on the trees, cicadas twanged, and the monotonous muffled sound of the sea that rose from below spoke of the peace, the eternal sleep awaiting us. So it rumbled below when there was no Yalta, no Oreanda here; so it rumbles now, and it will rumble as indifferently and as hollowly when we are no more. And in this constancy, in this complete indfference to the life and death of each of us, there lies, perhaps, a pledge of our eternal salvation, of the unceasing advance of life upon earth, of unceasing movement towards perfection. Sitting beside a young woman who in the dawn seemed so lovely, Gurov, soothed and spellbound by these magical surroundings—the sea, the mountains, the clouds, the wide sky—thought how everything is really beautiful in this world when one reflects: everything except what we think or do ourselves when we forget the higher aims of life and our own human dignity.

The thought is beautiful; it is profound; but it may also seem to us a little sappy, sentimental. Gurov seems poised on the verge of an epiphany, and indeed he is! But it is not the life-altering realization he expects. He is in love, though he doesn't know it yet. Gurov has never been in love. At this moment, he is simply a man sitting next to a "young woman who in the dawn seemed so lovely," but she is not yet *Anna.* The reverie brings us closer than ever to Gurov. But he can only see so far, we see, even when examining life as closely—as intimately—as he may well ever have up to this point in his life.

The third person subjective POV has allowed Chekhov a cut diamond's planes of perspective. The complexities of his character are prismed before him for us, not yet clearly understood, but invaluable in marching toward our discovery of Gurov's love. Here, at the end of the story, Chekhov squeezes one last bit of art out the seemingly simple third person subjective POV, making a move to loom large over the fate of both characters without ever necessarily leaving Gurov's perspective and yet managing to echo out beyond it:

> And it seemed as though in a little while the solution would be found, and then a new and glorious life would begin; and it was clear to both of them that the end was still far off, and that what was to be most complicated and difficult for them was only just beginning.

This short story is so well crafted that the subtleties of third person POV can be easily missed. For me, that is Chekhov's mastery in this story: *not* showing his genius. My advice? Read it again! And again and again and again!

THIRD PERSON OBJECTIVE

A contrast to the third person subjective POV Chekhov uses to tell the story of Gurov in "The Lady with the Pet Dog" is a story such as Hemingway's "Hills Like White Elephants" (Men Without Women), which is told almost exclusively in a distanced third person objective POV.

We pan into the story for a glimpse of "the hills across the valley of the Ebro [which are] long and white" before settling "[o]n this side" where "there "[is] no shade and no trees and the station [is] between two lines of rails in the sun." We focus on the American and the girl, Jig, sitting "at a table in the shade, outside the building." They're trying drinks while they wait for the "express from Barcelona" which "[will] come in forty minutes . . . stop . . . at this junction for two minutes and [go] on to Madrid."

Many students finish the story unaware that the situation centers around Jig's decision of whether or not to have an abortion. The word "abortion" is never used in the story, and the point of view in the story remains detached, *objective,* throughout except for a few vital moments when the perspective shifts to give us a quick, subjective insight through Jig: "The girl [Jig] stood up and walked to the end of the station. Across, on the other side, were fields of grain and trees along the banks of the Ebro. Far away, beyond the river were mountains. The shadow of a cloud moved across the field of grain and *she saw* the river through the trees" (italics mine).

"And we could have all this," she says. "And we could have everything and every day we make it more impossible."

Jig, as we get to see in this quick glimpse of what she sees, "just knows things." Her knowing is shown to us in the fertility of the valley, a hope "far away," the life of the river that she sees "through the trees," the "shadow of a cloud" that passes over everything.

But if we get to see this bit of what Jig sees, are allowed to feel for an instant what she feels, then why the objective POV? Why isn't the word abortion used? It is spoken of as "an awfully simple operation." Why not just say it? (Why not have Jig think about *it?*) Is "it" a trick? At the end, are we supposed to guess? Is the answer to the story, "Oh! They're talking about an abortion!" Obviously not. The story isn't a mere who-done-it, the point is not the surprise. So, what is the effect of not simply spelling out what the "operation" is?

Perhaps it's because the third person objective POV forces us to focus our attention on the actions and dialogue of the characters, giving us a seat at the station, as it were, to let us observe what the couple says and does for ourselves:

"It's really an awfully simple operation, Jig," the man said. "It's not really an operation at all."

The girl looked at the ground the table legs rested on.

The fact is we have no choice but to focus on what *they* choose to focus on; we are forced to hear and see what the trouble is between them for ourselves. The abortion is the combustible inner engine for the story, the central concern, the drive that puts their love to the test. But it is the tension of the operation that shows them for who they are. We are enabled to objectively experience their "love" for ourselves. We needn't be told.

Jig begins:

"And you really want to?

"I think it's the best thing to do. But I don't want you to do it if you don't really want to."

"And if I do it you'll be happy and things will be like they were and you'll love me?"

"I love you now. You know I love you."

"I know. But if I do it, then it will be nice again if I say things are like white elephants, and you'll like it?"

"I'll love it. I love it now but I just can't think about it. You know how I get when I worry."

"If I do it you won't ever worry?"

"I won't worry about that because it's perfectly simple."

"Then I'll do it. Because I don't care about me."

"What do you mean?"

"I don't care about me."

"Well, I care about you."

"Oh, yes. But I don't care about me. And I'll do it and then everything will be fine."

It is the very objectification of the abortion that throws the dialogue about love in which the American and the girl are engaged into stark relief. We might, at first, believe the man's protestations. But he protests too much! The man is slowly exposed for what he is, selfish and self-centered. He loves himself. But Hemingway doesn't need to tell us this, nor do we need Jig to explain that he's a heel or say how desperately she wants to stop traveling and trying drinks and settle down into a more complete relationship—to fulfill the possibilities of love that she's glimpsed in the white hills across the Ebro. There's no need. We have seen them for ourselves. We feel it. Actions, we find (again and again), do speak louder than words—they scream even while "sitting at the table . . . smil[ing]."

"Do you feel any better?" the American asks, coming back from carrying their bags around to the other side of the station, stopping to "[drink] an Anis at the bar" where all the other people are "waiting reasonably for the train."

"I feel fine," Jig replies. "There's nothing wrong with me. I feel fine."

THIRD PERSON OMNISCIENT

Strictly speaking, third person omniscient POV means all-seeing, all-knowing. When I think of an omniscient POV, I can't help but think of a God-like scope. In the third person omniscient, we may levitate above a scene or shift at will from one character's consciousness to another's—the author/narrator seems to know all. The writer may make pronouncements, predict futures. The author is an intimate part of the goings-on: a storyteller to be reckoned with, even when the reader momentarily forgets his or her presence.

In Isaac Bashevis Singer's short story "The Little Shoemakers," translated by Isaac Rosenberg (*The Riverside Anthology of Short Fiction*), our omniscient narrator tells a broadly inclusive tale of a family of shoemakers and the sons' journey to America to become successful shoe manufacturers themselves. The story spans generations of "The family of the little shoe-makers" who were "famous not only in Frampol but in the outlying distict—in Yanev, Kreshev, Bilgoray, and even in Zamoshoh." "Abba Shuster, the founder of the line" is reputed to have "appeared in Frampol some time after Chmielnitzki's pogroms"; his name is "recorded, on parchment, in the annals of the Frampol Jewish community." "His stone in the old cemetary had vanished, but the shoemakers knew a sign for the grave—nearby grew a hazelnut tree. According to the old wives, the tree sprang from Reb Abba's beard."

As the title suggests, the first part of the story goes on to establish a Genesis-like overview of lineage, establishing the descent of the shoe-maker's family line: "Reb Abba had five sons; they settled, all but one, in the neighboring towns; only Gretzel remained in Frampol. He continued his father's charitable practice of making shoes for the poor, and he too was active in the gravediggers' brotherhood.

> The annals go on to say that Getzel had a son, Godel, and that to Godel was born Treitel, and to Treitel, Gimpel. The shoemaker's art was handed down from one generation to the next. A principle was fast established in the family, requiring the eldest son to remain at home and succeed his father at the workbench. . . .
>
> As it is not our business to deal with all the generations of the little shoemak-ers, we will confine ourselves to the last three. Reb Lippe remained without heir till his old age. . . .

The story follows the line through Feivel to his oldest son, Abba, "named after the founder." This "Abba" was by far the best shoemaker in Frampol." Gimpel was the eldest of Abba's seven sons, and it is Gimpel who breaks with this long lineage of tradition. He tells his father: "I'm going to Amer-ica." Time sweeps by: "forty years pass"; Abba's house is burned to the ground—the place of his forefathers—and he takes to wandering, "staff in hand." Finally he goes to America where he is greeted by his sons who now "lived on the outskirts of a town in New Jersey. Their seven homes, sur-rounded by gardens, stood on the shore of a lake."

Here, at end, Abba realizes that his sons haven't forsaken him or their her-itage. "No, praise God, they had not become idolaters in Egypt. They had not forgotten their heritage, nor had they lost themselves among the unworthy."

The short story tells the tale of a family of shoemakers that spans gener-ations and continents. The narrator, who is relating all of this to us, is knowl-edgeable about everything concerning the family, aware of the parchment, "the annals," and the "old wives" accounts of events. The omniscient narra-tion soars through time, making record of the family tree, but at moments comes closer, to offer a third person objective account. In this instance, the narrator allows us a glimpse of Abba's evenings at home: "Evenings, when the sun was setting, the house would be pervaded by a dusky glow. Rays of light danced in the corners, flicked across the ceiling, and set Abba's beard gleaming with the color of spun gold." The omniscient POV goes so far as to allow the narrator to shift from seeing Abba's beard "gleaming with the color of spun gold" to dip into his consciousness, offering us an intimate third person subjective understanding of his thoughts: "[Abba] knew that the wide world was full of strange cities and distant lands, that Frampol was actually no bigger than a dot in a small prayer book; but it seemed to him that his little town was the navel of the universe and that his own house stood at the very center."

The breadth of this story seems to demand this sort of omniscience, allowing the narrator the sort of mobility he needs. We associate the omniscient POV more with early novels or tales than we do with the short story, but obviously it can work. "The Things They Carried" by Tim O'Brien (*The Things They Carried*) offers a contemporary consideration of the possibilities of a third person omniscient POV.

"The Things They Carried" alternates between a close third person subjective perspective from the POV of Lt. Jimmy Cross and an all-seeing third person omniscient POV told by an unseen narrator who has knowledge of all the soldiers who play a part in this story set in Vietnam.

The story begins in Lt. Jimmy Cross's third person subjective POV:

First Lieutenant Jimmy Cross carried letters from a girl named Martha, a junior at Mount Sebastian College in New Jersey. They were not love letters, but Lieutenant Cross was hoping, so he kept them folded in plastic at the bottom of his rucksack. In the late afternoon, after a day's march, he would dig his foxhole, wash his hands under a canteen, unwrap the letters, hold them with the tips of his fingers, and spend the last hour of light pretending. He would imagine romantic camping trips into the White Mountains in New Hampshire. He would sometimes taste the envelope flaps, knowing her tongue had been there. More than anything, he wanted Martha to love him as he loved her, but the letters were mostly chatty, elusive on the matter of love. . . .The letters weighed ten ounces. . . . At dusk, he would carefully return the letters to his rucksack. Slowly, a bit distracted, he would get up and move among his men, checking the perimeter, then at full dark he would return to his hole and watch the night and wonder if Martha was a virgin.

The narrative perspective then broadens. We step back from the specific example of the ten-ounce letters Lt. Jimmy Cross carries to weigh the "necessities" the other soldiers "humped" along on the march through the jungles themselves:

The things they carried were largely determined by necessity. Among the necessities or near necessities were P-38 can openers, pocket knives, heat tabs, wrist watches, dog tags, mosquito repellent, chewing gum, candy, cigarettes, salt tablets, packets of Kool-Aid, lighters, matches, sewing kits, Military Payment Certificates, C rations, and two or three canteens of water. Together, these items weighed between fifteen and twenty pounds, depending upon a man's habits or rate of metabolism.

After cataloguing each of these necessities, the narrator goes on to list the items each individual man carried: "Henry Dobbins . . . carried extra rations; . . . Dave Jensen . . . carried a toothbrush, dental floss, and several hotel-sized bars of soap he'd stolen on R & R . . . Ted Lavendar, who was scared, carried tranquilizers until he was shot in the head outside of the village of Than Khe in mid-April." The men are now referred to as "they." It isn't Lt. Jimmy Cross speaking, telling us these things. We're not quite sure who it is, but this *who* knows everything about Lt. Jimmy Cross and his men. The narrator knows that the bulk of the burden these men shoulder is the unweighed fear of death.

The omniscient POV the narrator assumes allows us to view the war both subjectively and objectively. We are made privy to Lt. Jimmy Cross's personal concerns, his "hope" for love, and the "distraction" he feels from the war, focused, as he is, on her letters. But we also understand, by noting the necessities of the other soldiers, that Cross is only one specific example of the "distancing" all of these soldiers employ. Ted Lavendar used tranquilizers to keep him "safe." Kiowa carries a Bible and his hatchet. The specific situation that Lt. Jimmy Cross finds himself in after Ted Lavendar is shot in the head outside Than Khe enables us to feel the story at a personal level. We empathize with Cross's guilt and remorse in failing his men. At the same time, the more objective aspect of the narration piles on the weight of understanding in the story, so that when Lt. Jimmy Cross burns the letters and "dispense[s] with love" and "form[s] his men] into a column to move out toward the village of Than Khe" we may see that his decision isn't necessarily the correct one. Yes, Ted Lavendar is dead, but they are men at war—other men will die as well. Cross, it seems, has simply discarded the weight of the letters to shoulder his full responsibility as a leader. But "dispensing with love" isn't *necessarily* the answer. Marching off to "burn Than Khe," he is as distanced from his place in Vietnam as he's ever been, albeit in a sort of opposite way. The higher plateau of perspective of the omniscient POV allows us a realization of which Lt. Jimmy Cross, trapped in his head and heart humping along in the steamy jungles, seems incapable.

The point of view is the distance that controls both our seeing and our feeling through characters. The possibilities for such seeing and feeling, though they may seem limited by the fact that we've enumerated them here, are virtually limitless. The designations of POV outlined here—first person subjective, second person, and a third person subjective, third person objective and third person omniscient—are offered as guidelines to consider when writing a short story. The writers own inventiveness, judgment, talent, and style will determine the only real boundaries.

Writing Exercises

1. Keeping in mind the examples of first person stories we've noted, try your hand at the opening of a story in the first person POV. Before you begin, ask yourself why this particular person is telling us his or her story. What it is about their voice that makes them unique? How is their speech distinctive? Where are they from—Alabama, or maybe Gloucester, a fishing town in Cape Anne, north of Boston? Employ their voice in having them describe a room or another character.

2. What does it take to tell a story in the first person plural POV, "We?" Can you think of a situation in which the narrator can speak for a group—maybe a class looking at the new kid who's just arrived that morning or a jury passing a verdict on some crime? You'll have to consider the why behind the group's telling the story. This is about *all* of them. How are they involved as a group? What characterizes them—and their collective voice—as our narrator?

3. In second person POV, try to write a short-short story like Hemingway's "Chapter XII." You might even go so far as to begin as Hemingway began his— "It happened right down in front of you. . . ."—and see where it leads.

4. Take the first few paragraphs of the opening to the first person story you tried above (or any story in any point of view that you've written). Now try writing those same opening paragraphs in second person, then try the same paragraphs in third, subject, objective, and omniscient. You'll find it isn't as easy as simply exchanging "I" for "We" or "You" for "He" or "She." Shifting the point of view may well change the story completely. Allow for this shift. You may find that you can't simply rewrite the opening paragraph of a story, but have to begin again entirely. If so, begin again! Consider the

allowances you've had to make in changing the POV. This exercise goes a long way in showing the strategic differences in points of view.

5. Complete a short story in any one of the third person points of view.

THE "WHY?" BEHIND THE POWER OF PLOT: SHAPING THE SHORT STORY

"Fiction is a lie," Eudora Welty writes in her essay "Place in Fiction" (*The Eye of the Story*) and in the first part of this book we found that we had to admit it was true. Even if we're telling a "true" story about our Great-Aunt Smyrna, we soon find ourselves having to make decisions about what aspects of the truth to include (Smyrnie, as we all called her, *was*, in fact, married twice, but the first marriage isn't vital to the vacation she took at Ruby Falls. So. . . .) Indeed, it comes as no surprise that stories are *illusions*. They are created; they are *made* of words on a page.

The word "made," though, seems to imply that stories are somehow pre-fabricated. I have the same trouble with talking about the *structure* of a short story. Talking this way makes me feel as if all we have to do as writers is conveniently fit our characters into a sort of jig that holds all the elements of the short story in place, nail them quickly up (not even bothering to take the time to drill for screws)—a real bang-up job—and be done with it. This would be an enterprise more fitting to the manufacture of picnic tables for a public works operation than to the crafting of one finely wrought oak conference table. "Shaped" allows for a discovery of form that will manifest itself from the necessities forced on the short story by the nature of its own telling. Our fine oak conference table may turn out to be recognizable to, say, a picnic table—the table, like the short story, is, after all, a *form*—but it is shaped by, and for, its own particular use. In a sense, although it is made, it has molded itself. The short story is shaped in much this way. And so even though the short story as a form will be recognizable, each particular story must stand structurally on its own, shaped to its own demands, as singly separate as Andre Dubus's "A Father's Story" is from Susan Minot's "Lust" or William Gass's "The Pederson Kid" is from Lydia Davis's "A House Besieged" or Joyce Carol Oates's "Heat."

To liberally paraphrase Sherwood Anderson, it is the shaping of the short story that wakes the writer screaming and kicking his or her covers off in the middle of the night. Much of the discussion in this section shadows process.

How can we write the beginning of a short story if we need to know the end first? Well, I don't think we can. Not a *finished* story. We must listen to our characters, and carefully consider their desires in crux. The moment in a story that we call an epiphany is often as much a discovery for the writer as it is for the characters involved. At a reading I heard Tobias Wolff give, he said that if his characters didn't discover something from the story how could he? Beyond the advice of listening to our characters to help us discover how to shape short stories, there are concrete ways of saying what we mean when we go to work molding any story. Motive, conflict, climax, resolution, and epiphany are the signposts that can help map our way to discovering how to "complete" the meaning of a story for ourselves.

Motivation

We are our desires. Aristotle's statement *feels* true, doesn't it? And it is this truth—our desires, any character's motivation—which powers a short story, casting the characters in a certain light and, in effect, shaping the form of the short story.

None of us does anything without a motive—a *reason.* We don't get up off the couch and go to the store unless we are driven there because we have run out of food, having cranked open the last can of Bumblebee tuna fish for breakfast. Nor can we continue to think of ourselves as honest if we cheat the cashier out of the extra $5.00 he or she accidentally counted back to us as change unless we can somehow justify it as luck, or perhaps our own little way of getting back at the system. If we stop in the parking lot counting our change, and then turn on our heels and march the money back inside, it may be because we, too, worked as cashiers at some point in our lives and we know at the end of the night when the register comes up short, it won't be the system that catches it, but Bob or Yolanda, Hamish, or our hero from John Updike's "A & P," young Sammy himself. When Aristotle says that *we are our desires,* it is these sorts of driving motivations that he has in mind. What we want or need and how we go about satisfying those wants and needs *show* who we are. We live by such desires; we are destined to be by such needs.

In fiction, as in life, motivation is the heart and soul of any character's action or inaction—even more so, because of the particular truth a short story sets out to portray. Aristotle's maxim holds true in determining the career our character pursues—book critic, cashier, owner of horses, saint— or something as seemingly inconsequential as the candy she may choose in line at the Stop and Shop, say Jolly Ranchers fortified with vitamin C over a Mounds bar, because she's just come from the doctor's office where she's learned, much to her joy, that she's pregnant. She eats two; she suspects its twins!

Without motivation, a character has no need to move, to act or react—enjoin, coerce, ridicule, praise, lie—and so if our characters lack strong motivations, chances are we won't have much of a story about them. No one will want to do anything; their need won't be strong enough to get them up off the couch and out the door. And—unless their *not* doing anything is exactly the point—the danger is there will be no impetus for a character's story to be told.

Characters want, they *need*, often desperately so, and this *motive*, rising in *conflict* with an opposing motive or obstacle toward a moment of crux, a *climax*, which has some *resolution, The End*, a "complete story," in Flannery O'Connor's words, in which "nothing more relating to the mystery of that character's personality could be shown through that particular dramatization," has classically defined the basic architecture of the short story.

Conflict, Climax, and Resolution

In class, I like to draw on the blackboard a simple paradigm for the classic composition of the short story:

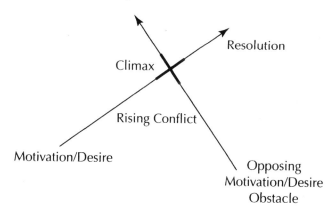

In his short essay included in *Fires*, "Creative Writing 101," Raymond Carver says: "Try as I might, I couldn't muster a great deal of interest or really understand this side of things, the stuff he [his first creative writing teacher, John Gardner] put on the blackboard." I have to admit such tell-tale mappings do make the spontaneity we feel when we read a great short story (or write a short story of our own!) feel mechanical. Revealing the "illusion" can make the course that we took for fun seem like drudgery, but in considering how we might shape the short story such models can help us to see how a fiction may come to be.

In thinking of these basic components of the short story—motive, conflict, climax, and resolution—I'm once again reminded of painting, in which a good composition is defined by a clearly marked contrast in values, that is, seemingly simple gradations of light and dark. Winslow Homer, the nineteenth-century American painter famous for his watercolors of Gloucester fisherman, the Adirondacks, and Prout's Neck, once said that his entire career as a painter could be characterized by his struggle to define such values. In shaping his or her own short story, the writer is faced with a similarly difficult (though apparently simple) endeavor—to set down clearly defined values, in the writer's case, motives, in juxtaposition to one another. It is this juxtaposition of "values" that creates the *conflict* that often delineates a short story.

Conflict in a short story is the ratcheting roller-coaster-car-like climb of motive set against motive, obstacle against desire—it is the friction, the energy generated by conflict, a character's battle with need, that hastens a short story forward. Conflict is not merely ACTION, which to borrow from one of my favorite TV shows when I was a kid, The Dukes of Hazard, I always think of as a corner-squeeling car chase, Bo and Luke Duke being pursued by Boss Hog and his boys. Action will race a story along for a while, but action should be a *re*-action to the effects of motive. Bo and Luke are being chased because they've vowed to put an end to Boss Hog's dastardly plan to rig (somehow) all the pool tables in town!

Climax in the story occurs when rising desires collide. In "A & P" the climax occurs when Sammy says, "I quit." In John Steinbeck's, "The Chrysanthemums," the climax occurs when Elisa sees her flowers, which the tinker who she gave them to has dumped on the side of the road. In "The Lady with the Pet Dog" by Chekhov the climax occurs when Gurov, with Anna in his arms, catches sight of himself in the mirror and realizes he's "fallen in love, really, truly—for the first time in his life." *Resolution* is the next logical step in how the climax is resolved—or goes unresolved. Sammy walks out the door of the store to "feel how hard the world is going to be to [him] hereafter"; Elisa ends up slumped against the car seat crying "weakly—like an old woman"; Gurov and Anna huddle together believing how "the solution" to their being forced to live apart "would be found." A resolution is an end for a story, but it is not necessarily *The End.* To revisit Flannery O'Connor's statement, the resolution makes a "complete story in which nothing more relating to the mystery of that [character's] personality could be shown through that particular dramatization."

And so, looking back at our blackboard diagram, even if we find we can't "muster a great deal of interest [for] this side of things," perhaps we can see how the simple drawing can help us better understand how clearly defined and conflicting motives can help to create a narrative in which we read to find out not only *what* happens, but *how* it happens, to *whom* it happens, and, most importantly, *why* it happens.

Story Versus Plot

In *Aspects of the Novel*, E.M. Forster defines a story as "a narrative of events arranged in their time-sequence." A plot, he writes

> is also a narrative of events, the emphasis falling on causality. "The king died and then the queen died is a story." "The king died, and then the queen died of grief" is a plot. The time-sequence is preserved, but then the sense of causality over-shadows it. Or again: "The queen died, no one knew why, until it was discovered that it was through grief at the death of the king." This is a plot with a mystery in it, a form capable of high development. It suspends the time-sequence, it moves as far away from the story as its limitations will allow. Consider the death of the queen. If it is in a story we say "and then?" If it is in a plot we ask "why?" That is the fundamental difference between these two aspects of the novel. A plot cannot be told to a gaping audience of cave-men or to a tyrannical sultan or to their modern descendant the movie-public. They can only be kept awake by "and then—and then—." They can only supply curiosity. But a plot demands intelligence and memory also.

This "why?" posed by plot is the character's motivation, which gives reason to events. Without reason, without the need to find out why (even if that need is "shown" to us inside the character's "secret life"), events remain stuck in "their time-sequence," powered along merely by actions that follow along "and then—and then—" like to the end of whatever happens next. This makes for a story, which is propelled along by events. The queen in the above plot longs for her dead husband. She is in deep mourning. And no matter what other concerns she may have—a funeral to attend, a prince or princess to look after, the responsibilities of state, being queen in a kingdom cast into a fit of chaos at her husband's death—the loss of her love compels her every thought and action, determining the reason behind her every move, ghosting her thinner and thinner because she cannot eat, the ache of emptiness hallowing her cheeks, until she too passes away—leaves her life behind to join her husband in the only way she now can, wedded once again by death.

The queen is dead; that's the "and then" end of events, but discovering the *why* behind her death allows us to deploy the rank and file of circumstances. The exploration of her grief uncouples us from the train of abutted actions. We may begin the plot with the day of the king's death, before wrinkling back in time to the morning of their first meeting when the queen was a girl of three, already with some inkling that she had been promised to this quiet boy with the chop of hair falling across his eyes, and then flash forward to the time the king as a young prince of fifteen first dared to kiss her (or maybe she made bold and kissed him!), in the garden, as they sat on the marble steps overlooking the silencing fountain. . . .

Maupassant's "The String" (in a translation from the French by Ernest Boyd, *The Collected Novels and Stories of Guy de Maupassant*) seems to me to be a near-perfect example of the way the "why?" works to determine the cause and effect of events on a character in the short story. Even though occurrences in "The String" are in fact related in chronological order, we can inspect the story engine of the "and then—and then—" to better understand the "why" of its happening to Maître Hauchecorne, the plot that actually makes it go.

Maître Hauchecorne is extraordinarily "economical like a true Norman, [who] thought that everything useful ought to be picked up." He's so frugal in fact that, when he sees a bit of string left lying in the road on his way to the square of the little town of Goderville with the rest of the peasants on market day, he bends down and picks it up, "painfully, for he suffered from rheumatism." But Maître Malandain, the harness maker, who's standing, arms crossed, in his doorway, has seen him do it. Maître Hauchecorne is embarrassed; he and Maître Malandain have "had a quarrel on the subject of a halter" and they remain in long-standing dispute, "being," as we're told, "both good haters." Embarrassed to be seen squirreling away a snippet of string, Maître Hauchecorne hides "his find quickly under his smock" and "pretends to be still looking on the ground for something which he [does] not find." He then continues on, without acknowledging his enemy, "his head thrust forward, bent double by his pain."

When it turns out that Maître Fortune Houlbreque of Manneville has lost his "pocketbook containing five hundred francs and some business papers," Maître Hauchecorne finds himself summoned to the mayor's office. Maître Malandain, who saw him stoop to pick up the pocketbook, has turned him in! Immediately Maître Hauchecorne understands. He's innocent; he can explain! It wasn't a pocketbook he picked up but a piece of string. And here it is! he says, voila!, and produces the unusable bit from his pocket. The mayor, as we may imagine, looks dubiously at him.

Even when the pocketbook is found and returned with the money in it, and Maître Hauchecorne's innocence is proven (he believes), no one buys his story of the string. They wink and laugh, laugh and wink, yuk it up more and more each time he tells his tale—compelling Maître Hauchecorne to relate his account of his innocence again and again.

At the end of the story, Maître Hauchecorne dies because no one will believe that he's not guilty of an "old trick." As a horse-dealer from Monvilliers explains when Maître Hauceconre "commences" (once again!) "to explain 'the affair' ": "Come, come, old sharper, that's an old trick; I know all about your piece of string. . . . One man finds a thing, and another man brings it back. No one is any the wiser, so you get out of it."

> He died early in January, and in the delirium of his death struggles he continued to protest his innocence, and to repeat his story:
> "A piece of string, a piece of string—look—here it is."

In "The String" Forster's understanding of plot is put to the test. Maître Hauchecorne is innocent of stealing the pocketbook—we know he's innocent, we saw him bend over and pick up the worthless snippet—the sequence of events bears that out, but there's a catch, a kick. As Maître Hauchecorne himself tells us:

> With his Norman cunning [he] was capable of doing what they had accused him of, and even of boasting of it as a good trick. His innocence seemed to him, in a confused way, impossible to prove, for his sharpness was well known. And he was stricken to the heart by the injustice of the suspicion.

Maître Hauchecorne's desire is to prove the spotlessness of his character. But the irresolvable conflict is the glut of his own inner guilt. The climax of his conflict is his realization that he is fully "capable of doing what they had accused him of, and even of boasting of it as a good trick." His innocence *seems* to him impossible to prove—indeed it *is* impossible to prove—because, at heart, Maître Hauchecorne is guilty of the crime. He is convicted by the answer to his own why.

The story of "The String," according to Forster's definition, might be the fact that Maître Houlbreque of Manneville's pocketbook was "stolen." We ask, "and then—and then—" to find out what happened until it is returned, but the plot reroutes us back to the the controlling why behind the actions of our primary character, Maître Hauchecorne, who was "wrongly" accused. His death, we discover, is inextricably rooted in his heart's desire to be a "cunning and thrifty Norman."

A story like James Baldwin's "Sonny's Blues" (*Going to Meet the Man*) exhibits the same principles of the importance of the why in creating a plot, but dissembles chronological events in favor of a structure that scans forward and back in an attempt to fathom the narrator's motive—his concern and responsibility for his younger brother, Sonny, arrested for heroin, who he "reads about . . . in the paper, in the subway, on [his] way to work. . . . [He] read it, and . . . couldn't believe it, and . . . read it again. Then perhaps . . . just stared at it, at the newsprint spelling out his name, spelling out the story . . . stared at it in the swinging lights of the subway car, and in the faces and bodies of the people, and in [his] own face, trapped in the darkness which roared outside."

Of course there are nearly as many examples of the performance of plot as there are short stories. We can't possibly catalogue all the variations here. But it does seem worth our while to consider the difference between plot in a short story and a novel, even though we have seen that Forster's principle of plot (included in his book, which, afterall, is entitled *Aspects of the Novel*) may be applied to either.

Plotting Short Stories Versus Plotting Novels

In *The Art of Fiction* John Gardner devotes a good deal of time to the plotting of the novel and in so doing creates a distinction in the structuring between the short story and the novel. "Though character," he writes, "is the emotional core of great fiction, and though action with no meaning beyond its own brute existence can have no lasting appeal, plot is—or must sooner or later become—the focus of every good writer's plan"; and that "Any narrative more than a few pages long is doomed to failure if it does not set up and satisfy plot expectations."

Gardner speaks of a plot that *works* in terms of "profluence" and says that "the conventional kind of profluence—though other kinds are possible—is a causally related sequence of events. This is the root interest of all conventional narrative. Because it is intellecutally and emotionally involved—that is, interested—the reader is led by successive, seemingly inevitable steps, with no false steps, and no necessary missing steps, from an unstable initial situation to its relatively stable outcome."

"A basic characteristic of all good art, then—all man-made works that are aesthetically interesting and lasting—" he goes on to write,

is a concord of ends and means, or form and function. The *sine qua non* of narrative, so far as form is concerned, is that it takes time. We cannot read a whole novel in an instant, so to be coherent, to work as a unified experience necessarily and not just accidentally temporal, narrative must show some profluence or development. What the logical process of argument is to nonfiction, event-sequencing is to fiction. Page 1, even if its' a page of description, raises questions, suspicions, and expectations; the mind casts forward to later pages, wondering what will come about and how. It is this casting forward that draws us from paragraph to paragraph and chapter to chapter. At least in conventional fiction, the moment we stop caring where the story will go next, the writer has failed, and we stop reading. The shorter the fiction, needless to say, the less the need for plot profluence. A story of three or four pages may still interest though it has practically no movement. And of course not all fiction need move at the same pace. Runners of the hundred-yard dash do not take off in the same way runners of the marathon do. If the opening pages of a thousand page novel would serve equally well as the opening pages of a short story, the likelihood is that that novel-opening is wrong. (This is not quite a firm rule, admittedly. A long novel may begin with great urgency, then gradually settle into its long-distance stride. But the writer's timing in his opening pages is a signal to his reader's expectations.)

Conventional novels depend for their life on this sequencing and postponed recognition of events, short stories less so. Still, as Gardner reminds us, "Plotting . . . however childish and elementary it may seem in comparison with the work of surgeons, philosophers, or nuclear physicists—must be the first and foremost concern of the writer." This concern is to "figure out a plot that will efficiently and elegantly express [the story]."

So, now, having noted the process that to varying degrees work to shape the composition of a short story—*motive, conflict, climax, resolution*—taking into account Forster's consideration between a story and plot as a way to get at the *why?* behind how to put a story together for ourselves, the question remains of exactly how the plot of a short story comes to be.

Certainly some pertinent considerations of this conversation on plotting spill over into our discussion on the fictional process—the how of getting the why of the plot done and the short story down on the page (which we will come to in Part Three). Short story writers, I believe, have a much different way of approaching their writing than novelists. Even though Gardner speaks of plotting as the writer's "foremost concern," there are many well-known and respected short story writers like Raymond Carver and Flannery O'Connor and Andre Dubus who, as Carver says, "had no idea where the story was going when [he] began . . . I wrote the first sentence and other sentences began to attach themselves." Carver believed this way of writing was "his secret" until he read Flannery O'Connor's essay "Writing Short Stories" in which she writes that she did pretty much the same thing in drafting "Good Country People" (*A Good Man Is Hard To Find*). O'Connor calls this ability to follow the felt tensions driving a character, "the habit of art," the title of Andre Dubus's essay on process, which is included later in this book. In his essay, Dubus emphasizes again and again that he does everything he can, not to plot, but to give up "control." He writes that when he has a story in mind "[he] gestate[s]: for months, often for years."

An idea comes to me from wherever they come, and I write it in a notebook. Sometimes I forget it's there. I don't think about it. By think I mean plan. I try never to think about where a story will go. This is as hard as writing, maybe harder; I spend most of my waking time doing it; it is hard work, because I want to know what the story will do and how it will end and whether or not I can write it; but I must not know, or I will kill the story by controlling it; I work to surrender. I know a political scientist who writes books. Once I told him that I try simply to go to the desk and receive what will come. He said he did the same. I said: "I thought you guys used outlines. Don't you already know what you want to say?"

No," he said. "It all happens at the typewriter. I never get any work done by thinking."

When writing a story, Dubus tells himself over and over again: "*Just follow the dots; become the character and follow; there will be a story.*" Dubus considers his stories less plots than "situations, and many of them are questions: *What if?* What would happen if a man's daughter accidentally killed a man by hitting him with her car, and did not stop but drove home and told her father?"

To offer a counterpoint to Dubus, I'd like to quote, Barry Targan, who wrote in an informal letter to me that Dubus's comments made him "a little nervous."

"True," he says,

good writing is an act of discovering, first in the writer and then in the reader. What you write should change you. But . . . there is planning in writing, although of course not the complete prefiguring of "formula" fiction. There is planning because there is PROCESS. You make a decision and that begets other kinds of decisions. You make a decision and then you act on it, and that's a kind of planning. In time inevitability develops. One of the most satisfying experiences in reading a story is the feeling of "Yes! Of course!" I think I know what Dubus means, but maybe a young writer might take this as too much "free association" or something like . . .

Maybe you could make a point that there are plenty of writers who do do a lot of planning, and more and more planning as they write themselves into the opportunities that they then have to manage. That's the fun of writing, the planning.

I believe Barry's point is well-taken. For a more thorough consideration of the concerns raised here by these and other authors, see Part Three, "Notes on the Fiction-writing Process."

To return to our reflection on the differences between the plotting of the novel and the plotting of the short story, we might deliberate Henry James's lament that novels must often end in death or marriage. The novelist has invented all these strands of plot and—at least in a conventional novel like Forster's *A Passage to India* or James's own *Daisy Miller,* contemporary novels such as Jane Smiley's *A Thousand Acres* or Charles Frazier's *Cold Mountain,* John Casey's *Spartina* or Alice Walker's *The Color Purple,* Anne Tyler's *The Accidental Tourist,* Pete Dexter's *Paris Trout*—they must be (somehow) knotted off, satisfied, or the reader will set the book down disgruntled, wondering what happened to who and how events turned out. (There is, I'm afraid, that remnant of the gaping caveman left in all of us.)

And yet most short stories don't end in such a tightly wrapped and neatly bowed fashion at all—though, more often than not, they do do *something.* Often, though, this *something* that is the end of a short story may feel to us less like a closing than the opening out of a new beginning!

Perhaps examining the endings of short stories will allow us some glimpse into how to finish shaping them—or perhaps even give us our start.

Meaning

I prefer to talk about the meaning in a story rather than the theme of the story. People talk about the theme of a story as if the theme were like the string that a sack of chicken feed is tied with. They think that if you can pick out the theme, the way you pick the right thread in the chicken-feed sack, you can rip the story open and feed the chickens. But this is not the way meaning works in fiction.

—*Flannery O'Connor, "Writing Short Stories"*

Let's consider again what Flannery O'Connor said about the conclusion of a short story. A story for her is "complete . . . when nothing more relating to the mystery of that [character's] personality can be shown through that particular dramatization."

Resolution is the term we are currently utilizing to suggest the completion of a short story. By resolution we mean an answer—not necessarily the right answer or the final word, no guaranteed solution—but a response to the climax of the conflict. Maître Hauchecorne dies; Sammy "saunters" out of the A & P; the the narrator of "Sonny's Blues" "hears" the music his younger brother, Sonny, plays and sends a scotch and milk to him on the bandstand. "[Sonny]didn't seem to notice it, but just before they started playing again, he sipped from it and looked toward me, and nodded. Then he put it back on top of the piano. For me, then, as they began to play again, it glowed and shook above my brother's head like the very cup of trembling." But close attention to O'Connor's words leaves the term resolution slacking. Resolution doesn't manage to take full account of the possibility for change in the primary character (if the narrative is designed in such a way as to lend change) or what is often a feeling of newly gained understanding on the part of the reader "relating to the mystery of that [character's] personality" that we experience when we've finished reading most short stories.

Three terms are bandied about to explain this mystery: *realization, denouement,* and *epiphany.* Close as they may be in definition, each has a slightly different shade of meaning. Realization, for instance, doesn't seem as life altering as epiphany (we realize we should have been at Dr. Watson's for our dental appointment at 3:00, not 4:00.), and denouement, the term Aristotle adopted, by which he "mean(s) the section from the start of the transformation to the end," technically designates the last third or so—the completion—of a drama. Both realization and denouement seem to act more quietly, more gently, bringing us closer to *change* perhaps, than they do in bestowing upon us the soul-altering shock Flannery O'Connor often uses to rock her characters into utter "completeness."

EPIPHANY

James Joyce seized the word epiphany from Christian doctrine—the epiphany was the moment when the Christ-child was revealed to the three magi—and held the flaming torch of it on high for literary purposes to mark such a revelation in a story such as his own "Araby." In this particular short story the young narrator, a boy lost in love with Mangan's sister, an older girl who hardly knows he exists, goes to the bazar to buy her a gift, but overhearing the shop girl talk to some young men, and seeing the place unveiled at closing time for what it is—a big drafty building with junk for sale—he suddenly realizes the futility of his mission, and of his "love," seeing himself clearly in that moment as "a creature driven and derided by vanity." Epiphany, by its very root, suggests that it is meant to signify more than any mere realization. Epiphany is not simply a showing forth, or even a revelation. Even for literary purposes the term retains its glow of mysticism. The moment of epiphany is less an intellectual than a felt moment, and the change it signals, no matter how seemingly subtle, is irrevocable.

To begin class discussion of the way epiphany works in a short story I use an exercise offered to me by Maxine Rodburg, director of the Writing Center at Harvard. Students are asked to consider the following two statements. The first, which I hope you'll recognize, is from Flannery O'Connor; the second comes from Eudora Welty:

Flannery O'Connor: I often ask myself what makes a story work . . . and I have decided that it is probably some action, some gesture of a character that is unlike any other in the story, one which indicates where the real heart of the story lies. This would have to be an action or a gesture which was both totally right and totally unexpected; it would have to be one that was both in character and beyond character; it would have to suggest both the world and eternity.

Eudora Welty: In going in the direction of meaning, time has to move through a mind. What it will bring about is an awakening there. Through whatever motions it goes through, it will call forth, in a mind or heart, some crucial recognition.

The exercise then poses the question, "What are these two writers talking about?", and asks the student to write two or three pages on the idea of epiphany, using examples from the stories we've read to try to come to terms with the idea behind the word.

In the heated discussion that inevitably ensues I'm less concerned that we come up with a "correct" definition than we give our thoughts on how short stories work at end a good stirring.

If the *beginning* of a conventional short story sets into motion a character's motivation in a given situation—say Maître Hauchecorne's picking up the snippet of string—and the *middle* of the story is the dramatization of conflict that leads to a climax, the resolution of which is *The End* of the short story, then it stands to reason that the end of the plot (for it to be a plot and not merely a story, according to Forster, to answer the "why?" and not simply satisfy the caveman's insistent "and then—and then—?") needs to take us beyond the simple cessation of events—the end of what happened (Maître Hauchecorne dies)—to *meaning*.

In "Writing Short Stories," Flannery O'Connor says she prefers the term "meaning" to "theme" when talking about a short story, and I agree. "People talk about the theme of a story," O'Connor writes, "as if the theme were like the string that a sack of chicken feed is tied with. They think that if you can pick out the theme, the way you pick the right thread in the chicken-feed sack, you can rip the story open and feed the chickens. But this is not the way meaning works in fiction." *Meaning* lets us talk about what the story has to say; what the story *says*, what the characters, and we as readers, have *experienced.*

To quote her in entirety:

Perhaps the central question to be considered in any discussion of the short story is what do we mean by short. Being short does not mean being slight. A short story should be long in depth and should give us an experience of meaning. I have an aunt who thinks that nothing happens in a story unless somebody gets married or shot at the end of it. I wrote a short story about a tramp who marries an old woman's idiot daughter in order to acquire the old woman's automobile. After the marriage, he takes the daughter off on a wedding trip in the automobile and abandons her in an eating place and drives on by himself. Now that is a complete story. There is nothing more relating to the mystery of that man's personality that could be shown through that particular dramatization. But I've never been able to convince my aunt that it's a complete story. She wants to know what happened to that idiot daughter after that.

Not long ago that story was adapted for a television play, and the adapter, knowing his business, had the tramp have a change of heart and go back and pick up the idiot daughter and the two of them ride away, grinning madly. My aunt believes that the story is complete at last, but I have other sentiments about it—which are not suitable for public utterance.

For O'Connor, when the man deserts the idiot daughter and drives off "nothing more relating to the mystery of [his] personality could be shown through that particular dramatization." The end is the instant of felt understanding of who he is, at heart, in essence. Forster's "why?" that powers the telling of the story has been fully realized and what happens to either of them after that isn't the point.

This is the story's *epiphany*.

Welty calls fiction a "lie"; Maupassant proclaims it an "illusion." Real life is full of vagaries, but not conventional fiction. Nothing in a traditional short story is random. Short stories, we find, exist for this moment of effect, and all the other elements of fiction work toward it.

In his essay "Against Epiphanies," which is included in his fine book *Burning Down the House*, Charles Baxter makes a strong case against a certain kind of epiphanic ending. The words "'I've had a major revelation,'" he writes, "typically fill me with dread." Baxter here, it seems to me, argues against *unearned* epiphany. "Suddenly, it seems, everyone is having insights. Everyone is proclaiming and selling them. . . . Everywhere there is a glut of epiphanies. Radiance rules." Epiphanies have become de rigueur; we have come to expect them and feel cheated in a story if we don't get one—even if the epiphany is merely "proclaimed" (i.e., told/expained) rather than being earned (i.e., felt, as O'Connor demands).

It is, I admit, a subtle difference. Certainly a judgement call is necessary here. But the gauge once again seems to be *feeling*. Unearned Epiphanies are often preceded by such exclamations as, "Suddenly Jane realized . . . " and

"Then Jesse knew. . . ." These signposts alert us that the epiphany or meaning is going to be told to us or explained. It might help us to go back and think again about O'Connor's "action or gesture" that triggers understanding. Such showing exacts feeling because it is born out of the character, because such an action or gesture is "both totally right and totally unexpected . . . both in character and beyond character, both totally right and totally unexpected," it comes from a deeper place than explanation can touch. Such signals are felt first and analyzed afterward.

At the end, I believe it is the idea that a story *must* have an epiphany that Baxter rejects—not the work earned epiphanies perform, though he admits to a "prejudice" against epiphanic stories. Baxter "[doesn't] believe that a character's experiences in a story have to be validated by a conclusive insight or a brilliant visionary stop-time moment." He lobbies for the anti-epiphanic story, which, he writes, "is perfectly capable of sneaking its own visionary eloquence through the back door." He does concede such stories have "been and probably will always be a kind of minority writing: quarrelsome, hilarious, and mulish. . . . Instead of a conclusive arrival somewhere, we end, or rest, at a garden of forking paths, or an apartment complex where no one knows how to start the car, but everyone has an opinion, possibly worthless, about the matter."

To explore some of these endings for yourself read Jorge Luis Borges's "The Garden of Forking Paths" (*Labyrinths: Selected Stories and Other Writings*), which Baxter alludes to above or stories that he examines in his essay such as Denis Johnson's "Car Crash While Hitchhiking" (*Jesus' Son: Stories*) or any of the short short stories by Lydia Davis in her collection *Break It Down*. I, too, encourage you to read James Alan McPherson's story "Elbow Room" in his collection by the same name, where the narrator self-destructs his own narrative in a dialogue with his editor who tries to force understanding and meaning on a story which, the writer tells us, he doesn't have the understanding to be able to write.

In any event, Baxter's objections should be kept in mind; for one thing, they keep us honest. The curtain has been yanked back, and Charles Baxter is staring straight back at us. If it is to go beyond pat realization, epiphany must reveal the "mystery" or character in conflict. Pat endings or simplistic moralizations, summaries of emotion, and quick fixes may be termed epiphanies, but they will never punctuate good stories with meaning. Stories that are guilty of such failings will read like the contrivances they are; they will not convince us with the earned effects of true "illusion." They will not feel complete. Such endings are more in keeping with the taste of Flannery O'Connor's aunt.

Writing Exercises

1. Compare the architecture of several short stories. Choose three and draw a paradigm of how each is shaped. Do the three stories you've chosen follow the diagram I've drawn? Consider the differences and similarities of each.

2. Now try the above exercise with one of your own stories. Map out a story you've written. Then answer these questions: Is the motive in your story clearly defined? Is there a clearly drawn conflict? Where does the climax of the story occur? How is the climax resolved? Is there an epiphany? Has the epiphany been "earned"? In your own estimation, is your story "complete"? If not, where does the diagram you've drawn reveal a weakness?

3. "The king died and the queen died," according to Forster, relates a story; "The king died and the queen died of grief" transforms the story into a plot. The difference, as Forster describes it, is that "in a story we say 'and then—and then—' [and that] in a plot we ask 'why?'" In consideration of the above definition, is the story you have outlined a story or a plot? In a page or two engage the reasoning behind your answer by keeping strictly to the terms of Forster's definition. Use specific examples from your own story to prove your point.

4. Try your hand at the epiphany exercise. What are O'Connor and Welty *really* talking about? Reckon with them in three or so pages and offer your own understanding of epiphany. This exercise works best if you use specific instances from stories you've read to help test and explore your thinking.

"THE LESSER ANGELS OF FICTION": SETTING AND TIME

"Place," Eudora Welty writes in her essay "Place in Fiction" (*The Eye of the Story*),

> is one of the lesser angels that watch over the racing hand of fiction, perhaps the one that gazes benignly from off to one side, while others, like character, plot, symbolic meaning, and so on, are doing a good deal of wing-beating about her chair, and feeling, who in my eyes carries the crown, soars highest of them all and rightly relegates place to the shade.

And yet place, or setting as we'll call it and time, must be given their due—lesser angels though they may be. Without them we wouldn't have a story! Let's consider each separately.

Setting

"Where we are is who we are, Miss Moore always pointing out," says Sylvia, the irrepressible narrator of Toni Cade Bambara's "The Lesson" (*Gorilla, My Love*) a short story about a bunch of children from "the slums" who take a field trip to Fifth Avenue to enter FAO Schwarz's grand toy store only to find they've touched down in a world where a "toy sailboat" costs "one thousand one hundred and ninety-five dollars." They are shocked and are ripe for an awakening about their own place on the planet—whether Sylvia wants to learn Miss Moore's pointed lesson or not: "Not that I'm scared [of going inside], what's there to be afraid of, just a toy store."

Even for a lesser angel, the setting in "The Lesson" seems to be doing a lot of wing-beating, a veritable flurry of fluttering. And here we can quickly see a few of the jobs setting may be responsible for in a short story. Setting can work as a *backdrop* for the character's actions, a stage like the showroom floor of FAO Schwarz; it can help create a certain *atmosphere,* happy and seemingly carefree as Sylvia and her friends harass the cab driver all the way downtown and then, suddenly, somber, as they come face to face with the price tags in the windows of the toy store; setting enhances *believability*—we recognize FAO Schwarz, whether we've ever been to the toy store or not. A "real" place (even if it were made up!), a store on Fifth Avenue in Manhattan that is stocked with thousand dollar toy sailboats and three hundred dollar microscopes, a paperweight for four hundred and eighty dollars, makes us believe in the characters and their reactions. They've come to FAO Schwarz from a place where "thirty-five dollars could buy new bunk beds for Junior and Gretchen's boy . . . and the whole household could go visit Granddaddy Nelson in the country . . . pay for the rent and the piano bill too." Setting, as we see plainly in "The Lesson," can power a story as *motive.* As Miss Moore says, "Where we are is who we are." And as an integral part of the story's *situation,* setting may also help create the conflict of the story—in effect becoming part of the plot. It may also act as a *metaphor,* significantly enhancing—deepening or expanding—the meaning that takes place on its "stage."

SETTING AS BACKDROP

Setting as backdrop is the most basic way in which place works in a short story. Setting in this case simply *sets* the stage where the characters interact and the conflict of the story takes place. When the curtain rises on a story such as Hemingway's "Hills Like White Elephants." (*Men Without Women*), we see before us "The hills across the valley of the Ebro . . . long and white . . . the station . . . between two lines of rails in the sun . . . the warm shadow of the building and a curtain, made of strings of bamboo beads . . . The American and the girl . . . at a table in the shade, outside the building. . . ." Setting here acts as a lesser angel in that its job is relatively straightforward. The story has to take place somewhere. So now the stage is set, and now the girl, Jig, can ask, "What should we drink?"

SETTING AS ATMOSPHERE

Beyond the work it does as backdrop, place can help create the mood of a short story and help us connect with a character's emotional state. John Gardner details a writing exercise in description that we can employ for ourselves to help us get a feel for the significance of setting in creating the atmosphere of a short story.

> Describe a barn as seen by a man whose son has just been killed in a war. Do not mention the son, or war, or death. Do not mention the man who does the seeing. (The exercise should run to about one typed page.)

Many students want a rainy day, a weepy, cloudy afternoon, say, to make their job (they think) easier. They want the sky to cry. The point is the lean of the barn, the dark maw of its double-door, "boards, straw, pigeon manure, and ropes, the rhythms of . . . sentences, his angle of vision" should all add to the writer's desire to "'tell the truth'; that is, to get the feeling down in concrete details." The "images of death and loss that come to him are not necessarily those we might expect." As Raymond Carver says in "On Writing" (*Fires*), even "commonplace things and objects" can be "endow[ed] with immense, even startling power."

The danger, as Carver goes on to warn us, is that

> If the words are heavy with the writer's own unbridled emotions, or if they are imprecise and inaccurate for some other reason—if the words are in any way blurred—the reader's eye will slide right over them and nothing will be achieved. The reader's own artistic sense will simply not be engaged. Henry James called this sort of hapless writing "weak specification."

Consider again the sections on character and point of view. In a particular point of view, we may feel anything the character feels, see anything the character sees, tastes, smells, senses, and hears. The setting can be made to expose the character by revealing what he or she is feeling, etc. about his or her surroundings. The very choice of what is observed—much less how it is described—draws for us the portrait of that character.

This use of setting as mood works in a further removed, objective point of view as well. In "Hills Like White Elephants" the descriptions appear fairly flat; Hemingway does not unduly call attention to the depiction of the "hills across the valley of the Ebro" or flag the fertility on the "other" side of the Ebro. "On this side," we know, "there [is] no shade and no trees . . ." But subconsciously we have been alerted to a stark difference. We are left with a feeling about the place where the American and the girl Jig find themselves sitting in "the warm shadow of the building"—strategically placed "between two lines of rails in the sun." They now have "forty minutes" until the express from Barcelona arrives. "It stopped at this junction for two minutes and went on to Madrid." The atmosphere of the story has lent an edge of expectancy to the timed conversation to come.

It's important to note that, even as setting in "Hills" is serving as the static, painted background that surrounds the stage upon which events take place at the station, the hills ("They don't really look like white elephants. I just meant the coloring of *their skin* through the trees.") [italics mine] are growing forward to take on more important roles in the story as well, here as atmosphere. The wonder of setting—as with each of the other elements of fiction that compose a short story—is that it performs a multiplicity of jobs all at once. The facets of setting enumerated here are not put into operation one by one in single file, as I have listed them to better help us note their particulars. As Gardner said of putting the elements to use, there must be "profluence." The writer creates his story, not element by element, but in a "single coherent gesture, as a potter makes a pot; or as Coleridge put it, he must copy, with his finite mind, the process of the infinite 'I AM.'" We'll return to concept of exercising the elements in a "single coherent gesture" in Part Three, Notes on the Fiction-writing Process. For now, let's be content with sounding the dimensions of setting at play in a short story. Setting, as we have seen, drapes a backdrop about the stage of the story upon which the characters may act, as well as, as we see in "Hills" (or any of a host of short stories), splash on the atmospheric lightning bolts and scud clouds and sunnyness of mood. Less obvious, perhaps, is when setting goes to work to quietly convince readers of the truth of a story by creating the illusion of a real place on the page.

SETTING AND BELIEVABILITY

Recall the quotation from Flannery O'Connor in Part One, "Fictional Truth and Significant Detail," where we're given a more complete consideration of the theory that stands behind the curtain working the levers of believability in creating the "vivid and continuous dream" that is a "true" short story. In "Writing Short Stories," O'Connor writes "Fiction is an art that calls for the strictest attention to the real—whether the writer is writing a naturalistic story or fantasy." In fact, as we noted before, O'Connor

> would go so far as to say that the person writing a fantasy has to be even more strictly attentive to concrete detail than someone writing in a naturalistic vein— because the greater the strain on credulity, the more convincing the properties in it have to be.

By creating a world chock-full of concrete significant detail—"a clamor of bells that set the swallows soaring" and "the rigging of the boats in the harbor sparkl[ing] with flags," "the streets between houses with red roofs and painted walls, between old moss-grown gardens and under avenues of trees, past great parks and public buildings," a world inhabited by "old people in long stiff robes of mauve and grey, grave master workmen, quiet, merry women carrying their babies and chatting as they walked," such as Ursula Le Guin does in "The Ones Who Walk Away from Omelas" (*The Wind's Twelve Quarters: Short Stories*), the writer convinces us of the realness of the place, despite the "strain of credulity" we may begin to feel when we realize this place, Omelas, seems too good to be true: "But I fear Omelas so far strikes some of you as goody-goody. Smiles, bells, parades, horses, bleh. If so, please add an orgy. If an orgy would help, don't hesitate."

Ironically, in this particular short story, it is the narrator's exposure of the city of Omelas as *un*believable that transforms it from feeling real to being true:

> Do you believe? Do you accept the festival, the city, the joy? No? Then let me describe one more thing.

The narrator confesses to a

> basement under one of the beautiful buildings of Omelas, or perhaps in the cellar of one of its spacious private homes [where] there is a room. It has one locked door, and no window. A little light seeps in dustily between cracks in the boards . . . The floor is dirt . . . The room is three paces long and two wide: a mere broom closet . . . In the room a child is sitting. It could be a boy or girl. It looks about six, but actually is nearly ten. It is feeble-minded . . . It picks its nose and occasionally fumbles vaguely with its toes or genitals, as it sits hunched in the corner. . . .

We find—and we are not surprised—that "They all know it is there, all the people of Omelas" and that "They all know that it has to be there. Some of them understand why, and some do not, but they all understand that their happiness, the beauty of their city, the tenderness of their friendships, the health of their children, the wisdom of their scholars, the skill of their makers, even the abundance of the harvest and the kindly weathers of their skies, depend wholly on this child's abominable misery." It is this place, the room in the basement where the child is kept, that makes the city even more real to us—*believable*—than it was before. The narrator asks:

> Now do you believe in them? Are they not more credible?

We may be horrified to find we aren't surprised at all. Though the specific details we were offered did make the city believable, we couldn't help but feel it was too good to be true. It is this shadow side of Omelas that makes the place more than real; it makes it *true,* even if it is a fantasy, and whether we like it or not.

It is the thousand dollar sailboat in Bambara's "The Lesson" or the "two lines of rail in the sun" in Hemingway's "Hills Like White Elephants," the "curtain made of strings of bamboo hung . . . to keep out flies" that bring both stories to life in our mind's eye. Such significant details of setting make the made-up mirage shimmer of our stories as actual as the skyscrapers in Manhattan that we *know* rise above FAO Schwarz.

SETTING AS SITUATION

A real surprise about the dimensions of setting at work in a short story might be the way setting may be the origin of tension inherent in a given situation— in effect, forcing the hand of the story. In "Hills Like White Elephants" the scene set is one of waiting and transience. "It was very hot and the express from Barcelona would come in forty minutes. It stopped at this junction for two minutes and went on to Madrid." The stark contrast of the "hills across the valley of the Ebro" that are "long and white" and the barrenness on their side of the river where "there [is] no shade and no trees and the station [is] between two lines of rails in the sun" which is offered to us in the first paragraph draws the division of the couple's predicament, whether we know it yet or not. They are stuck at a crossroads with time on their hands, and they are going to have to talk—no matter how many drinks they "try." Jig is pregnant, and her companion, the American, wants her to have an abortion: "I know you wouldn't mind it, Jig. It's really not anything. It's just to let the air in."

The place where these two characters have paused—waiting at a crossroads station for the train that will take them to Barcelona—occasions this slice of their lives, the "forty minutes" of the story that is all we'll ever know about them, and the conversation that ensues, born of the situation they find themselves set in, will put their love to the test. Jig and the American are stalled at a crossroads in their relationship as well. Soon the express will arrive to whisk them away into the rest of their lives. The setting forces us to feel the impending arrival of the train—and the pressure of the lifelong life or death decision to be made.

SETTING AS MOTIVE

When we advance to setting as motive, uniting it with the power that drives our characters, our lesser angel sheds her hummingbird flutters for the wings of an eagle, soaring higher and higher.

Where we are is who we are. For Sylvia in Bambara's "The Lesson" there is no escaping that fact: she lives in the "slums," whether or not she bows to concede the truth of her home. This certitude drives the lesson of place she learns at FAO Schwarz.

John Steinbeck's "The Chrysanthemums" (*The Long Valley*) opens with a broad cinematic shot of the Salinas Valley, and, at first, the setting seems a mere staging or perhaps an atmospheric coloring of mood:

> The high grey-flannel fog of winter closed off the Salinas Valley from the sky and from all the rest of the world. On every side it sat like a lid on the mountains and made of the great valley a closed pot. On the broad, level land floor the gang plows bit deep and left the black earth shining like metal where the shares had cut. On the foothill ranches across the Salinas River, the yellow stubble fields seemed to be bathed in pale cold sunshine, but there was no sunshine in the valley now in December. The thick willow scrub along the river flamed with sharp and positive yellow leaves.

Such description conforms exactly to what we expect of our lesser angel. She has her part to play, relegated to the "shade" as Welty says she may be. When called on to perform, it's true, she fulfills her role beautifully—we clearly picture the Salinas Valley, the "black earth shining like metal where the shares had cut" and the "yellow stubble fields [seemingly] bathed in pale cold sunshine," the "flam(ing) . . . sharp and positive yellow leaves" of the "willow scrub along the river." We acknowledge the story's boundaries, a great valley surrounded by mountains, lidded by the "high grey-flannel fog of winter" that isolates this place "from the sky and from all the rest of the world." We *feel* that remove, for sure! Certainly the setting does justice to itself as a stagelike backdrop for the characters to play out events to come, while, at the same time, invoking the atmospheric pathos of solitude, the emotional vacuum created by lifelong containment in the "closed pot" of the valley where the story takes place.

From this broad perspective, we advance closer with each succeeding paragraph. We view "Henry Allen's foothill ranch" with its orchards and cattle before our focus finally fixes on Elisa Allen, our primary character, at work behind her fence tending to her flower garden. And now the story can begin, though the setting has already set the motive in motion.

Subsequent readings of "The Chrysanthemums" reveal one possible reason for waiting to introduce Elisa until the fourth paragraph of her story: The Salinas Valley, and the careful time taken to describe it, prove vital to our understanding of Elisa's desire *to get out* of the story—to prove her strength as a woman beyond the enclosed compound of her flower garden, behind which she nurses her capabilities and bides her time, not to *escape* exactly, but surely to leave for a better place where she could fulfill her capabilities. Or so she believes. . . .

Elisa's roots grow deeper in the soil of the valley even than her precious chrysanthemums that she nurtures behind the confines of her fenced garden. She, too, is a product of that small square of fertile loam, that particular patch of "black earth."

Elisa appears strong: "She was thirty-five. Her face was lean and strong and her eyes were as clear as water. Her figure looked blocked and heavy in her gardening costume, a man's black hat pulled low down over her eyes, clod-hopper shoes, a figured print dress almost completely covered by a big corduroy apron with four big packets to hold the snips, the trowel and scratcher, the seeds, and the knife she worked with. She wore heavy leather gloves to protect her hands while she worked." "Her face was eager and mature and handsome; even her work with the scissors was overeager, overpowerful. The chrysanthemum stems seemed too small and easy for her energy." She swipes the hair in her view and "[leaves] a smudge of earth on her cheek doing it." Their home she cares for is a "hard-swept looking little house with hard-polished windows, and a clean mud-mat on the front steps."

Watching while her husband Henry makes a deal over thirty head of cattle with some men, "strangers," she "[takes] off a glove and put[s] her strong fingers down into the forest of new green chyrsanthemum sprouts that [are] growing and the old roots. She spread[s] the leaves and look[s] down among the close-growing stems. No aphids [are] there, no sowbugs or snails or cutworms. Her terrier fingers destroyed such pests before they could get started."

When Henry arrives home from striking a deal—"I sold thirty head of three-year-old steers. Got nearly my own price, too."—he marvels at her gift for growing the flowers. "You've got a gift with things," Henry says. And then he adds: "I wish you'd work out in the orchard and raise some apples that big."

At the mention of this invitation to come out from behind her fence and apply her "gift," Elisa's "eyes sharpen." "Maybe I could do it, too. I've got a gift with things, all right. My mother had it. She could stick anything in the ground and make it grow. She said it was having planters' hands that know how to do it."

"Well, it sure works with flowers," Henry replies.

Elisa seems ready to take on the world. And yet the world outside the range of mountains that surround the Salinas Valley is a big place, scary. The garden is a safe haven; it is known territory. Though she seems sure that she could "do" what Henry asks, she qualifies it, implying some doubt in herself, by saying "maybe."

The truth we are to discover about Elisa is that she is as strong as she appears to be, and as capable, we're sure, but she is native to this soil—this earth—grown and pruned to fit her place as a woman in the Salinas Valley. She is a product of her world. Her job is to keep the house (even the mud mat is "clean") and she raises giant flowers—it is worth noting here that Elisa, at thirty-five, remains childless.

When an outsider—"a big stubble-bearded man [sitting] between the cover flaps"—rattles up in his "old spring-wagon, with a round canvas top on it like the corner of a prairie schooner," the advertisement for his services hand-painted on the sheets, "Pots, pans, knives, sisors, lawn mores, Fixed," we are not worried for Elisa. We have grown as sure of her as she appears to be of herself.

And yet, after a brief conversation in which the tinker, in an obvious ploy to interest Elisa in his services—or so the reader sees, though Elisa perks up like a watered plant at his attention—shows an interest in her chrysanthemums, she ends up fawning before him. She asks the tinker if he's ever "[heard] of planting hands?" Of course, he hasn't. But Elisa is on a roll. This outsider, this man of the world, has shown an interest in *her* "wares"—the giant flowers that are the blossom of her womanly strength. On her knees in the dirt gazing intensely up at the tinker, her "breast (swells) passionately, and she spills out to him her trapped desire:

> Elisa's voice grew husky. She broke in on him, "I've never lived as you do, but I know what you mean. When the night is dark—why, the stars are sharp-pointed,

and there's quiet. Why, you rise up and up! Every pointed star gets driven into your body. It's like that. Hot and sharp and—lovely."

From such an uncharacteristically emotional display on the part of Elisa, we might not be at all surprised if she acted like the woman she appears to be and pulled the tinker to earth with her and satisfied her fantasies before legging up on the plank seat beside him to travel, as he does, "from Seattle to San Diego and back every year." But Elisa does neither. The doubt of the "maybe" we heard from her earlier lingers. What Elisa does is safely send one of her chrysanthemums with the tinker to give to "a lady down the road a piece," whom he has told her about. He drives away with the flower in a little pot she has given him to carry it in along with a whole litany of directions for the woman if she is to grow such successful chrysanthemums of her own. Elisa is left "[standing] in front of her wire fence watching the slow progress of the caravan":

> Her shoulders were straight, her head thrown back, her eyes half-closed, so that the scene came vaguely into them. Her lips moved silently, forming the words, "Good-bye—good-bye." Then she whispered, "That's a bright direction. There's a glowing there." The sound of her whisper startled her. She shook herself free and looked about to see whether anyone had been listening.

Of course, the tinker's pitch worked; he made his "sale." He needed a few pots to mend, and he quickly invented the woman "down the road" to gain Elisa's favor. He wasn't the least bit interested in Elisa or her "smelly" flowers. But Elisa has taken her "act" of sending a chrysanthemum on its way out of the valley as proof of her strength.

Immediately afterward, she takes a bath to prepare for the dinner Henry is taking her to in town to celebrate "his" deal. "In the bathroom, she tore off her soiled clothes and flung them into the corner. And then she scrubbed herself with a little block of pumice, legs and thighs, loins and chest and arms, until her skin was scratched and red. When she had dried herself she stood in front of a mirror in her bedroom and looked at her body. She tightened her stomach and threw out her chest. She turned and looked over her shoulders at her back."

In this scene, stripped of her gardening "costume" of men's clothing, the hat and heavy gloves, Elisa seems to positively glow with pride in herself as a woman; she *throws* out her chest and *looks* at herself, it would seem, admiringly. She dresses in her "newest undergarments and her nicest stockings and the dress which was the symbol of her prettiness." She blooms as beautiful as one of her own grand chrysanthemums.

But when Henry arrives home and "[stops] short and [looks] at her," exclaiming: "Why—why, Elisa. You look so nice!" a strange exchange ensues:

> "Nice? You think I look nice? What do you mean by 'nice'?"
> Henry blundered on. "I don't know. I mean you look different, strong and happy."
> "I am strong? Yes, strong. What do you mean by strong?"
> He looked bewildered. "You're playing some kind of game," he said helplessly. "It's a kind of play. You look strong enough to break a calf over your knee, happy enough to eat it like a watermelon."
> For a second she lost her rigidity. "Henry! Don't talk like that. You didn't know what you said." She grew complete again. "I'm strong," she boasted, "I never knew before how strong."

Strong enough to break a calf over your knee, happy enough to eat it like a watermelon? Not exactly the sort of comment that would send most of us tittering. And yet, for Elisa this compliment of her strength confirms for her the truth of the attribute she has most hoped for in herself—the power she'd like to believe she's exerted in sending a potted flower rooted from the soil of her garden out into the world. If her chrysanthemum can survive on its own, prove itself outside of the wired-in garden, beyond the valley, then maybe Elisa could too.

On her way to dinner in town with Henry she immediately recognizes the speck on the road. Elisa *knows* before the car can even draw close enough for her to see that it is her flower, which the tinker has dumped out while he was rattling along "to keep the pot." "He had to keep the pot," she says. "That's why he couldn't get them off the road."

Elisa discovers she is more than merely disappointed in the fate of her flower. As the "roadster turn[s] a bend. . . . she [sees] the caravan ahead. She [swings] full around toward her husband so she [can] not see the little covered wagon and the mismatched team as the car pass[es] them." She does not look back.

Elisa is reduced to asking Henry if they can "have wine at dinner." To which Henry replies, "Sure we could. Say! That will be fine." Elisa then appears to rally, to gain back a bit of the grit she has shown: she asks about the prize fights in town to which Henry earlier jokingly offered to take her. "[D]o the men hurt each other very much? . . . I've read they break noses, and blood runs down their chests. I've read how the fighting gloves get heavy and soggy with blood." Henry goes shocked. He looks at her. "What's the matter, Elisa?" he asks. He's already noted that she's "changed" again. He offers to take her to the fights if she wants to go.

But Elisa doesn't want to go. She "relax[es] limply in her seat. 'Oh, no. No. I don't want go,'" she says. "'I'm sure I don't.' Her face (is turned) away from him. 'It will be enough if we can have wine. It will be plenty.' She [turns] up her coat collar so he [can't] see that she [is] crying weakly—like an old woman." Elisa is devastated. No longer can she blame her place on anyone but herself. It's true; the Salinas Valley is a man's world: Elisa lives on "Henry Allen's foothill ranch." A man in the world of this story may wander around at will beyond the boundaries of the mountains "following the nice weather," as the tinker does, though he tells Elisa, "It ain't the right kind of life for a woman" when she "wishes . . . women could do such things." The men do not observe the limitations by which Elisa lives her life.

Elisa, in her garden outfit appears manlike, but it is as a woman that she takes her pride, lives to show her strength, her *gifts*. In sending her chrysanthemums with the tinker she has glimpsed the "brightening" of possibility for herself. Proud of what she's done in sending her flower out into the world—having sent this part of herself beyond the bounds she herself has known, perhaps all her life (no clue hints at a knowledge of the outside)— seemingly confident, she is in this momentously quiet scene where she recognizes what the tinker has done all but destroyed. Her resolve, her root-deep idea of herself and her capabilities, her dream, has been rooted out, yanked up, only to be revealed as a fantasy of escape, her belief in her strength all been dashed. And by what? A vagabond tinker casting away one flower? No, Elisa has been laid as bare as "the black earth [left] shining like metal where the shares [have] cut."

Elisa can no longer kid herself. She has, for the first time, clearly seen and admitted to herself who she is, a woman of thirty-five who has been irrevocably shaped by her place—she cannot escape that station, no matter how strong she tells herself she is. The seed of doubt planted inside her has long since matured and borne its poisonous fruit; this "maybe I could do it to" doubt is the reason she must so insist on her strength. At end, she may seek revenge on men, perhaps want to see them bloodied and punished by watching them bash and beat each other senseless, but, for her, that's just another excuse—at end, the limits she observes aren't about men and she knows it. She could've climbed up onto the seat of that wagon. She *could* leave! The fence is not a cage; though she is certainly caged behind it.

Elisa surely has the desire to escape herself, the motive, but not the will. It simply isn't *in* her. Doubly sad because it is not her fault, Elisa must remain—she realizes—behind the safety of her fence, tending to her flowers, on her husband's farm—both motivated and damned by her place, which, as it turns out, is less the pot of the Salinas Valley than it is the lid she keeps on her own heart's desire.

SETTING AS METAPHOR

Back at the train station in Hemingway's "Hills Like White Elephants" (*Men Without Women*)—so long as we have them waiting around for forty minutes we may as well put them to work for us!—the "girl [Jig] stands up and [walks] to the end of the station."

> Across, on the other side, were fields of grain and trees along the bank of the Ebro. Far away, beyond the river, were mountains. The shadow of a cloud moved across the field of grain and she saw the river through the trees.
>
> "And we could have all this," she said. "And we could have everything and every day we make it more impossible."
>
> "What did you say?"
>
> "I said we could have everything."
>
> "We can have everything."
>
> "No, we can't."
>
> "We can have the whole world."
>
> "No, we can't."
>
> "We can go anywhere."
>
> "No, we can't. It isn't ours any more."
>
> "It's ours."
>
> "No, it isn't. And once they take it away, you never get it back."
>
> "But they haven't taken it away."
>
> "We'll wait and see."

This exchange between Jig and her companion, the American, unveils the metaphorical nature of setting. By metaphor, I simply mean the interpretation of figurative meaning that lies beyond the literal representation. (We'll discuss the complexities of this element, including simile and symbol, in detail in the next section.) Literally, in "Hills Like White Elephants," the hills are, just that, hills; the river flows as water between banks; the shadow that blots the field of grain is a cloud. We have our scene, our *setting*. Jig, however, obviously sees in the hills, river, and field shadowed over by a cloud something that the man doesn't; by what she says she draws our attention to and focuses it on the figurative relevance of what she sees in these things, what they *are* for her. She looks "across, on the other side" and recognizes in these physical things something else, something more.

In them, Jig recognizes a view of what *could* be—she glimpses the fertility of the field of grain clouded over (perhaps by this dark, floating question of whether she should have an abortion, the shadow that is passing over their relationship), the life of the flowing river, the purpose in its current, the dream of possibility held by white-distant mountains. She may see in her view an Elysium vision of completeness, all the possibilities for their life together—as man and wife?, father and mother?—a place for them that would be a paradise of their love. Jig can see their love growing, can imagine a life for the two of them that jumps off the tracks of the existence they simply share as companions now. She is tired of the traveling to see new places and try new drinks: "And we could have all this . . . And we could have everything and every day we make it more impossible."

Literally, of course, they cannot have the valley. They can't buy the river; they can't take the mountains with them in one of their world-tour-stickered and tagged suitcases. The conversation that they hold throughout the story clearly draws a line, contrasting the literal and figurative. Jig, in a previous scene, has imagined the mountains as "white elephants" to which the American replies, "I've never seen one." Jig tries to back off, invoking the simile: "They don't really look *like* white elephants. I just meant the coloring of *their* skin through the trees" (emphasis mine). Her clarification of what she *really* means is ambiguous: In the second sentence is she referring only to the elephants, is it their skin, or has she doubled back, contradicting her denial by reemphasizing the fact that the hills *are* white elephants—the pronoun "their" personifying the hills?

We need not come up with one answer. The doubling of possible meanings or interpretations is what's important. Jig realizes their prospects in the view across the Ebro stretched out before them, but the man remains glued to the actuality of his chair, sipping his beer, focused on the fact of Jig's pregnancy and what to *do* about it. "But I don't want anybody but you," he says and, "It's really an awfully simple operation, Jig . . . It's not really an operation at all . . . I know you wouldn't mind it, Jig. It's really not anything. It's just to let the air in." As the story progresses, the setting takes on the mass of metaphorical implication. The stake between the characters is made rather obvious to us by the stress placed on their separate places in which they find themselves, though they inhabit the same location. The girl sees fertility, prospects for their love; the man has "never seen" a white elephant, and he will not try to imagine one. He refuses to see anything in his surroundings other than the tracks that will take him to a destination where he can solve his "worry."

Hemingway often spoke of what he called the "iceberg principle" of writing. He wrote, he said, so that most of the story lay under water with only the top ten percent left exposed on the surface. His idea was that the story took on the mass from what was left *unsaid*. The ten percent of the setting shown in "Hills Like White Elephants" assumes the portentous size of the ice we feel hunkering just below the surface when we read the story, whether we are immediately alert to the metaphorical implications of the setting at work on us or not—the bulk of the story that we must, like Jig, imagine for ourselves.

Obviously we could recount favorite stories that are not as reliant on the intricacies of setting as the short stories I've illustrated here as examples of place—backdrop, atmosphere, believability, motive, situation, and metaphor. It's so obvious that—beyond noting the possibility—I am not going to pursue that avenue further. Not employing setting in a short story is not the point of this section. The point of this section on setting is that though the physical setting of a short story may well be, as Welty says, a "lesser angel," it can still play a vital role in a short story, not merely remain static as a stage upon which the other elements, like plot, do their thing. In fact, without setting's flurried "wing-beating," a story might never make it off the ground, much less soar beyond the place we believe it to be.

Time

To begin our talk about fictional time, I'd like to touch back to the quotation from Eudora Welty I first cited to start us thinking about the idea of epiphany in a short story.

> In going in the direction of meaning, time has to move through a mind. What it will bring about is an awakening there. Through whatever motions it goes through, it will call forth, in a mind or heart, some crucial recognition.

Fictional time is not real time. Fictional time, like the constructs of character or setting in fiction, is *illusory*. Fictional time strives to give the reader the impression or felt-meaning of time, but the truth of time—which is however long it takes us to sit down and read the particular short story, perhaps thirty minutes to an hour—has little to do with the months that are added up and totaled in a fifteen-page story like Chekhov's "The Lady with the Pet Dog." (In fiction, O'Connor says, two plus two always equals more than four.)

How, then, is time told in fiction?

SCENE

In going in the direction of meaning, time has to move through a mind. . . .

It has occurred to me that in this passage Welty is making a reference to scenes when she says "time has to move through a mind." Fictional time can be enacted by the dramatization of events that clock together as experience in a short story.

In Flannery O'Connor's short story "Everything That Rises Must Converge" (*Everything That Rises Must Converge*), we "stand before the hall mirror" with Julian and his mother as she prepares to go to her "reducing class." She tries on her new hat—"a hideous hat" with "a purple velvet flap [that] came down on one side of it and stood up on the other; the rest of it was green and looked like a cushion with the stuffing out"—while Julian stands behind her, with "his hands behind him, appear[ing] pinned to the door frame, waiting like Saint Sebastian for the arrows to begin piercing him."

"Maybe I shouldn't have paid that for it," his mother says, "No, I shouldn't have. I'll take it off and return it tomorrow. I shouldn't have bought it."

Julian "raise[s] his eyes to heaven. 'Yes, you should have bought it.' He [says]. 'Put it on and let's go.'"

O'Connor slants the story into motion by creating a scene. The dramatization of this event establishes the immediate felt-time of the story (even if events are related in past tense). Such a showing—as we have discussed throughout this book—allows the reader a character's perception of events—and consequently of the passage of time—as they prepare to leave the house for Julian's mother's reducing class. The scene, related from Julian's third person subjective point of view, privileges us to what he feels and thinks—it is Julian who uses the word "hideous" to describe his mother's new hat. The result: we are able to *experience* their interaction for ourselves. Time moves forward in as natural a way as possible. In scene time is, perhaps, as true as it can ever become for us. We are there, going through the motions with the characters. In this manner, scene functions as the primary offering of experience. Scene, as a direct showing of time, is the concrete foundation upon which the straw-bricks of fictional time are laid.

SUMMARY

The scene above sets "Everything That Rises Must Converge" into motion, but the story begins with summary:

> Her doctor had told Julian's mother that she must lose twenty pounds on account of her blood pressure, so on Wednesday nights Julian had to take her downtown

on the bus for a reducing class at the Y. The reducing class was designed for work-ing girls over fifty, who weighed from 165 to 200 pounds. His mother was one of the slimmer ones, but she said ladies did not tell their age or weight. She would not ride the buses by herself at night since they had been integrated, and because the reducing class was one of her few pleasures, necessary for her health, and *free,* she said Julian could at least put himself out to take her, considering all she did for him. Julian did not like to consider all she did for him, but every Wednes-day night he braced himself and took her.

Summary buys us the fictional time to be brought up to speed in the story. In this particular instance, it provides the reader with a block of necessary information, a sort of *survey* of significant times, that influences the scene we are about to experience for ourselves. This brief of the past exists outside of their present trip to the Y. Summary puts fictional time in perspective— creates a context for events—and can leap years, weeks, an hour, summers, or a day, in a single paragraph; or, as it is engaged here, can be a beginning and offer us a panoramic (though pertinent) view of the history of and between the characters.

FLASHBACK

Flashback reveals another useful manipulation of fictional time the writer may adopt, in which we telescope from one scene into another scene or pos-sibly into a summary of an event or events usually in the past, though it is easy enough to imagine a flash*forward* as well.

As Julian and his mother walk through their dilapidated neighborhood— the "houses . . . bulbous liver-colored monstrosities of a uniform ugliness though . . . this had been a fashionable neighborhood forty years ago . . ."— on their way to the bus stop, his mother recalls her girlhood and the place their family once occupied, a far cry from the position they find themselves in now:

"I remember going to Grandpa's when I was a little girl. Then the house had dou-ble stairways that went up to what was really the second floor—all the cooking was done on the first. I used to like to stay down in the kitchen on account of the way the walls smelled. I would sit with my nose pressed against the plaster and take deep breaths. Actually the place belonged to the Godhighs but your grand-father Chestney paid the mortgage and saved it for them. They were in reduced circumstances," she said, "but reduced or not, they never forgot who they were."
"Doubtless that decayed mansion reminded them," Julian muttered.

And then Julian flashes back, effortlessly bridging across the transition, "He never spoke of it without contempt or thought of it without longing."

He had seen it once when he was a child before it had been sold. The double stair-ways had rotted and had been torn down. Negroes were living in it. But it remained in his mind as his mother had known it. It appeared in his dreams reg-ularly. He would stand on the wide porch, listening to the rustle of oak leaves, then wander through the high-ceilinged hall into the parlor that opened onto it and gaze at the worn rugs and faded draperies.

Flashbacks are a good and useful technique, necessary even, and—as we've seen here—introduced with mastery can be used fluidly, the reader hardly noticing that he or she is being carried back through time, to layer the motivation of characters. The trouble I've found is that beginning writers will sometimes crutch along through stories leaning too heavily on flash-back as a way to tag in motivation without, perhaps, having sought first to show motivation to the reader in a scene.

Make no mistake about it, finding the right scene to dramatize desire is hard work. Earned flashbacks—flashbacks like this one in "Everything that Rises Must Converge" that *work* (that word again!)—do not inadvertently stall out the tension invoked by direct interaction of characters. Not only that. Flashbacks by their nature call attention to themselves as a device and so threaten to pop the bubble of believability a true fiction strives so to create.

A smooth transition leading into a flashback is a must for the serious writer. A working transition paves the way from the present moment of the story into the past. A door-jangling transition that announces its entrance into the story might begin *Julian remembered that house.* The sentence cer-tainly gets us from the current conversation about the mansion to Julian's recollection of it—the sentence is adequate, but it doesn't very well slip us into the remembrance. O'Connor, simply by invoking the contradiction in the remembrance and thereby creating in it a tension, earns *profluence:* "He never spoke of it without contempt or thought of it without longing." The transition in this case doesn't merely serve as a joiner, but actively weds two conflicting thoughts or desires, smoothing them together *seamlessly,* a workshop word, into the movement of the story as a whole. The motive is in effect spurred forward and this transports us "effortlessly" and "fluidly," through time.

SLOW MOTION

Slow motion is the technique in the handling of fictional time that enables the writer to practically freeze-frame an important moment in a story so that the reader may absorb the significance of every nuance of what happens. In "Everything That Rises Must Converge" we slow for the significant moment of impact after Julian's mother has bestowed a shiny penny upon the little black boy. The boy's mother, who has been sitting on the bus smoldering like an active volcano at this condescension, finally erupts:

> The huge woman turned and for a moment stood, her shoulders lifted and her face frozen with frustrated rage, and stared at Julian's mother. Then all at once she seemed to explode like a piece of machinery that had been given one ounce of pressure too much. Julian saw the black fist swing out with the red pocketbook. He shut his eyes and cringed as he heard the woman shout, "He don't take nobody's pennies!" When he opened his eyes, the woman was disappearing down the street with the little boy staring wide-eyed over his shoulder. Julian's mother was on the sidewalk.

Now, we know that the *explosion* must have happened in the blink of an eye—a purse swung by an enraged big woman moves *fast*. But it is a critical moment—the cumulative, climax of events, the "crucial action or gesture" of the story that O'Connor writes about in her understanding of "what makes a story work"—and slow motion closely focuses our attention so we don't blink and miss the uncoiling of significance. The art of it is that in the machinery's flying apart we hardly notice that time has slowed at all; rather, we feel we have expanded into the moment.

Writing slow motion seems to come naturally enough to most writers. Slow motion concentrates closely on frames of events. The trick is not to slow things down heedlessly. The moment, or event, must warrant the lag, otherwise—as with flashback—it will run up a yellow flag, cautioning the reader as to the use of a means; unless, of course, the pricking of the reader's consciousness is exactly the purpose—as it is in Tobias's Wolff's story "Bullet in the Brain," which places us under the "mediation of brain time" after Anders is "shot in the head," affording us the "leisure to contemplate the scene that, in a phrase [Anders] would have abhorred, 'passed before his eyes.'"

Writing Exercises

1. Try John Gardner's exercise in pertinent description: "Describe a barn as seen by a man whose son has just been killed in a war. Do not mention the son, or war, or death. Do not mention the man who does the seeing. (The exercise should run to about one typed page.)"

2. To explore the metaphorical nature of setting take an old hat idea, such as that of a family tree or the river of life and make new the intended

metaphorical understanding through a description of a particular setting. Do not explain away the power of the meaning. *Show* us!

3. Describe the setting of a story you're writing that reveals its emotional landscape.

4. Look at a painting such as Van Gogh's "A Night in Arles" or one of the photographs from a work like James Agee's and Walker Evans's *Let Us Now Praise Famous Men,* and strive to capture in writing the atmosphere of the scene.

5. Believability in fiction is in the details. Set a specific place, for a particular character in a given situation—an operating room or a hardware store, a dress shop or toy store like FAO Schwarz—using as much concrete and specific detail as practicable without calling undue attention to the act of the description. (Unless, of course, such undue attention is exactly the point: a sports-crazed thirteen-year-old boy whose father has promised to buy him one item for his birthday walking into a sports store like MVP Sports might go into foaming conniptions detailing the cornucopia of choice in basketballs alone.)

6. Create a setting that acts as the situation for a story, as Hemingway does in "Hills Like White Elephants."

7. Give the lesser angel of place wings as a story's motive: A young woman with magazine-cover good looks is working as a hair dresser in a beauty shop in the small town of Salt Rock, West Virginia. . . .

8. Practice the separate techniques of the workings of fictional time by performing specific exercises that highlight each stratum: (a.) write a short, showing scene that shifts a story into gear; (b.) create a summary that covers a large block of time, such as a childhood worth of summers spent at a camp in the Adirondacks; (c.) flashback (perhaps working a transition from the direct scene above), consider well the transition that lands us wherever we end up!; (d.) slow the motion of a meaningful moment.

9. More full-length short stories have been born out of the following exercise than any other I've asked my students to do. Perhaps it works so well because giving fluidity to these four aspects of fictional time illustrates the natural ebb and flow between the experience of scenes and other ways of controlling the tempo of a short story. Write a short unified piece, like the example I tailored of Flannery O'Connor's short story "Everything That Rises Must Converge," which begins with a summary and then shifts into the forward motion of a direct scene, makes a seamless transition that carries us into a pertinent flashback, and ends in slow motion.

"THE CONNECTEDNESS OF ALL LIVING THINGS": METAPHOR

I find it interesting to note that in *The Poetics* Aristotle ranks "facility with metaphor" as "by far the most important point . . . in the use of each of the mentioned types . . . including compound and foreign terms." *Facility with metaphor:* "This alone," he writes, "is a sign of natural ability, and something one can never learn from another: for the successful use of metaphor entails the perception of similarities."

Perhaps it's true that writers think in "the perception of similarities" in much the same way that I imagine a physicist's brain, as a sort of given, working like a compass, a slide-rule, a scale, or a plumb, that is more disposed to weigh, vector, gauge, measure, and compare the properties of energy and matter in the natural world. This is more than a way of seeing; it is a way of *being.* Such a bent may well be predetermined; we call such propensities *abilities,* or *talents.* But most would-be writers I've known come equipped with a sort of double-vision, which is the recognition of a parallelism; it is what, in large part, has made them want to become writers in the first place. Assuming this desire as a given, any would-be writer will benefit greatly from a better understanding of metaphor and how to put such perceptions to work in imagining the similarities in a short story.

The Writer's Muscle

I have always thought of metaphor *metaphorically* as the short story writer's muscle, the bulking up of strength we can gain in our prose by making, as Flannery O'Connor has said, "the concrete work double time."

Whether or not we've fully recognized the hills across the Ebro that Jig says "don't really look like white elephants. I just meant the coloring of their skin through the trees," or the lid of fog that pots Elisa in the Salinas Valley in "Chrysanthemums," shutting her off "from the sky and from all the rest of the world," or the wind that whispers like the very voice of God around Luke Ripley as he feels for the pulse of the boy his daughter has hit with the car in "A Father's Story," it is metaphor—or to give the term a complete consideration—the entire scope of figurative language, including simile and symbol—which may help fill out a short story's hints of possibility earned by its showing. As we discovered in our reading of setting as metaphor in Hemingway's "Hills Like White Elephants," such showing sounds a radar alert to possible figurative meanings massed below the surface of the story.

Figurative Language

I have invoked the overarching term *metaphor* to head this section but, strictly speaking, there are three variations on figurative language: *simile, metaphor,* and *symbol.*

SIMILE

A simile conjures a likeness between two apparently dissimilar things and is announced by *like* or *as.*

In William Faulkner's "A Rose for Emily" (*Collected Stories*) the following description of Miss Emily is not a simile; it strictly relates an observation:

> [S]he entered—a small, fat woman in black, with a thin gold chain descending to her waist and vanishing into her belt, leaning on an ebony cane with a tarnished gold head. Her skeleton was small and spare; perhaps that was why what would have merely plumpness in another was obesity in her.

So far, the narrator has simply observed for us as accurately and in as much significant detail as is warranted by first impression a picture of Miss Emily's literal condition. She is simply "a small, fat woman in black." We note the facts of the gold chain she wears and the ebony cane, upon which she *leans.* The gold head of the cane is *tarnished.* From this significant detail, we might surmise she uses the cane a lot and has been using it for some time, and that, given her condition, she leans upon it *heavily.* In the two lines that follow, however, simile is put to good use in lending a more pronounced and unpalatable emphasis to Miss Emily's "obesity."

> She looked bloated, *like* a body long submerged in motionless water, and of that pallid hue. Her eyes, lost in the fatty ridges of her face, looked *like* two small pieces of coal pressed into a lump of dough as they moved from one face to another while the visitors state their errand [italics mine].

Wow! we say. "Gross!" The simile—the striking likeness the narrator has drawn between a live body and a long-drown one, between skin and dough, eyes and lumps of coal—goes beyond mere factual description. The comparison fleshes out our understanding of Miss Emily's fatness. Miss Emily isn't cutely chubby; she's "bloated," and the image of a body, waterlogged and drained of color, flashes uncomfortably to mind.

In Cynthia Ozick's "The Shawl" (*The Shawl*), "Rosa [does] not feel hunger" on the forced march to a Nazi concentration camp: "she [feels] light, *not like* someone walking but *like* someone in a faint, in a trance, arrested in a fit, someone who is already a floating angel, alert and seeing everything, but in the air, not there, not touching the road" (italics mine). The likeness of simile here elevates the felt-truth of the narration from what Rosa is actually doing, "walking" to the after death state of a "floating angel," which is "not like someone walking." The simile makes us feel the truth of the subconscious beyond our literal consciousness that Rosa is starving.

When simile is done well, it strikes a chord of truth—the comparison drawn by *like* or *as* adds, enlightens, or resonates, a believable connection. But when a simile is off, ugh! *Gong!* The discordance struck by a false simile may leave us shaking our heads or busting out a guffaw—and we're not laughing with the writer.

"Winners of the 'worst analogies ever written in a high school essay' contest" hung posted above the copier of the Expository Writing Program at Harvard. A few doozies:

> Her hair glistened in the rain like nose hair after a sneeze. (Chuck Smith, Woodbridge)

> John and Mary had never met. They were like two hummingbirds who had also never met. (Russell Beland, Springfield)

> McBride fell 12 stories, hitting the pavement like a Hefty Bag filled with vegetable soup. (Paul Sabourin, Silver Spring)

Similes by their very nature of the risk they take in going beyond concrete description in comparing something actual in a short story to something outside the story draw attention to themselves, and so they must be true. A true simile has the power to awaken us to a deeper connection and to round out a flat description. But a false simile obscures and unnecessarily complicates the very description it is trying to enhance.

METAPHOR

Robert Boswell's long short story "The Darkness of Love" (*Dancing in the Movies*) is most importantly about Handle, a black New York City police officer, who fears that he has become a racist because he has begun to scrutinize black men more than whites. In an attempt to come to terms with the turmoil he feels, Handle takes time off from his job and retreats to the rural home of his wife's, Marilyn's, parents in Tennessee. Once there, though, Handle realizes a deeper dissatisfaction: he's in love with his wife's younger sister, Louise. In the beginning of the story, Handle recounts a tale told by his wife's family that, he says, "before he'd met his in-laws [Marvin and Annalee] . . . shaped his opinion" of them:

> Their old dog, Hoot, had gone blind. Marvin speculated it stemmed from eating inky cap mushrooms, but Annalee insisted age had blinded the yellow dog. Too old to adjust, Hoot would become confused in the big yard, howling until someone came after him. He began shitting in the living room and lifting his leg on the furniture. Marvin couldn't bear the thought of putting Hoot to sleep. He'd found the dog as a pup, cradled in the boughs of the purple magnolia that marked the northeast corner of their property. Who put the dog there and why, they never discovered, but Marvin attached significance to finding a puppy in a tree. Annalee finally solved the problem. She made a trail with bacon grease from the front porch to the old barn where he liked to pee, to the thick grass near the purple magnolia where he liked to shit, and back to the porch. The old dog ran this circle the last two months of his life. When he finally died, Marvin insisted they bury him under the purple magnolia. Annalee dug the hole and buried the dog. The tree promptly died, leaving Marvin to speculate on the connectedness of all living things. Annalee argued that she may have severed the taproot while digging the grave, but Marvin ignored her.

On a literal level, the family tale that Handle recounts characterizes Marvin and Annalee for us as well as it did for Handle. We get to see for ourselves their love and kindness for Hoot in the way Annalee devises a trail of bacon grease "from the front porch where he liked to pee, to the thick grass near the purple magnolia where he liked to shit, and back to the porch"; we can't help but grin at the oddness of Marvin's "finding a dog in a tree." The "significance" that Marvin attaches to this aspect of their family tale, the very fact that they all make so much of it—in the recounting of it, Marvin, Annalee, Marilyn, and Louise each have their scripted family part to play, telling and retelling the story of Hoot every time they gather together, a sort of touchstone for who they are—is crucial to our understanding of them as individuals as well as to the workings of their relationships with one another and to our sympathy to their interdependence as a family. It is Marvin who recognizes for us the figurative importance of the story beyond the fact of its telling. After he buries the dog under the magnolia tree in whose boughs he discovered him, the tree in turn dies. This cause and effect leads Marvin to "speculate on the connectedness of all living things," waving away Annalee's literal explanation that she must have severed the taproot when she was digging Hoot's grave.

The tale serves as a *metaphor.*

The story of Hoot is an event in their lives, and their recounting of it around the supper table, for instance, waiting for Louise to speak her part in the story after she and Handle have secretly made love—of course, she can't, she won't, Louise sits mute, her very silence speaking of her failing in her family part—works as a dramatic scene in the story, but our figurative understanding of what the tale means transcends its happening. "The connectedness of all living things" that Marvin gives serious consideration is a story that represents the interdependence of all life, not just of the dog Hoot and this magnolia tree, but each of us to each other, and to other living things as well. Members of a family depend on each other in this way; it is their very "connectedness" that makes them a family, and when a family members is lost—or family members lost, as Handle and Louise lose themselves here at end to *the darkness of love*—the tap root may be cut, and the family withers. We recognize the felt-sameness. The metaphor acts out a larger truth—a rock-in-a-pond-like impact splash that ripples out to touch all of us.

The basic difference between a metaphor and a simile is that the metaphor *is* the thing it is being compared to rather than simply being *like* it.

SYMBOL

Symbol differs from simile and metaphor in that a symbol is an object or sign that assumes its own meaning. A cross is a symbol that bears the weight of its own significance regardless of the dramatic action of the story. Symbols can also be created inside a story. Consider the white doll that Marilyn's grandmother gave her in "The Darkness of Love." The characters in the story are black, and Marilyn has had a dream in which white dolls with blue eyes rain from the sky. Handle thinks it a "beautiful nightmare." But Louise sees the symbol: "We all have white dolls in us, whether we like it or not." Whites have influenced the characters. The doll becomes the symbol of that influence.

A Word of Advice About the "Fancy Stuff"

In his essay "The Writer's Workshop," included in *On Writing Short Stories,* Frank Conroy says that the greatest "failure" he finds in the writers he teaches at the renowned University of Iowa Writer's Workshop is that they try to "write over their heads." "Most writers," he says,

> began writing as an extension of their love of reading. They were excited by books even as children, perceiving a kind of magic going on in narrative which they were eventually drawn to emulate. As they grew older they simply plunged into literature and became used to reading over their heads. They *eagerly* read over their heads. When, as adults, they try to write they are often as much preoccupied with magic—effect, simile, metaphors, mood, etc.—the fancy stuff—as

with meaning. They are intoxicated with the seemingly endless power of language, an intoxication that can be dangerous. For while it is true that reading over one's head is good, writing over one's head is very bad indeed. An almost certain guarantee of failure, in fact.

Of course, it is this *magic,* the *fancy stuff,* that attracts many of us to writing in the first place. We get a charge out of unearthing symbols or unfolding the hidden agenda betokened by metaphorical connections in a short story or novel—this is the *real* stuff, we think, Literature!—and we, too, want to pack our short stories with the impact realization of such hidden discoveries.

Metaphors (similes and symbols) are the most natural things in the world! We don't need a professor of literature to help us feel them, nor as writers do we need to overburden a scene with the weight of symbolism merely for the sake of symbolism. The best metaphors are born naturally out of a story. When Hemingway's Jig looks off across the Ebro, given who she is, given where she finds herself with the American at this crossroads of their relationship, both physically and spiritually, because of their very situation, she can't help but yearn for the lushness of promise she sees before her. Jig is this close and that far away from realizing her "dream": "And we could have all this. . . ." The metaphor of fertility is captured by her state of mind. We feel the conflict between her view, the very real possibility for their love in the fleshing out of the hills, and what the man, in all his "reasonableness," his practiced practicality, *sees* for "real."

In "Writing Short Stories," Flannery O'Connor discusses how "in good fiction, certain of the details will tend to accumulate meaning from the action of the story itself, and when this happens they become symbolic in the way they work." She tells the story of how she wrote a now-often-taught short story called "Good Country People" (*A Good Man Is Hard to Find and Other Stories*), "in which a lady Ph.D. has her wooden leg stolen by a Bible salesman who she has tried to seduce." Though stated so starkly, O'Connor acknowledges the story may seem nothing more than "a low joke," this story "does manage to operate at another level of experience, by letting the wooden leg accumulate meaning," so that " . . . finally, by the time the Bible salesman comes along, the leg has accumulated so much meaning that it is, as the saying goes, loaded. And when the Bible salesman steals it, the reader realizes that he has taken away part of the girl's personality and has revealed her deeper affliction to her for the first time."

Though O'Connor concedes the "accumulation of meaning" that the wooden leg amasses in her short story, she is careful to caution us about proclaiming the wooden leg a *symbol.* Her reservations are good for beginning writers to hear:

If you want to say that the wooden leg is a symbol, you can say that. But it is a wooden leg first, and as a wooden leg it is absolutely necessary to the story. It has its place on the literal level of the story, but it operates in depth as well as on the surface. It increases the story in every direction, and this is essentially the way a story escapes being short.

Now, there is, obviously, some question as to how all this comes about. O'Connor readily admits that she didn't sit down thinking "I am now going to write a story about a Ph.D. with a wooden leg, using the wooden leg as a symbol for another kind of affliction." She "doubts . . . if many writers know what they are going to do when they start out." O'Connor tells us that "one morning [she found herself] writing a description of two women that [she] knew something about, and before [she] realized it, [she] had equipped one of them with a wooden leg." Then the Bible salesman appeared! O'Connor says she "didn't know he was going to steal that wooden leg until ten or twelve lines before he did it, but when I found out that was what was going to happen, I realized that it was inevitable." She writes: "This is a story that produces a shock for the reader, and I think one reason for this is that it produced a shock for the writer." O'Connor cites Jacques Maritain, French philosopher and critic, in terming such a seeming miracle of process "the habit of art," an idea we will return to and continue to explore in Part Three, Notes on the Fiction-writing Process.

For now, let me leave you with a bit of avuncular advice about employing metaphors (simile, symbol, and figurative language) in your short stories: First do the hard, honest work of capturing character; invest that character with motive and place your character in a setting that reflects or informs his or her situation; then, as the story begins to take shape, seek to sound its depths—all the prospects suggested at by the churning mesh of its other elements at work—by capitalizing on the metaphorical possibilities which have presented themselves naturally in the course of telling the story. Make a habit of this and the *fancy stuff* will take care of itself!

Writing Exercises

1. The power of successful simile relies on making believable comparisons fresh by offering your reader a true, unexpected, though not shocking, understanding of two dissimilar things being compared. To begin this exercise, recount a worn simile, a clichéd likeness such as—Old Billy was sharp as a tack! Or, perhaps, Old Billy was dumb as a doornail! Your job: *Make It New Again.* Create an original, true simile that preserves the intended meaning of the cliché you've recalled.

2. In a paragraph or so, attempt an extended metaphor. Begin with a notion such as *the river of life* or a *family tree.*

3. Locate a metaphor that you have unveiled in a recent story you have read and unveil it the way I tried to do in the family story of Hoot in Robert Boswell's "The Darkness of Love." In two or three pages draw every imaginable connection the metaphor makes to inform the story as a whole.

4. Locate a possible symbol in a short story you've read or in a short story that you've written. In two or three pages make the most of its symbolic significance.

5. Employ an outside symbol in a scene (such as a cross).

6. Create a symbol that is brought to life by the scene in which it takes place (such as Marilyn's white, blue-eyed dolls in "The Darkness of Love").

THE WRITER'S SIGNATURE: VOICE

It is akin to style, what I'm talking about, but it isn't style alone. It is the writer's particular and unmistakable signature on everything he writes. It is his world and no other. This is one of the things that distinguishes one writer from another. Not talent. There's plenty of that around. But a writer who has some special way of looking at things and who gives artistic expression to that way of looking: that writer may be around for a time.

—*Raymond Carver, "On Writing" (Fires)*

Voice

To begin our in-class discussion on a writer's voice in my course "The Craft of Stories," I have my students try their hand at a second writing exercise offered to me by Maxine Rodburg. In this exercise, students write a *pastiche*—"a time-honored literary tradition, a high compliment—one writer writing in living imitation of another." I ask them to choose two writers from the syllabus whose work we've read. Then I have them rewrite a scene from a story by Writer A written in the voice of Writer B. Then they compose the reverse: a scene from Writer B written in the voice of Writer A.

The exercise is much tougher than it may seem at first—as well as a whole lot more fun! To make the assignment work, we not only have to think carefully about the fundamentals of a writer's style which we read at work on the page—the "particular and unmistakable" way he or she chooses language to create sentences to build the blocks of paragraphs that he or she uses to shape his or her short stories—we must also consider the writer's vision, his or her unique view of the world, "that special way of looking at things" for which he or she has found "artistic expression." "It is his [or her] world," as Carver says, "and no other."

Voice, we discover in our struggle to successfully complete a pastiche, is "akin to style . . . , but it isn't style alone." Voice includes style, but is more than style, beyond style. Voice accounts for the sum of all the writer becomes on the page, and, though chances are that a writer's voice will be recognizable in most of his or her short stories, a complete comprehension of any writer's voice is not ultimately determined by any single story, but in the totaling, or as is the case with contemporary writers, a subtotaling of their work. Style lends expression to voice, but voice has to do with things outside of strict stylistic concerns such as the sorts of characters a writer writes about and the particular places in which his or her stories are likely to be set, etc. Voice suggests the concerns and themes that most preoccupy a writer, and brands our perception and expectation of any writer's work as evidently different as John Steinbeck's stories are from Cynthia Ozick's, or David Foster Wallace's prose is from Jamaica Kincaid's, or the concerns and characters of Dagoberto Gilb are from those of Susan Minot, or the Catholic writer Andre Dubus's treatment of his faith is from the Catholic writer Flannery O'Connor's, makes Jim Harrison's world seem another planet from Virginia Wolff's.

Such an accounting of differences makes individual writers stand separate—as round and as real as the characters about which they write. Such notable differences in voice also allow room on the field for other writers besides Shakespeare, who most writers are readily willing to concede is the greatest writer of us all. Voice allows for the breadth of vision shown by William Faulkner and Toni Morrison in their collected works and makes way for Sarah Orne Jewett to write well about what Henry James called her "tiny subject" in Maine in *The Country of the Pointed Firs* as well as for Edward Abbey to write expansively about the canyons of the west, echoing out his concern for global ecological ruin in *The Monkey Wrench Gang*. Each of us has a voice, as individual as Faulkner's or Morrison's, Jewitt's, or Abbey's. Such differences in vision, our very individuality as writers, grant us permission to write—to test our "special way of looking at things" and the means we've found of "giving artistic expression to that way of looking" against the writers who have gone before us. If we're successful enough in matching the two, then we may hope our work "may be around for a time." For literary writers, this longevity is the coin of the realm.

William Blake's voice was hardly heard in his own lifetime, but his "Tiger, Tiger, Burning Bright" still lights up our nights, as well as our imaginations. And that piece will brighten the lives of our children's children, too.

Reading the pastiches we've written out loud in class often turns hilarious. Imagine a dose of Flannery O'Connor's violently retributory redemption played out in Chekhov's patently anti-moralistic story "The Lady with the Pet Dog." The philanderer Gurov sits with one arm draped over a chair enjoying a slice of watermelon after he and the "inexperienced youth," Anna, who is now sobbing, "treat[ing] what [has] happened" in their having consummated their adulterous affair "in a peculiar way, very seriously, as though it were her fall."

> Suddenly, a seed stuck in Gurov's throat. He gasped. Choking, he grabbed his throat. His eyes bulged. He staggered up, the chair he'd been lounging in slapping sharply back against the floor. A tide of darkness seemed to be sweeping her from him. "Anna," he thought. "Darling, sweetheart!" "Help, help!" The shout echoed in his closed mind. And then, a second before he lost consciousness and the lights grew dim, he caught sight of himself in the vanity mirror and saw himself and Anna together clearly for the first time. "My, God!," he thought. I'm in love with her! With that, Gurov pitched forward and died.

I imagine you get the point. I've more or less simply stolen a few of O'Connor's sentences from her short story "Everything That Rises Must Converge" and put them to work in melding two scenes from Chekhov's "The Lady with the Pet Dog." The exercise does reveal something of the impending pressure of consequence on certain moral questions in O'Connor's work, which seems a vital recognition to understanding her voice. Whichever writers we choose to pair, the results always prove instructive, even if, merely through failing, we discover for ourselves just how difficult even apparently simple voices such as O'Connor's are to capture. It proves as tough as Hemingway always said it would be to write "one true sentence," particularly in imitation of a singular style that invokes someone else's "unmistakable" view of the world.

Style

WHO WE ARE IN OUR PROSE: THE LEARNING OF A WRITER

Each of us as a writer has his or her own style—whether we recognize our writing yet as such or not. Our prose inks the page as originally and uniquely as our own rolled thumbprint. Yet much of the struggle of becoming a writer is the work that goes in to figuring out how to render our very own particular and unmistakable way of looking into words. At first, this may seem to pose a paradox: how can you have a style but not yet fully comprehend it? Coming into our own style seems to me a lot like growing up. We spend much of our adolescence going to school, taking courses in algebra or lessons on the piano, studying the science of bicycle frames or the genus and species of plants, trying to figure and then, in turn, fulfill that which our interests and talents have already predicted we would (if we listen to them) someday be. Similarly, it takes time—years and years in the case of some fiction writers—for us to find out *who we are* in our prose.

A notable example is Joseph Conrad who was off sailing the high seas, getting a glimpse of such places as the Congo, and didn't get around to finding and fulfilling himself as a writer by publishing his first book, *Almayer's Folly,* until he was thirty-seven, though in the next thirty years of his life he managed to give voice to twenty-seven volumes of fiction (Jerry Allen Introduction to *The Great Short Works of Joseph Conrad*) Of course, there are the rather glaring exceptions to this sort of slow maturation process—Hemingway and Fitzgerald wrote most of their distinctive works early on in their careers, in their twenties and early thirties. These writers had been famous for years by the age Conrad was when he published his first book—his famous works like "Heart of Darkness" still in his future.

I find it interesting to note, as Joan Didion does in her essay "Last Words," which first appeared in *The New Yorker* and was reprinted in *The Best American Essays 1999,* that in contrast to Conrad's late success and long career as a writer, Hemingway by 1961, barely in his sixties, had lost the ability to compose even one sentence for a contribution to a ceremonial volume for John F. Kennedy. I am not suggesting any correlation between early success and suicide or ruin; I am making a case for the young writer to be patient, not only in being discovered, but also in discovering himself or herself in prose. Early success is not always the blessing it may at first seem. The *writing* is the thing, and being "discovered" may not be all it's cracked up to be. As Frank Conroy writes in "The Writer's Workshop" (*On Writing Short Stories*), "Success has ruined more writers than failure." *There will be time. . . .* In the case of some writers, time may be exactly what it takes.

Individual style—though obviously determined by innumerable factors—is undoubtedly influenced by the authors we love to read. As writers, we do not exist in a vacuum. We do not have to invent language—though we may coin new words or terms—or come up with the fact of paragraphs—though we may well give new definition to structures and possibilities for shaping them into our own work. And so, perhaps the best advice anyone can offer to the young writer is to direct him or her to read and read widely.

Either on his or her own, or through college courses of study, or with the help of a writing workshop, beginning writers *must* read (note that I mean *must,* a word I have studiously avoided throughout this book—reading is the one thing *all* writers do!) to discover those writers who seem to speak directly to him or her. In a question and answer session with a group of undergraduates at the University of Virginia in 1957 (*Faulkner in the University,* edited by Gwynn and Blotner), where he was then writer-in-residence, William Faulkner cited Joseph Conrad as well as Thomas Beer, who wrote *The Mauve Decade,* a writer few of us have ever heard of, as influences on his own prose style. As Faulkner himself said: "Yes . . . I got quite a lot from him [Beer]—was to me [*sic*] a good tool, a good method, a good usage of words, approach to incident. I think the writer, as I said before, is completely amoral. He takes whatever he needs, wherever he needs, and he does that openly and honestly because he himself hopes that what he does will be good enough so that after him people will take from him, and they are welcome to take from him as he feels that he would be welcome by the best of his predecessors to take what they've done."

In this same question and answer session, Faulkner is asked another direct question that is pertinent to our point: "Mr. Faulkner, do you think that a writer can teach young writers?" To which he replies, in a passage I use often in teaching beginning writers:

> I don't think anybody can teach anybody anything. I think that you learn it, but the young writer that is as I say demon-driven and wants to learn and has got to write he don't know why, he will learn from almost any source that he finds. He will learn from older people who are not writers, he will learn from writers, but he learns it—you can't teach it. Then I think too that the writer who's actually hot to say something hasn't got time to be taught. He's too busy learning—he knows what he wants—his instinct says to take this from this man or that from that man. That he's not—he hasn't got time to sit under a mentor and listen to try to learn.

I think Faulkner's absolutely right in that, no matter how helpful a mentor or a book on the writing of the short story, college courses, or writing workshops may prove to be, a writer must be *demon-driven* in an all-out effort to *learn* all he or she can for him or her self. The education of a writer is a tricky business. I've often heard the aspersion that The Writer's Workshop at Iowa, for instance, produces a certain type of writing. And there seems always to be the danger of the mad scientist, ego-maniac mentor who simply wishes to produce clones who write the sorts of fiction that he or she writes, whether experimental or traditional. But I haven't really found this to be true, or if occasionally true, certainly not rampantly factual. Writing teachers, on the whole, are good folk who profess a deep down love of writing and reading and have the student's best interest in mind. Intelligent by nature, they rarely attempt to pigeonhole a writer or a writer's style. Most are genuinely concerned with the student writer's work, even if understandably preoccupied with their own efforts to write—most creative writing teachers are, after all, *writers* first.

Of course there are the horror stories. I've heard from the director who hired a "writer" who made up an entire list of publications in order to land a job teaching fiction. He taught for nearly a semester before he was found out and asked to leave, though the students knew him for a fake long before he got the boot. And there is, and always will be, jealousy among the ranks of publishing creative writers and students of creative writing; a hierarchy of who has books and who's been reviewed and where so-and-so went to school or teaches and what press published them. Writers act human, too. And success, we may be dismayed to learn the hard way, is not always bestowed on those (including ourselves!) who we feel are the most deserving—writers who have worked hard and long and honestly at their craft. We complain that those writers who leap frog us in our "careers" as writers knew someone or that they had a trust fund and so didn't have to teach a four/four load at the community college like we do. Hard work, we learn, this lesson of life, is no guarantee of anything, and certainly not of best seller success. But, at heart, most of us realize that this is our problem. Again: *Writing is the thing.* Writers write. Period. And writing as well as we are able offers its own tangible reward. An audience of eternity awaits—read Blake!—"*Tiger, tiger, burning bright . . .* "—no matter what earthly awards are bestowed on us in the here and now.

As to the education of a writer, there can be no rules, no absolutes, just as there are no rules or absolutes in the writing of fiction. I would simply state the obvious: the great majority of writers publishing today have college degrees and most of those have sought masters' degrees, most likely M.F.A.s. (Master's of Fine Arts). A quick look through the AWP (Associated Writing Programs) catalogue gives the addresses and contract numbers of the many graduate programs in creative writing in the United States. And, even though an M.F.A. is a terminal degree—meaning a capstone degree in the field of fine arts—there are by now a host of universities that offer a Ph.D. with creative dissertation, upping the educational ante for writers who wish to make their living teaching. Fifteen years ago a handful of undergraduate programs boldly offered an English Major with a writing emphasis. Today, a few schools like Susquehanna University, where I teach, offer an undergraduate major in creative writing.

Things have certainly changed since Faulkner's day! This book is not the place to argue the relative merit of such a system, though I can't help but say that a country with a greater percent of the population than ever before educated in the art of writing and close reading can't be a bad thing, whether or not every graduate of every writing program in the country goes on to become a great writer, such as Faulkner, or even an Ophrah Winfrey anointed author-of-the-moment. Obviously, they won't. Though, to be fair, neither will every graduate of business school go on to be a Bill Gates, nor every graduate from pre-med actually become an M.D., much less a neurosurgeon. For a better understanding of the good reasons behind why we have such a proliferation of writing programs in the United States read *The Elephants Teach; Creative Writing Since 1880* by D.G. Myers. And for a truly engaging discussion of the merit of the education of a writer, read John Gardner's *On Becoming a Novelist,* in which he discusses "The Writer's Nature," "The Writer's Training and Education," "Publication and Survival," and "Faith." Suffice it here to say that a sort of demon-driven reading is at the heart of learning for a writer who is making the noble attempt to fathom his or her own style, whether or not he or she chooses to attend a writing program; it has always been so, even for Mr. Faulkner.

In his journals, Henry James writes with admiration of Balzac. In her essay "Reading as a Writer: the Artist as Craftsman" (included in *On Writing Short Stories*) Joyce Carol Oates notes Sylvia Plath's method of becoming a writer, scrutinizing authors as disparate as Frank O'Connor, Wallace Stevens, and James Thurber and tells us how Frost pored over the poems of Thomas Hardy until he'd "absorbed . . . the cadences of Hardy's language . . . into his soul" and how Chekhov "revered Tolstoy as he did no other writer," nearly opposite as they were "as artists, and as visionaries." Eudora Welty came into her own as a writer with her own voice in Mississippi as a winning fan of Faulkner's. Carver often expressed the debt he felt to Chekhov, as have many other contemporary writers such as Francine Prose. I myself will never forget the first time I read Jayne Anne Phillips's collection of short-short stories *Sweethearts,* Andre Dubus's "The Pretty Girl," Larry Woiwode's novel *Beyond the Bedroom Wall,* Isaac Babel's *The Red Calvary and Other Stories, The Stories of Breece D'J Pancake,* or the knock-out delivered by the short story "Sonny's Blues" by James Baldwin. Each writer must seek to find the writer or writers he or she can call his or her own and "take whatever he [or she] needs" from them.

The late Richard Marius, a well-known historian, novelist, and the former director of the Expository Writing Program at Harvard, from whose extremely fine book on essay writing, *The Writer's Companion,* I have taken the title for *A Short Story Writer's Companion,* and in whose memory it has been written, once told me how Gordon Lish saw Marius as he passed by his editor's office door at Knopf and called out to him with a grin in his voice, "It's all in the sentences, Richard!" Beyond the influence other writers have on us and who we find we've become in our prose, *It's all in the sentences!* is the solid bedrock block of truth we discover again and again about style, a rallying cry to mind the fundamentals we find put into practice time and again in our reading. Sentences and the words they're born of are everything to the writer. Care and attention must be paid to mastering the fundamental building blocks of prose, what, in their famous book Strunk and White have forever-named *The Elements of Style.*

In an effort to think through the makeup of our own style—in an attempt to sound our own voice—let's turn back to the basics of language, sentences, and paragraphs, the elements of which we find any writer's signature composed.

LANGUAGE

In "On Writing" (*Fires*) Raymond Carver tells of the three-by-five cards that he kept posted on the wall next to his desk. One of the cards read: "Fundamental accuracy of statement is the ONE sole morality of writing. Ezra Pound." "It is not everything by ANY means," Carver cautions, "but if a writer has 'fundamental accuracy of statement' going for him, he's at least on the right track."

The words we use in our writing must be the right words—the exact words. There is a huge difference between the verbs *walked* and *skipped* or *jumped* and *lunged.* One action does not work interchangeably for the other without significantly altering the meaning of the sentence. Only one of these words can be correct given the appropriate mood and specific objective of movement that needs to be conveyed. It is of course the writer's job to make sure the word fits.

I often turn to poetry to make the point of choosing the right word for the specific work any word performs in any particular sentence, bringing a few poems to class that we pass around and then read out loud. Short stories are no less attentive to language than poems—*nothing in a short story is random*—but the even more demanding brevity of a poem pushes the poet to pressure, not only the exact meaning of a word, but its every syllable through tighter and tighter coils of rhythm, rhyme, and form (if the poet is indeed practicing such poetics) toward a purer, if a somewhat seemingly more obscure, distillation of intended meaning. In poetry, each word works to *be* rather than to explain. The imperative of length and line says there's no time!

Below follows "Pied Beauty" by Gerard Manely Hopkins, a delightfully personal understanding of which is offered to us by Franklin Burroughs in his essay "Compression Wood," which first appeared in *The American Scholar* and was reprinted in *The Best American Essays of 1999.*

Glory be to God for dappled things—
    For skies of couple-colour as a brinded cow;
    For rose-moles all in stipple upon trout that swim;
Fresh-firecoal chestnut-falls; finches' wings;
    Landscape plotted and pierced—fold, fallow, and plough;
    And a'll tra'des, their gear and tackle and trim.

All things counter, original, spare, strange;
    Whatever is fickle, freckled (who knows how?)
    With swift, slow; sweet; sour; adazzle, dim;
He fathers-forth whose beauty is past change:
                   Praise Him.

Go ahead! Don't be shy. Read it again. Read it out loud!

Besides the good fun we're having in letting the poem roll happily off of our tongues, the reliance of each word on the next, their combined lilt and musicality—*Glory be to God for dappled things—Fresh-firecoal chestnut-falls; finches' wings—With swift, slow; sweet, sour; adazzle, dim*—the powerful building effect of the poem as a whole to the cumulative punctuating point—"Praise Him."—becomes obviously relevant. Yank a word, slight a single syllable, a stress or emphasis, and the poem falters, the rollicking rhythm flags, an image becomes vague—not *couple-coloured,* a perfect description of *brinded* (read *brindled*), but uniformly (and inaccurately) *coloured*—and, as a result, the poem halts; meaning, merely taken aim at, is missed and goes wide of the bull's eye its well-chosen language now boldly marks.

We can see the same hard-won relevance of words in any sentence of any of the stories excerpted for discussion thus far in this book. These words are discovered, chosen, discarded, honed, then polished like brightwork, before finally being published (and then perhaps groaned over by the writer who reads the wrong word or an awkward phrasing in print). In my writing classes, I like to say, "Short stories aren't written; they are rewritten." Most writers I know work and rework draft after draft after draft of their stories—sentence by sentence—striving to secure every word until it holds fast as those of "Pied Beauty."

Sentences

"It's all in the sentences, Richard!"

Sentences form the basis of communication between writer and reader. On their own, most words lack direction; sentences give language work to do, specific jobs to perform.

In a workshop, taking care with specific sentences in a student's work, I often make reference to the Fundamental Principles of Sentences offered in *A Writer's Companion:*

> Sentences make statements or ask questions. We learn to make sentences naturally when we learn to talk because we have to make statements if we are to be understood by members of the community where we live. Although some people imagine that they do not speak in complete sentences, we in fact nearly always do unless we are answering a question or adding information to a sentence we have already made. To say that a sentence is complete is only to say that it makes a comprehensible statement.
>
> Most sentences make their comprehensible statements by naming a subject and by making a statement about that subject. Clauses, phrases, and other kinds of modifiers may amplify the basic statement just as harmonies may amplify the theme of melody. Everything in the sentence should serve the basic, central statement. When you write a sentence, you should know exactly what the basic statement is. Are you telling how somebody acts? Are you explaining that something exists in a certain way? Are you saying that something happens? If you do get confused with one of your sentences, stop and ask yourself what is the most important statement you are trying to make in that sentence. Name the subject, and as simply as you can, tell what you want to say about it. Once you have arrived at that thought, revise the sentence so that it clearly conveys what you want to say.

The basic tenants of sentences set forth in *A Writer's Companion* pertain to all forms of writing, fiction writing as well as essay writing, the composition of formal reports, business memos, e-mails to friends, information found on Web pages, and advertising copy. Sentences strive to clearly and concisely (even beautifully!) communicate a statement or question.

Spoken sentences, though they may make as Marius suggests "comprehensible statements," are mere kin to written sentences. This is where the *striving* I've written of earlier comes in. It has been my experience that sentences come into being through revision, endless revision. In writing, I don't merely want to say what I think I've said, but what I've meant to say! When writing we can't splay our hands or shrug *You know what I mean* or use the questions of companions to help us zero in on our point.

Written sentences, writers may say, are *tightened*, by which we mean they are closely edited—*discovered, chosen, discarded, honed, and polished, before finally being published (and then perhaps groaned over by the writer who reads the wrong word or an awkward phrasing in print)*—in much the same way as are the individual words that go into composing them. This discovering on the part of the writer is part of the process of making good sense out of the chaos that can be thought through as a sort of talking out loud on paper. Writers work at their sentences until, finally, like finding the fit of a particular word in a poem like "Pied Beauty," they're confident each statement or question will stand on its own without confusing or misdirecting the reader—that is, that the intended statement or question has been *communicated.* If written well enough, the reader may never even notice the painstaking work the writer has put into making his or her sentences function just so.

Henry David Thoreau, although not known as a writer of short stories, is one of the preeminent stylists in American Literature. Much to his credit, he is also read as one of the most natural. In his Introduction to *Walden and Other Writings by Henry David Thoreau,* Joseph Wood Krutch makes note of the careful crafting that went into each sentence of the titular work: "From careful studies of the much that survives of Thoreau's notes, first drafts and revisions, we now know that *Walden* was composed with infinite care and polished again and again, but one of the charms of the book is the fact that it seems so informal, so spontaneous and so easy."

Krutch writes of Thoreau that "no one was ever a more careful workman":

Every journal was often rewritten again and again, and many of the perfect phrases in *Walden,* which seem so spontaneous were, we now know, polished and repolished until often the first version becomes almost unrecognizable. A journal entry includes the flat statement "I have traveled some in New England, especially in Concord," but in *Walden* it is transformed into the paradox "I have traveled a good deal in Concord." An early version of an even more famous passage begins with a sentence which sounds almost like sociologist gobbledygook "a stereotype but unconscious despair is concealed under what are called the amusements of mankind." It becomes instead "the mass of men lead lives of quiet desperation."

In a letter to a friend he once wrote: "Don't suppose that you can tell it precisely the first dozen times you try, but at 'em again. . . . Not that the story need be long, but it will take a long time to make it short." Or again: "Nothing goes by luck in composition . . . The best you can write will be the best you are. Every sentence is a result of a long probation. The author's character is read from title page to end. Of this he never corrects the proofs." Of no writer was it ever more true that the style is the man.

There is, as Thoreau proves, quite something to a writer's turn of phrase. Mere sentences on a page—though they may well communicate the intended idea—"I have traveled some in New England, especially in Concord"—do not necessarily possess the enigmatic power of the paradoxical proclamation: "I have traveled a good deal in Concord." Such repolished phrasings show us something of Thoreau's love and care for his work and the intensity and precision with which he strove to re-create his understanding of life, in the woods, or otherwise: "The greater part of what my neighbors call good I believe in my soul to be bad, and if I repent of any thing, it is very likely to be my good behavior. What demon possessed me that I behaved so well?"

Marius, in his chapter on "Writing Sentences," states twenty or so "principles of writing good sentences." I'm sure you've heard some of these principles paraphrased before: "Be direct!" "Use the active voice." "Combine thoughts to eliminate choppy sentences." "Begin most sentences with the subject." "Be economical with adjectives!"

Marius's book is well worth having on your shelf.

Buy it and mark it up, or—at the very least—borrow it from your local library and take careful notes, go after it, *learn* the stuff, even if you were never taught. Practice usage and experiment with punctuation until both become second nature. Such ingraining is a must for mastery.

This is not to say the same as saying that the successful short story writer need be a starched-stiff, ruler-wielding grammarian. I imagine that we've all met up with that one English teacher—my bane Mrs. Dalton in the eighth grade—who bedeviled us (me!) with the diagramming of sentences. I remember how angry and frustrated I used to feel; I still remember the sting of the D she slapped me with. I must admit that when I was in the eighth grade direct objects meant nothing to me—the slashes and dashes, the hang man at the end of a dangling participle, less than nothing—*hang it all!* Mrs. Dalton's mistake, I still feel, was in teaching that writing is grammar. For years afterward, I felt I was a "bad" writer. But writing isn't grammar. Just as handwriting isn't writing. As spelling isn't writing. Though, as students, we are often made to understand that these things make a writer. Sentence fragments, for instance, are not an outright crime to be categorically condemned. Though such fragments may be grammatically incorrect, they can have an interesting effect. Used purposefully, such ungrammatical uses can *work*. Grammar serves writing; handwriting (or the computer) serves writing; spelling serves writing, though misspelling words will certainly not serve the writer well, nor, will a sentence, befuddled, by, commas (sic!). We've all read deadly uninteresting writers who never miss a comma or misspell a word, and we may have sat beside the beaming child whose cursive was held up for all the class to see. That kid got the A for *writing*.

This, of course, does not excuse the young writer or the growing-old writer from knowing his or her stuff. We may use a sentence fragment intuitively in the steeling heat of composition. But at some point in the process we come to the red light flashing and bell clanging crossroads of accepted usage—and we should at least recognize what we've done (whether or not we can diagram it on a blackboard) so as to make the all-important choice of whether or not it does what we want, and whether or not the effect is worth the risk of stopping the Mrs. Dalton's of the world in their tracks. ("A SENTENCE FRAGMENT!" And he calls himself a writer. HA!) It might help those of us who have had our difficulties with punctuation and run-on sentences to know that when Faulkner first began to publish there were professors of English who railed against his writing as incompetent. But make no mistake. Let's not let ourselves off too easily. There can be no excuses. As Carver said, "Don't complain, don't explain." To gain mastery of our craft, we must, as the Russian writer Isaac Babel has said, "know everything"—even, unfortunately for some of us, how to spell.

Paragraphs

It *is* all in the sentences, certainly, but those sentences—individual statements or questions—are strung together with other sentences to make paragraphs. Paragraphs become the blocks we use to build our short stories.

Paragraphs are constructed in one of two ways. As Marius points out in his chapter on paragraphs, in one type of paragraph, removing any single sentence—like pulling a word from a sentence—disrupts the meaning of the paragraph as a whole. The second type of paragraph is controlled by a general statement. The sentences that follow refer back to the first. Reordering those sentences has little to do with the overall idea of the paragraph.

The 4th Edition of *The Writer's Companion* offers the following illustration of the two types of paragraphs. In the first type of paragraph each sentence relies on the next:

First Sentence
+
Second Sentence
+
Third Sentence
+
Fourth Sentence
+
Fifth Sentence

This sort of paragraph in which each sentence is reliant on the one before in its development, can be shown in numerous short stories, here in Lorrie Moore's "Four Calling Birds, Three French Hens" from her collection *Birds of America:*

> Poor Jack: perhaps she had put him through too much. Just last spring, there had been her bunion situation—the limping, the crutch, and the big blue shoe. Then in September, there had been Mimi Andersen's dinner party, where Jack, the only non-smoker, was made to go out on the porch while everyone else stayed inside and lit up. And *then,* there had Aileen's one-woman performance of "the house-work version of Lysistrata." "No Sweepie, No Kissie," Jack had called it. But it had worked. Sort of. For about two weeks. There was, finally, only so much one woman on the vast and wicked stage could do.

The first sentence makes a general statement and each of the following sentences develops that idea in sequence, each example building on the next, creating a sort of equation, which, in the last sentence, draws a sort of sum of meaning from the sequencing of sentences before.

In the second type of paragraph, as Marius notes, "the first sentence is a general statement followed by a list of detailed statements that support the generalization." The order here isn't necessarily sequential. Changing the order of the sentence would not necessarily affect the intent, or sum meaning, of the paragraph.

First Sentence
+   +   +   +   +

Moore uses such a paragraph in the same story, just a few lines down from the above example:

> The birds had become emboldened, slowly reclaiming the yard, filling up the branches, cheeping hungrily in the morning from the sills and eaves. "What is that *shrieking?*" Aileen asked. The leaves had fallen, but now jays, ravens, and house finches darkened the trees—some of them flying south, some of them stay-

ing on, pecking the hardening ground for seeds. Squirrels moved in poking through the old apples that had dropped from the flowering crab. A possum made a home for himself under the porch, thumping and chewing. Raccoons had discovered Sofie's little gym set, and one morning Aileen looked out and saw two of them swinging on the swings. She'd wanted animal life? Here was animal life!

In this paragraph, I think it's safe to say that we can more or less rearrange the order of these sentences without significantly altering the paragraph's meaning. In reordering the sentences, we might begin:

The leaves had fallen, but now jays, ravens, and house finches darkened the trees—some of them flying south, some of them staying on, pecking the hardening ground for seeds. "What is that *shrieking?*" Aileen asked. The birds had become emboldened, slowly reclaiming the yard, filling up the branches, cheeping hungrily in the morning from the sills and eaves. Here was animal life! She'd wanted animal life? A possum made a home for himself under the porch, thumping and chewing. Squirrels moved in poking through the old apples that had dropped from the flowering crab. Raccoons had discovered Sofie's little gym set, and one morning, Aileen looked out and saw two of them swinging on the swings.

Moore has done a fine job of crafting the original paragraph, and I don't mean to suggest that I would change one word of what she's written. But it is fun to note how easily we can rearrange the above sentences without misrepresenting the general idea of the paragraph.

The wide use of cutting and pasting by writers who use personal computers reveals much of how paragraphs work in a short story. In shaping a story, I've often found I can move paragraphs (or even entire scenes) to gain or heighten effect and to clarify meaning. Moving paragraphs often shows me whether or not the sentences they contain are necessary. Moving paragraphs in this way helps me test the tension or direction of a piece.

In the draft stage, I find a write a lot, usually in long blocks. It's only when I go back to what I've written, either later that same day or the next morning, that I begin to hone in on the meaning I begin to see emerging from a story by dividing these blocks, at the same time editing the sentences, so that each block becomes a sort of step. At this stage I am not afraid of cutting away pages and pages—reams if need be. I imagine this is something like the sculptor faced with a Volkswagen-sized block of ice. Inside that block, she begins to see . . . a merman! . . . and from the moment she imagines him there begins to shape toward freeing the feeling of him from the ideal posed in her mind—chipping and chiseling at the block, knocking off chunks and raining showers of ice, until the basic figure shows itself. Only then does she sculpt more carefully, precisely—giving the merman a great walrus's mustache, detailing the knuckles around his forked fishing spear, casting his eyes with the haughtiness of the likes of Poseidon.

In workshop, I have found that if a story has gone wrong, we can often locate the problem in a particular paragraph. It might be as simple as noting that the first few paragraphs in a draft were simply a sort of warm up for the writer. The conflict isn't established until the second paragraph on page three. Cutting the other paragraphs and beginning on page three focuses the story and may help the writer make his or her emerging intent more clear.

Paragraphs make more manageable the process of revision. Working paragraph by paragraph offers writers a close, step by step process by which we may examine the work we've done, while looking forward to the work we may do. Paragraphs can be mapped out, each paragraph drawn to reveal the objective of its group of sentences. From this map the writer may read for himself or herself if the step set out is a necessary one.

How long should a paragraph be?

A paragraph could be a single word, Yes!, or it could run on for several pages. (Read Cormac McCarthy!) Keep in mind that it's easier for your reader—and for you as a writer—to keep track of the development of a short story if each step is set out clearly. These steps are your paragraphs. We can almost always find a good place to separate long blocks of text. Often when we divide long blocks of text the transitions are natural, the *flow* is there. All it takes to make such a simple break and gain clarity is to punch the return key. If only all aspects of writing could be so easy!

Writing Exercises

1. Write a pastiche. Choose two writers. Then rewrite one scene from a short story by Writer A using the voice of Writer B. Next write the reverse: a scene from Writer B using the voice of Writer A. Keep in mind that you may have to change the scene to allow for a writer's vision. As Carver says, "Voice is akin to style . . . but it isn't style alone." My favorite part of this exercise is hearing them read aloud.

2. Read a few poems by Gerard Manley Hopkins (or any other poet). In two or three pages, note the interdependence of language.

3. Choose one word that interests you. Find out as much as you can about this word. Look it up in the dictionary, note every possible shading of meaning. Go to the library and use the Oxford English Dictionary to investigate the origin of the word. Use this word in separate sentences in which you explore its shades of meaning and usage. Can you create a new, sensi-

ble use for this word, based on its accepted meaning? (For example: "A flood of cars and trucks *rivered* by the city.") Use this word as creatively as you can in a paragraph, writing a sort of prose poem that depends not only on the meaning of the word, but on its sounds and syllables. Write a mini-essay of one or two pages centered on this word.

4. During the course of a week, collect one word you read or hear misused. Listen or read for that word when it is used perfectly (even if unexpectedly).

5. In the vein of Hemingway, write one "true" sentence.

6. Consider the job of a random sentence in any paragraph.

7. Write a strong declarative sentence.

8. Write a weak declarative sentence.

9. Write a complex sentence.

10. Compose two sentences necessarily joined by a semicolon.

11. Edit the following sentence: He was going to the store.

12. Rework these sentences so that they become possible: *Racing down the stairs, she jumped into the taxi* or *Standing beside the pool, he dove in.*

13. As we did in the section on Shaping the Short Story, map out the development of a few paragraphs. Which of the two general types do they fall under?

14. Reorder the sentences of a paragraph in which the sequence isn't vital.

15. Create your own new paragraph by writing out from under the opening sentence of an ordered paragraph. Concentrate on making your order as vital, while at the same time different from, the original paragraph as possible.

16. Consider the job of a single paragraph in a short story as a whole. Type out the chosen paragraph and annotate it, making as many connections as possible to the other concerns and possibilities of the story. In two or three pages make sense of the web of connections of which a close investigation of this particular paragraph has made you aware.

17. Remove a paragraph from one of your own stories. Can you move it? How does the missing paragraph reveal itself as being necessary?

I rewrite to be reread.

—*André Gide*

It is a fact that fiction writing is something in which the whole personality takes part—the conscious as well as the unconscious mind. Art is the habit of the artist; and habits have to be rooted deep in the whole personality. They have to be cultivated like any other habit, over a long period of time, by experience; and teaching any kind of writing is largely a matter of helping the student develop the habit of art. . . .

—*Flannery O'Connor, "Writing Short Stories"*

I gestate: for months, often for years. An idea comes to me from wherever they come, and I write it in a notebook. Sometimes I forget it's there. I don't think about it. By think I mean plan. I try never to think about where a story will go. This is as hard as writing, maybe harder; I spend most of my waking time doing it; it is hard work, because I want to know what the story will do and how it will end and whether or not I can write it; but I must not know, or I will kill the story by controlling it; I work to surrender.

—*Andre Dubus, "The Habit of Writing"*

THREE

Notes on the Fiction-writing Process

Just as there are no rules for the writing of fiction or the use of its elements, there is no easy right or wrong when it comes to the process of composing a short story, of *getting the work done.* How the writing comes to be is entirely up to the individual writer. Hemingway stood when he wrote and so does Rita Dove. Thomas Wolfe, who was six foot four inches tall, composed longhand on yellow legal paper upon his desk, the top of the refrigerator in his Brooklyn apartment. He hand-numbered each page written in his giant's scrawl, ripped it off and tossed it over his shoulder—literally thousands of pages piling up on the floor. He'd wait until he was finished with the day's (or night's) work before he'd gather them up and read them back through in order. Jean Toomer and Mark Twain dreamed up some of their best work in bed (separate beds!), as did Walker Percy, Edith Wharton, Colette, Proust, and James Joyce, so John Updike tells us in the introductory essay that accompanies Jill Krements's *The Writer's Desk,* a book of photographs of writers in their workplaces.

In an excerpt from that book, which I first came across in the December 1996/January, 1997 issue of *Civilization: The Magazine of the Library of Congress* (The accompanying essay is by John Updike.) Richard Ford tells us that his "'desk' is more of a concept than a thing. It's like the 'Belize desk' at the State Department; an idea more than a place you actually sit at. 'Ford's writing at his desk.' That could mean a lot of things. It could mean on an airplane or a Greyhound bus, or in a rental car or a rented house. It could mean in the Hotel L'Abbaye (though it could *not* mean at an outside table at the Deux Magots). Like Emerson's giant, I carry my desk with me." A photograph of E. B. White shows him sitting in rolled shirt sleeves on a wooden bench at a bare desk before a manual typewriter in a cabin. Notably, the only other furniture in the room is a trash barrel. The cabin, if we can trust the view through the window beside him, looks out across the water to a line of pristine shore, and makes his "office" seem as it is set up on stilts, surrounded by water and completely cut off from the demands and annoyances of the modern world. The photograph shows White at work in what many of us would think to be a sort of idyllic spot to get our work done, though in the accompanying text he reveals that "a girl pushing a carpet sweeper under my typewriter table has never annoyed me particularly, nor has it taken my mind off my work . . . in consequence, the members of my household never pay the slightest attention to my being a writing man—they make all the fuss they want to. If I get sick of it, I have places I can go." We should all have such a place to go!

I once read that Annie Dillard isolates herself in one of those awful metal tool sheds that she's converted into an office to get her writing done. Kurt Vonnegut stays in his pajamas. I could swear I read somewhere that Cheever dressed in a suit and tie to ride the elevator of his apartment building down to the basement. Once there he promptly removed the suit and tie he'd just put on and hung them on the coat rack. He would then clack away at his typewriter in his boxer shorts, smoking up a storm, until 5:00 in the evening when he would once again don his suit and tie for the elevator ride back up to his apartment.

I don't mean to give the impression that most writers are idiosyncratic or even odd in their work habits. The truth is most probably aren't. A poll of writers might well find that many of them get up at a reasonable hour, have breakfast, and sit down to write for, let's say, an average of about four hours. Most writers write because they wish to (often desperately so!), and writing for most writers is a joy to which they quickly, directly, simply, and easily get to.

Here, I want to sound again the epigraph from John Gardner with which we rang in Part One: "To the great artist, anything whatever is possible. Invention, the spontaneous generation of new rules, is central to art. And since one does not learn to be a literary artist by studying first how to be something different from a literary artist, it follows that for the young writer, as for the great writer he hopes to become, there can be no firm rules, no limits, no restrictions. Whatever works is good. He must develop an eye for what—by his own carefully informed standards—works." And there we have it: whatever works in getting writing done *works*—and wherever and however it works, too!

All beginning writers have to do is put themselves to the task of discovering, perhaps through trial and error, or by achieving some notable success—completing, say, their very first short story!—a process of writing that works best for them.

Short story writers have a lot to say when talking about the process of their writing. I've always enjoyed and found useful the *Conversations with Series* from the University of Mississippi Press. Each book in the series collects the interviews with writers like Eudora Welty, Norman Mailer, John Edgar Wideman, John Gardner, Toni Morrison, Flannery O'Connor, Franz Kafka, James Baldwin, and Grace Paley. Wonderful also are the volumes of *The Paris Review Interviews: Writers at Work*. I keep the 1st and 2nd series in the bookshelf beside my desk. Interviews included in the 1st Series give a good idea of the range of each volume: E. M. Forster, Frank O'Connor, Dorothy Parker, Nelson Algren, Francois Mauriac, James Thurber, William Faulkner, Robert Penn Warren, Georges Simenon, Francoise Sagan, William Styron, Thornton Wilder, Truman Capote, Angus Wilson, Joyce Cary, and Alberto Moravia. Both sets of interviews allow us to find out how the writers we most admire work. It's also a great introduction to writers we may not have read.

Other books directly address our concern with process, from Peter Elbow's *Writing without Teachers* to the volumes of *The Best Writing on Writing* edited by Jack Heffron. David Michael Kaplan has written a book entitled *Revision: A Creative Approach to Writing and Rewriting Fiction,* and Jay Woodruff has edited *A Piece of Work: Five Writers Discuss Their Revisions.* There is no lack of discussion on the topic, which is as it should be. Everyone seems to want to know how writers write.

I've found this avid interest in how writers write asked of many of the authors whose readings I've attended over the years—Tobias Wolff, Evan Boland, Andre Dubus, Jayne Anne Phillips, Richard Ford, Jill McCorkle, Robert Stone, Tom Perrotta, Margaret Atwood, Tony Hoagland, and Richard Bausch to name a very few. Indeed, it has been my own experience that wherever I give a reading, afterward when the floor is opened to questions, the first question I'm most often asked is "How do you write?"

The interest in the answers to these questions is surely genuine. The aspiring writer or avid reader looks up at the Writer standing before the podium, published book in hand, and perhaps can't help but believe that he or she has some keep on the keys to the kingdom to literary success. Certainly, we believe, there's some magic to writing—is it this thing called *inspiration,* or some trick, beyond talent and hard work and the gift of learning that a good creative writing teacher may offer? Perhaps if we too sharpened up number 2 pencils with our uncle's old tusk-boned pocket knife or switched to yellow legal pads and climbed up on a chair to write on top of the refrigerator or shucked our job and moved back to our little "postage stamp of soil" in Mississippi where we were born or got up at four in the morning or scribbled out chapters on the subway on our way to Wall Street or stayed up all night carousing or spent more time in bed or left America to live in Paris, then we would be writers too. . . .

Well, we admit, probably not.

The trick is to take what you can from someone else's process. Composing with a feather quill dipped in ink might just work for you—it did for William Blake—or go so far as to sing your "verses," as he did. You might try writing everyday. Or it could be impossible for you to work everyday. You may well work best in the solitude of an empty cabin at a spare desk stilted island-like in the middle of a lake or you might have trained yourself, as Richard Bausch told me he has, to write everyday—anywhere at anytime, under any conditions: at the kitchen table while the kids are eating or even Christmas morning sitting on the couch surrounded by the rip and flutter of wrapping paper being stripped off all the goodies. I like writers and writing, and so I am always intrigued—fascinated even—with how other writers get their writing done whether or not I change the way I work one iota.

I myself write everyday. *I believe in the discipline of writing.* For me, that means setting the alarm for 5:45 AM every morning. I've made it a habit, as soon as the alarm goes off, to jackknife straight up in bed like a sprung cadaver. I stumble into the bathroom where I splash cold water in my eyes. I fumble on my glasses and dress in sweats and a sweater, t-shirt and shorts, depending on the weather. Shoes, sandals, or sneakers. The coffee in the kitchen has been automatically brewed. I fill a cup, take my first sip—black, bitter black, a caffeine-volted jump-start! The first thing I do is log in on my journal; this morning I signed in at 6:02, yesterday at 6:04. I work until 10:00.

Of course I'm crazy! Boring too! What was it Virginia Wolff said, that the writer's life must be without event so that they can work?

I also work out everyday—either run or lift weights—immediately after I've finished writing and had a quick breakfast. (I've known lots of writers who held to this sort of schedule—Hemingway wrote from "first light until noon, or a little before, and then would exercise his body." Andre Dubus kept a similar regimen of writing and exercise before he lost his leg in a terrible accident, but even after that he would wheel his chair around the parking lot of his church. Finally he had a ramp built so that he could wheel out his door, down thirty yards or so and back—"wheelchair sprints" he called them. Henry James used to walk after he wrote. May Sarton did, too.)

Unlike Richard Ford, I have a desk; my desk is (relatively) neat. It is worth remarking on the desk itself. I bought it from a crafty old antique dealer here in central Pennsylvania by the name of Joe Herman. He gave me a deal. When you ask him the price of a piece, he always starts his bidding by cudding around a wad of chewing tobacco, "Would ten thousand dollars be too much?" The desk is one of those giant partner's desks. Basically, it's two old-time school teacher's desks—you know the kind, oak desks with all the drawers and the sliding pieces of wood that pull out for a typewriter— covered by a single solid piece of oak. The top of my desk measures fifty-four inches wide by sixty-six inches long! Two people can work at this desk at the same time. Or you can compose on one side and edit on the other. You can do any damn thing you want with a desk this big—if you've got a space big enough to keep it. Fortunately, we do, in the basement, which, because of the way the house is set, has windows all around that look out over the yard and the line of spruce and (if I crane my neck a bit) the ridge of blue hills that rise on the other side of the Susquehanna River. If I crane the other way I can see the steeple of the chapel at Susquehanna University.

My office is not spare like E. B. White's empty island-unto-itself cabin. My space, like my son Samuel's room, as my room was when I was a boy, is chock-full of photographs and paintings of people and places. Stuff: rocks I've found, an old canoe paddle, a gorgeous blue and black butterfly (*Thaumantis diores*), postcard paintings of Winslow Homer's "Leaping Trout" and Michelangelo's "The Creation of Man," Modigliani's "Portrait of Woman in Hat," and, still in the Styrofoam box they were returned to me in, the ashes of my English Mastiff, Sax, which I saved to cast when we moved to Pennsylvania from Cambridge but cannot bring myself to throw out. I love to canoe and I have a photograph set out next to my laptop computer, that I took paddling solo from the stern, looking forward out over a wild Adirondack lake. I like being borne along by that picture; it gives me something to look forward to during the blight white of winter when the Susquehanna River is all frozen solid or clogged with great chunks of ice. The wall behind me is covered with notes and maps for the novel I'm working on. I like to see the entire story along a time line spread before me, such a telltale mapping also helps me keep track of my characters. It helps me to be able to take them all in at a glance.

The bookshelf against the opposite wall is stuffed to toppling. Nearly every book on writing that I don't already own is checked out of the university's library—all of the *Paris Review Writer's at Work Interviews* and the entire The University of Mississippi's *Conversations With series*, numerous short story collections—Lorrie Moore's *Birds of America*, Richard Bausch's *The Fireman's Wife*, Gina Berriault's *Women in Their Beds*, Harold Brodkey's *Stories in an Almost Classical Mode*, Chaucer's *The Canterbury Tales*, John Barth's *Lost in the Funhouse*, Sandra Cisneros's *Woman Hollering Creek*, Reginald McKnight's *White Boys*, Rick Moody's *The Ring of Brightest Angels Around Heaven*, the *Yellow Wallpaper and Other Writings* by Charlotte Perkins Gilman, among a host of others—anthologies like Richard Ford's *The Granata Book of the American Short Story* and John Updike's *The Best American Short Stories of the Century*, and other books like *Talks With Tolstoy* and *Theory of Fiction: Henry James* edited by James E. Miller, Jr., and *How to Write* (which most assuredly is not meant to tell you how to write!) by Gertrude Stein, *The Poetics of Aristotle* translated by Stephen Halliwell. Until a week ago when I had to return them I had over sixty books from interlibrary loan on the Adirondacks, where the novel is set. Scribbled index cards from my reading are spread out over the top of the desk.

All this, of course, is about *me* and the where of how I work. I have found (how can this come as a surprise? but it did, it does) that I'm no different as a writer than I am as a person, which is to say I'm no different as a person than I am as a writer. I write. That's just what I do, what I love to do. Truly, even if I knew I would never publish another word, I would get up tomorrow morning at 5:45 and write a short story. I write and therefore I am a writer. I like a schedule and feel comfortable knowing I have a place to do my work. I write everyday, just like I work out everyday.

Not that elbowing out the time to get the writing done is ever easy, or making time to write isn't a sacrifice—I started getting up at 4:00 AM in college when I had to go to school all day and had a job after classes were over. I'll never forget summers when I used to work on my cousin's farm. I got up at 4:00 because we had to be at the shop to start lugging pipe for irrigation at 6:00 (a blessing in some ways, so much cooler than would be by 10:00). We worked until 6:00 or 7:00 or 8:00 at night. We worked until whatever had to get done was done. I stumbled home, somehow managed to stand through a shower, and dropped into bed. My wife Sarah gets the credit for my being able to continue to find time to write through the blur of two newborns—my son, Samuel, and my daughter, Isabel. No, getting the writing done is never easy. We will always have other responsibilities—a job, a family, the promises we make to others that makes us part of a community—but I have a gut feeling that it would be much more difficult *not* to write, even under such extreme circumstances.

Perhaps, reading this, you may sit back and snap your fingers: it's dawned on you that you need structure in your life! A schedule! *Discipline!* That's the key! Tomorrow you'll try getting up at 5:45 and magically. . . . Or, more likely, you'll read this and say, Tom Bailey's a nut. The guy's uptight. He should get a life.

I knew a fellow at Iowa who wrote exactly (so far as I could ever tell) once a year. I mean he simply stood up from dinner at The Mill one evening and said he was going home to write a story. And he did. As I remember, it was a good story too. And Louise Gluck, who was our neighbor when we lived in Cambridge, tended to the needs of her flower garden all through the spring until one day . . . she wrote and wrote and wrote and wrote, poem after poem, until they were all out, her next book!

I would only caution, as Hemingway says in his interview for *The Paris Review,* that you don't "kid yourself" that you're writing when, truth be told, you're not writing anything at all. "So as not to kid myself," Hemingway said he kept track of his daily output of words, recording them, George Plimpton tells us, "on a large chart made out of the side of a cardboard packing case and set up against the wall under the nose of a mounted gazelle head . . . 450, 575, 462, 1250, back to 512, the higher figures on the days he puts in extra work so he won't feel guilty spending the following day fishing on the Gulf Stream."

I see value in Hemingway's enforcing an accounting on himself and his work. Of course counting page numbers is just one sort of accounting, and not even the most important one for a writer—writing 512 words a day does not guarantee they're good words, the right words. Anyone who is literate, I dare say, could sit down for an hour and blast out two pages worth of words. I once wrote five hundred pages toward a novel in a single semester. I wrote very quickly, as you might imagine, just trying to spill out the story. Somewhere along the way I became caught up in the number of pages I was writing. Then came my day of accounting, beyond the total number of pages I'd written, when John Vernon, my mentor when I was working toward my Ph.D. at the State University of New York at Binghamton, had to read those five hundred pages. (Sorry, Jack!)

What I learned from the experience is five hundred pages is just that, five hundred separate pages, unless they turn in on themselves in important and believable ways. In my case, I'd simply written out and out (and out and out and out). Five hundred? I could have written five thousand! There was nothing to stop me! I may have had some interesting characters, and there may have been a vital scene or two, but as a novel? It was an . . . *and then, and then* story (to touch back Forster's definition of the difference between a story and a plot). It simply did not work.

So, counting words or page numbers, at least in my experience, isn't everything by any means, and it may well amount to nothing at all. But I've already admitted that I still log in first thing every morning, writing the date, day, and time in my journal, before I begin, just as I used to punch the time clock at my first regular job which came with my turning fifteen, a pot washer at, yes, you guessed if you still recall our fictional student, Jack, in Part One, The Buffet Royale.

WRITE A SHORT STORY!

So, you still want to write a short story? My guess is that you've found the most difficult part is simply getting started. Let's consider the entire process, from beginning to drafting, to rewriting, and polishing.

How to Begin

How to begin? How do we go beyond merely exercising the individual elements of the short story in order to "shape simultaneously (in an expanding creative moment) . . . characters, plot, and setting, each inextricably connected to the others . . . making a whole world in a single coherent gesture, as a potter makes a pot?" As Gardner goes on to tell us that Coleridge "puts it," the answer is that "[the writer] must copy, with his finite mind, the process of the infinite 'I AM'".

The elements of the short story—as we've noted again and again—do not work alone. A short story *works* by calling upon the elements all at once. But how is this possible? There's so much to *consider.* The contorted effort that can be the writing of our first short story seems to me something like a first tennis lesson where we've paid someone to help us to simply (or so we thought) make contact with the ball. The pro tells us to (1) turn sideways to the net and (2) to take our racket back, (3) to bend our knees, (4) to keep our eyes on the ball, (5) to step forward, and (6) to swing, emphatically reminding us (7) to "watch the ball!," and (8) to connect just in front of our front foot, and (9) to follow through with the head of the racket, and (10) pointing it past where you want the ball to go.

No sweat, right?

Trying our best, we turn, take back, bend, watch, step, swing, connect, and follow through. We look up to see the effect of our stroke. Where's the ball? The pro is tapping his foot; he glances at his watch. Tick, tick, tick. And then the ball plops back onto the court—only it's the court behind us, over the fifteen-foot fence. Foul ball. Strike one. Though, entangled as we've become in our own ten-step effort, it may feel like we're out of our league. There's just too much to consider. Making a single coherent gesture out of all these separate instructions seems the most difficult thing we've ever done.

It is the practice of process, I have discovered, having sprayed entire hoppers of balls onto adjoining courts, having written more than my fair share of unsuccessful short stories, that makes such a successful gesture even remotely possible. Through the process of drafting and revision, the elements, merely hinted and hacked away at in draft after draft, slowly become defined and refined. We go from clodding about the court axing away at the ball to competent players fluidly rallying backhands and forehands crosscourt and down the line.

In Gardner's analogy a writer creates a story as a potter makes a pot. The comparison parallels his point that the elements are to be employed all at once—the lump of clay rises spinning on the wheel shaped by the pressure of the potter's hands. The thumbs press in and slowly widen out, a pot is shaped. The techniques the potter has been taught have been employed at once—in a single coherent gesture. In that moment of rising there was no time to think, only to act, to *do*. But the bowl that's been raised could as easily go back into the slop bucket as into the fire of the kiln to be glazed. Once again, I'm insisting on the *if-at-first-you-don't-succeed* prospects of process. I am drawing a distinction between the first draft of a short story—in which all the elements are invoked at once in an effort to "tell a story"—and the process of revision—in which the separate elements may be reworked (again and again and again and again if ·necessary) to function flawlessly in a complete short story. The glaze, then, that the potter paints on to fire the pot in the kiln comes after the single coherent gesture has been successfully made. To me, this is like the *polish* with which the writer buffs his or her short story for publication. Beginning is simply the first step in the process.

Getting started on a story means *drafting*. Let us, then, begin.

Drafting

If I were giving you your first tennis lesson, I would simply tell you to turn sideways with your racket back and watch the ball. Then I'd bounce a ball to you. Chances are it might still go over the fence behind you. We would try it again. And then again. You can only focus on one thing at a time, and the most important thing you can focus on is the ball—afterall, the object is to hit the ball.

Let me turn you sideways with your racket back. Short stories, as we've discussed, are most importantly about character. *We are our desires.* Every character wants or needs something. Consider such a character. Name their desire. Now, simply ask yourself why they can't have what they wish for or need. That's your basic conflict. Now, keeping your eye on that problem (the ball!), write a draft of the story in which your character struggles to satisfy the specified desire.

And if this draft goes wide of the mark, write another. And if that one goes straight up and bounces down two courts over, write another.

Exercises that put into practice the individual elements of craft are useful. Beginning writers can use them to develop confidence and to become aware of the workings of craft. But, in my opinion, there's no substitute for simply swinging away, draft after draft.

To return to Gardner's analogy: Drafting has always seemed to me like working the air bubbles out of the clay you hope to shape into that bowl to glaze. I don't believe we know what we have to say until we begin to see the words that materialize on the page. Andre Dubus agrees with the political scientist he meets in his essay on "The Habit of Writing" who says, "It all happens at the typewriter. I never get any work done by thinking." And Frank O'Connor, the Irish short story writer, whose book *The Lonely Voice,* remains one of the most well-respected commentaries on the short story form said in an interview for the *Paris Review:*

> "Get black on white" used to be Maupassant's advice—that's what I always do. I don't give a hoot what the writing's like, I write any sort of rubbish which will cover the main outlines of the story, then I can begin to see it. When I write, when I draft a story, I never think of writing nice sentences about, "It was a nice August evening when Elizabeth Jane Moriarty was coming down the road." I just write roughly what happened, and then I'm able to see what the construction looks like. It's the design of the story which to me is most important, the thing that tells you there's a bad gap in the narrative here and you really ought to fill that up in some way or another. I'm always looking at the design of the story, not the treatment.

In our earlier discussion on the difference between plotting the short story and the novel, we noted that in his essay "On Writing," Raymond Carver said he was shocked after reading Flannery O'Connor's essay "Writing Short Stories" in which she revealed that when she began to write "Good

Country People" she didn't know "there was going to be a Ph.D. with a wooden leg in it" and that she "merely found herself one morning writing a description of two women [she] knew something about, and before [she] realized it, [she] had equipped one of them with a daughter with a wooden leg," and that, more, when she brought in the Bible salesman she had "no idea what [she] was going to do with him," and that "[she] didn't know he was going to steal that wooden leg until ten or twelve lines before he did it, but that when [she] found out that this was going to happen, [she] realized it was inevitable." Carver couldn't believe that "[O'Connor], or anyone for that matter, wrote stories in this fashion. [Carver] thought this was [his] uncomfortable secret, and [he] was a little uneasy with it. For sure [he] thought this way of working on a short story somehow revealed [his] own shortcomings."

Carver goes on to relate how he "once sat down to write what turned out to be a pretty good story, though only the first sentence of the story had offered itself to me when [he] began it":

> For several days I'd been going around with this sentence in my head: "He was running the vacuum cleaner when the telephone rang." I knew a story was there and that it wanted telling. I felt it in my bones, that a story belonged with that beginning, if I could just have the time to write it. I found the time, an entire day—twelve, fifteen hours even—if I wanted to make use of it. I did, and I sat down in the morning and wrote the first sentence, and other sentences promptly began to attach themselves. I made the story just as I'd make a poem; one line and then the next, and the next. Pretty soon I could see a story, and I knew it was my story, the one I'd been wanting to write.

I like the idea of starting out with a single sentence in mind. I also admire Flannery O'Connor's courage in sitting down to write not even knowing that there was going to be a Ph.D. with a wooden leg in her story. And I believe absolutely in Maupassant's advice to "Get black on white," which Frank O'Connor wrote by.

I once wrote a "pretty good" short story called "Crow Man," about a black field hand in the Mississippi Delta who comes under the influence of a white pilot, a crop duster from Ohio. Though I was born in the Delta, grew up spending a part of every summer there, and even worked driving a tractor as Jasper does, watching out from under the cow shed as crop dusters dove down over the telephone wires and swooped across the cotton fields, raining pellets on top of me, I had no idea where this story came from. I had not planned to write it nor had I ever thought about the characters before. It was born in a single draft in four solid hours of typing one morning and except for minor revisions and clarifications was hardly rewritten at all. After I finished that morning, I buried it in my filing cabinet for three months before I dared take another look at it! But when I did pull it out I found myself reading it straight through from beginning to end as if I were reading someone else's story! For me, that is always the truest mark.

In my experience, such stories are gifts. Another story I wrote, "Snow Dreams," included at the end of this section alongside its galleys for publication, was no gift. I *earned* this short story, which grew nearly as painful and difficult for me to write as the tragic story of it was to tell. A father goes hunting with his two sons and accidentally shoots one of them. When he sees what he's done, he turns the rifle on himself. The son who's left—his younger son—finds his father and his brother. It is this character who brings meaning to the piece. "Snow Dreams" took me a year and half to write, and although I didn't work on it every single morning, I worked on it more mornings than not. When I finished telling it, the story turned out to be only fifteen pages long, though at one point it was as long as thirty-five or forty pages.

It took me draft after draft to discover how to tell the tale—to uncover the necessary levels of perspective. The question that plagued me after having written the first section was: How I could bring meaning to the piece if my narrator died? I began by trying to tell a story about a father who accidentally shoots his only son and then takes his own life. Over time, I learned that the father had a second son. It was this shift in perspective to the younger son's point of view that led me to understand the meaning of the story I'd been attempting to write and which enabled me to write it. So, even though I'd known from the outset the basic story—what happened at the end—finding out how and why it happened to these particular characters took some doing.

All this goes back to what I've said that I repeat over and over to the students in my short story workshops: *Short stories aren't written; they are rewritten.* So, now that you have a draft, let's think about how to realize its potential.

Rewriting

To be sure, there are nearly as many ways in which writers compose their drafts as there are writers who draft them. But if there is any act of process upon which contemporary writers can agree, I believe it would have to be the importance of rewriting.

Most writers I know rely on rewriting to shape their work. When asked in the same *Paris Review* interview noted above if he rewrote his stories,

Frank O'Connor nodded, "Endlessly, endlessly, endlessly. And keep on rewriting, and after it's published, and after it's published in book form, I usually rewrite it again. I've rewritten versions of most of my early stories and one of these days, God's help, I'll publish these as well." And he did, too. "Guests of the Nation" (*Collected Stories*) is one of the finest stories he rewrote and republished, and it is worthwhile to check out both versions and compare them. A few of the changes are subtle indeed, but perhaps more instructive for being so seemingly slight. *Why bother?* we might ask. But then we wouldn't be thinking as seriously as Frank O'Connor who proves his determination to make every word right, no matter what it takes.

Another worthwhile comparison is between Raymond Carver's "The Bath" and the much expanded and elaborated-on short story he fleshed out on its bones, "A Small, Good Thing." Here we see not only the care and determination to change particular words, but the courage to write what, in effect, becomes a new story.

PRACTICAL ASPECTS OF REWRITING

Beginning writers often have the impression that rewriting means simply changing the choice of a word or correcting mistakes in grammar, removing or adding commas, etc. Veteran writers have learned the hard way that rewriting might be better termed "reworking." Often a story (or novel or essay) must be completely reimagined, sometimes abandoned. We rewrite not merely to correct our grammar (though of course this is a part of revision), we rewrite to zero in on the story we're trying to bring to life. Much to the dismay of my students, I like to flip a draft over and show them the blank back page. This, I say, is all that *has* to be there.

But how can we go about making the page blank again? How do we separate our original intent from the will of the story? In the following essay, "The Habit of Writing," which he first wrote for *On Writing Short Stories,* Andre Dubus discusses his method of "receiving" a story. My friend, Tom Perrotta (author of *Bad Haircut,* a collection of stories, and the novels *Election, The Wishbones,* and most recently, *Joe College*), has called this essay of Dubus's typically (for Dubus!) "idiosyncratic." I know what Tom means—the idea of a male writer "gestating," especially an ex-Marine like Andre, or of his declaring his make-no-bones-about-it Catholic view of "receiving" a story as an act of grace remind us indeed of vintage Dubus. The universal value for all aspiring writers is communicated to us in the way in which Dubus makes his idiosyncratic journey as a working writer particularly accessible to each of us.

As you read through this essay, note the sorts of things Dubus did to make his stories new again—from keeping a journal, to exercising his body after writing each morning, to talking to folks in his workshop, to reading his work aloud on tape, to "listening" closely to his characters, writing "vertically" instead of "horizontally." It would also be beneficial if at all possible to read a few the stories he mentions here before you begin. "A Father's Story," "The Fat Girl," and "Anna" can all be found in his *Selected Stories.*

ANDRE DUBUS

The Habit of Writing

I GESTATE: FOR MONTHS, OFTEN FOR YEARS. AN IDEA COMES TO ME FROM wherever they come, and I write it in a notebook. Sometimes I forget it's there. I don't think about it. By *think* I mean *plan.* I try never to think about where a story will go. This is as hard as writing, maybe harder; I spend most of my waking time doing it; it is hard work, because I want to know what the story will do and how it will end and whether or not I can write it; but I must not know, or I will kill the story by controlling it; I work to surrender. I know a political scientist who writes books. Once I told him that I try simply to go to the desk and receive what will come. He said he did the same. I said: "I thought you guys used outlines. Don't you already know what you want to say?"

"No," he said. "It all happens at the typewriter. I never get any work done by thinking."

The Zen archer does not release the arrow; he concentrates, breathes; the arrow releases itself, and the target draws it to itself.

I gestate, and when I am blessed, I am working on one story while another is growing in me. I begin to see characters' souls, sometimes their faces. I give them bodies and names. That is all I need, for most of my ideas are situations, and many of them are questions: *What if?* What would happen if a man's daughter accidentally killed a man by hitting him with her car, and did not stop but drove home and told her father? When I see the first two scenes, I begin writing. This truly means that the first two scenes show themselves to me. I may be watching a movie or driving my car or talking with a friend, and here come the scenes. It means it is time. The story is ready for me to receive it. Then I must write, with the most intense concentration I can muster.

In 1979 I was at someone's house, at a party, and I met a lawyer. By then I had been writing for a quarter of a century, since I was seventeen years old. He asked me what was the hardest part of writing. I said: "I just learned what it is. Concentration. I don't mean ridding the mind of bills and heartbreak and other things. I mean absolute concentration on one word. Becoming the word."

"I'm a Zen archer," he said, "and lately my concentration has been bad."

We talked about pitchers, how sometimes they lose concentration during a game, and can't get it back. And he said: "In this country, they'll forgive you for losing concentration while writing a story, or trying a case, or pitching a baseball, or shooting an arrow. But there's one place they won't: in bed. They'll always say 'You don't love me.'"

I repeat this because it's funny and profound. If we can lose concentration—and we do, we do—performing a natural act that animals can perform as easily as some of them kill, and if we lose concentration performing this with one we truly love, two lovers in harmony in body and spirit, how can we expect anything while writing but a very difficult and intense struggle simply to concentrate on discovering one word after another, and putting them on a blank page till the page is no longer blank? And filling a page with words means nothing of itself. We have to make those words into human beings, while writing the story; and if we do it well enough, that reader will remember these fictional people, as if they actually walked the earth, and entered, however briefly, the reader's life. Anyone who wants to write should read Joseph Conrad's Preface to *The Nigger of the Narcissus;* I have read nothing better about writing prose, giving life to imagined characters.

I told the lawyer *concentration* because of a story I was working on then. It's called "Anna." A few years earlier, I'd read in the *Boston Globe* about a man who robbed a bank in Boston, then went to a phone booth and called his girl-friend in Florida to tell her about it; she asked him where the phone booth was, then whispered to her boyfriend to go next door and call the Boston Police; then she kept the cuckolded bank robber on the phone till the police came. I wrote this in my notebook, and wrote: "story of betrayal." In those days I was still planning stories. I only wrote one of them, in 1968 or 1969, exactly as I had planned it, and it was dead long before I put the final period on the page; I had not given free will to the young woman in the story I dropped into the waste-basket. So I knew stories would never become what I planned them to be and that, with draft after draft, they would tell me what they were. I usually wrote five or six drafts; generally the first draft was ter-

rible and several only showed me what the story was not, and generally what
it was not was precisely what I had thought it would be. A novella, *Adultery,*
took seven drafts, four hundred typed pages (I write in longhand, then type)
to get the final sixty pages. This was foolish, or seems foolish now, but perhaps I needed it for those twenty-five years before I confronted "Anna,"
which threw me on my back, then raised me up to a new way of working.

Of course I have to plan some things. With "Anna" I had to plan a robbery. I went to see my pharmacist, told him what I was doing, and asked him
how much money someone could steal from a drugstore. He said very little
from his, because he had regular customers who charged everything; but he
said that from a drugstore on a highway, especially one that sold money
orders, a robber could get two thousand dollars. So I made up a drugstore in
a shopping center on Route 1, north of Boston, not far from Haverhill, where
I live, and where Anna and Wayne lived, a young, unmarried couple, he a
maker of hamburgers at Wendy's, she a clerk at a convenience store. But I
planned too much, still, after a quarter of a century, believing these things
would happen. Even though, in my late twenties, I had written a novel, *The
Lieutenant,* and my protagonist had broken my heart when he failed to climb
one more rung on the moral ladder; even though character after character in
stories had broken my heart, doing things I wished they would not. The
young man in "Anna," because he had no money, had only a hunting knife
as a tool for their first robbery of the drugstore. I planned how later he would
get a gun. They lived upstairs in an apartment building and on the ground
floor was a widow. She would kill herself with gas from the stove. He would
smell the gas and go into her apartment, open the windows, and find, in her
bedside table, a pistol she had chosen not to use. He would escalate, robbing
now with a gun, robbing several places, and Anna, in fear and maybe good
conscience, would betray him to the police. I actually wrote all of this nonsense in my notebook; writing it down makes it feel like it must happen.
That is why I call it nonsense.

The story is in Anna's point of view. I began it slowly, writing about her,
then moved to the robbery. But it was very difficult for me to become her. I
kept telling friends: "As far as I know, I don't know anyone who's commit-
ted armed robbery." I kept writing, trying for those five pages a day, but each
day I felt as though I were watching Anna from a distance, and I could not
get inside of her, become her. Then one day or night I decided to try a different approach. I told myself that next day at the desk I would not leave a
sentence until I knew precisely what Anna was feeling. I told myself that
even if I wrote only fifty words, I would stay with this. By now Anna and
Wayne had robbed the drugstore and had driven to a liquor store in their own

town, but the store was closed, so they went to the neighborhood bar where they were regulars.

At my desk next morning I held my pen and hunched my shoulders and leaned my head down, physically trying to look more deeply into the page of the notebook. I did this for only a moment before writing, as a batter takes practice swings while he waits in the on-deck circle. In that moment I began what I call vertical writing, rather than horizontal. I had never before thought in these terms. But for years I had been writing horizontally, trying to move forward (those five pages); now I would try to move down, as deeply as I could.

I always stop writing for the day in mid-sentence, a trick I learned from Ernest Hemingway when I wrote a paper about him while I was a college freshman. That was his method, and his advice to writers: stop in mid-sentence, while it is going well (I stop in mid-scene too), then exercise your body and forget the story and let the subconscious do the work. On that first morning of vertical writing, I read the half-sentence, with Anna and Wayne in the bar, hunched my shoulders and leaned toward the page one more time, then slowly dove. Very slowly. I worked on feeling all of her physical sensations. There are probably too many tactile details in that story, there are probably too many in every story I've written since "Anna," but that is the only way I can work. And something happened, in that bar with Anna.

I did become her, through her senses. *You must know what a glass of beer feels like in her hand,* I told myself; *you must know everything.* While they stood at the bar, I learned this: she truly loved Wayne. Now, I was excited. I had not written many words, and suddenly I knew that this was a story about two people who loved each other. It was not a story of betrayal. Walls fell down and everything was open: I knew nothing of what would happen next, and that was frightening—though simple to solve—but it was wonderful, it was elating, I was both lost and free. There were no more plans. The widow remained in the story, but there would be no suicide, no gun, no more robberies. Now what?

They were still in the bar. *Just follow them home,* I told myself, and since then I have believed that you can write a story simply by becoming a character and following that character home. Or through a day or a night. Who among us is not a story, or several of them, every day? So I went home with Anna and Wayne. Next day I woke with her, felt her bad hangover, went to work with her. Then what? I followed her home. Now, when working on a story, I keep telling myself: *Just follow the dots: become the character and follow; there will be a story.* So that night after work, Anna and Wayne went to the mall. Her hangover was still bad. They bought things. They went home and carried the things upstairs: a record player, a television set, a vacuum cleaner. They left the things and walked to the bar. They had not bought food or beer; I *noticed* that; I did not plan it. They had forgotten their nearly bare refrigerator. On the way to the bar they walked past a car dealership. I almost wrote that, through the large windows, the new cars showed them what they would never be able to buy, showed them the economic futility of their lives. But I decided not to point this out; maybe a reader would notice. I was still following the dots: they went to the bar because of their hangovers, and the spiritual fatigue caused by the mall's stimulation, and by their spending money on dead yet good things that would give them comfort but not hope. In the bar they drank, then went home, where in bed they sadly talked, knowing now that they could never get everything. And then I knew it was a story about America too, about the things we are expected to buy and love, and the things that are supposed to give us equality with other Americans, and fulfill our souls. Next day Anna took their clothes to the laundromat and washed them. The story was done. I had written slowly every day, and in one draft it was done.

Because I wrote it vertically; if I had written it horizontally, I would have discovered in the first or at least an early draft that it was not a story of betrayal, or even a story about robbers. In the fifth or sixth draft I would have written the story as it wanted me to. When I have finished a story in longhand, I read it into a tape recorder. Doing this makes me see things I had not seen before, probably because reading aloud is a physical act that heightens my concentration. Remember: before each day's work I read the manuscript from the beginning; so, by the time I have finished a story, I have read sentences as many as a hundred times or more. While reading aloud I change things: often I cut or compress. The day after I record the story, I listen to it, and usually have a few changes to make, but not as many as when I read it aloud. Then it is ready to type. When I wrote horizontally, I wrote an average of three stories a year, in a good year. Writing vertically, I still write three stories a year, in a good year.

My stories often stop; I think this happens less since I began writing vertically. While I was writing horizontally about sixty-five percent of my stories stopped, and would not move. I do not believe in forcing a story. If it stops, it is telling me that I am not seeing it or hearing it. I could force it, impose action on it, but it would be false. So I lay it aside, and start another story, and wait for the motionless story to put itself into motion and to tell me it is moving now, and I should turn to it. A story called "The Fat Girl" stopped after the young woman's roommate put her on a diet and she lost weight. Simply stopped. I put it in a drawer. A year or more later I was walking on a small town sidewalk when those words came into my mind, from the air, the sky, from God knows where: *Get her married.* That night I wrote, and the next day, and the story was done.

I gestate. In 1985 I wrote a story, "A Father's Story," which came in one longhand draft, one tape recording, then a typed draft. I don't remember how many weeks or months I spent writing the story, but the work truly began years before I wrote the first sentence. I used to walk, fast and happily, for five miles, for conditioning and peace of soul and clearing of clutter from my mind. On one of these walks, an idea came: *Write about a man of faith. Make him a good-field no-hit infielder who plays triple A ball and knows he will never play in the major leagues.* When I got home, I wrote that in my notebook. Much later, months, maybe a year, while I was on my conditioning walk, another idea came: *What is the morality of a hit-and-run accident? I know the civil law; but what is the moral obligation, if you have accidentally killed someone? Can you flee?* I wrote that in my notebook. At least a year later—oh, I miss those conditioning walks, now that I am in a wheelchair; they gave me transcendence and opened me to the voices—another idea came: *Why not make the man of faith not a ballplayer but the father of a hit-and-run driver?* I wrote that in my notebook and it felt right.

Now I did have to think. Unlike my government, or American voters, or both, I believe I have to give jobs to my characters. I also had to decide whether the driver would be a son or a daughter. An instinct told me to make her a daughter, because the father may treat her differently than he would a son. I did not know how, or even if he would treat her differently. It was an instinct, and I have faith in those. Nearly absolute faith, when the instincts are about writing. So: a father and a daughter, and a false start. I gave the father a convenience store with a coffee and lunch counter; probably he had a wife and other children; I don't remember. Nor do I remember why he did not work as a character. I was interested in his owning this store where police officers from his small town would come to drink coffee; they would be his friends—casual ones, but still friends—and he would be concealing his daughter's crime from them. But the story stopped, and I laid it aside. I do not understand these things; I think part of my work is not to understand. Not long ago I wrote a story called "All the Time in the World." Again and again, it stopped about midway through, when the woman in the story met a man whom she would love and marry. All I wanted to do was write a story about how and why a man and woman met each other. But when the man—Ted Briggs—entered the story, it stopped. He was a slender, angular man; I gave him the body of a man I knew. One day, while I was not writing the story, I saw him differently: he was a broad and strong man with a cane and a limp from a knee wounded in Vietnam, and an alcoholic who no longer drank. This new body gave Ted Briggs something richer: he was a man, wounded in body and spirit, and from this I got another story I wrote later, "Falling in Love," about Ted when he was drinking and taking erotic love too easily. With Ted's new body and soul, "All the Time in the World" moved dot after dot after dot.

I imagined a new man for "A Father's Story": I used the body of a man who owned a riding stable where I used to bring one of my daughters for Sunday afternoon lessons, in the 1970s, when she was in high school. I gave this man the riding stable. Now he had a body and a job. And I took away his wife, made him a divorced Catholic, so that his faith would be action: he will not remarry and he tries to be celibate, and almost perfectly is. His children are grown, and he lives alone, and I gave him a priest as his best friend.

But I was not ready to begin. He had a name, Luke Ripley, and work, and he went to daily mass and cared for his horses. It was time for me to immerse. I read William James's *Varieties of Religious Experience.* Then I reread Kierkegaard's *Fear and Trembling:* this was in the winter of 1983 while I was teaching at Bradford College in Haverhill. I asked a woman friend, a philosophy teacher, if she would like to team-teach *Fear and Trembling* in an open seminar, without grades or credit, and she said she would. We somehow announced this seminar, saying we would meet one night a week, for as long as all of us wished. Then we started, and students came to the classroom; I don't remember how many times we met, only that, for the last night, the woman and I met with one female student in the neighborhood bar. Now I was ready, and the story did not take a long time to write; I finished it in April. A blizzard came one school day that April, canceling classes. At my desk, while snow blew outside, I knew my story was ending. I stopped, in mid-sentence, mid-scene. Next day the sky was clear, but I called the registrar and told her I wasn't feeling well and could not teach, and I went to my desk. I had to know how this story would end. And that day it did end, and in its closing lines, I knew.

Nearly everything in that story surprised me. I had planned how the accident would happen. That was all. The story is in the first person, and I knew that its beginning would have to establish, for a reader, that Luke was a man of faith. All I had to work with was his going to daily mass, and his nearly perfect refusal to make love out of wedlock, therefore his refusal to date women, and to consider marriage forbidden by the Catholic church. I had nothing more.

But on the first page Luke took my pen and moved: he talked about his solitary life, about his rituals of loneliness, about God, and his priest friend, and his marriage and children. I kept telling my wife: "He won't stop talking. *Nothing* is happening, and I can't make him shut up." That was at times when I was away from the desk, and worrying about those words in the notebook on the desk, but I should not have been worrying, or thinking about Luke Ripley. This is hard work: trying to free yourself from thinking about what you have written that day and will write tomorrow.

I taught two classes every weekday afternoon, and that freed me. At night I had homework, reading novels and stories for the literature classes; and my wife and I always, on weeknights, went to a movie or watched one on video. Then there was sleep. Of course the day after the April blizzard, I could no longer wait, and I went to my desk. I should not have worried about Luke talking on and on; for at the desk, I did not worry. I *was* him, I spoke; I also listened to him. But not from a distance, the kind I had had from Anna till I began to write vertically. No, I listened to him as he listened to himself. I will paraphrase E. M. Forster because I don't remember where I read this: How can I know what I think about something till I hear what I have to say about it? This is profound, I believe, and universal; when we speak from the heart, with no plan, no point to make, we discover truths we did not know that we knew. So at the desk Luke's talking filled me, surprised me, and I was one with it and with him.

I believe "A Father's Story" was twenty-six typed pages, and for the first thirteen of those—in longhand, slowly, vertically—Luke Ripley talked. Finally he stopped and told the story of the accident, and his daughter coming home to him. Then I could tell my wife: "He's finally stopped talking; something is finally *happening*." There is a strong wind blowing that night, in the story, only because one night I woke up to go to the bathroom and outside a strong wind was blowing and I thought: *I should put wind in a story.* Near the end of the story's action, I began, while writing, to see images: Luke and his daughter riding horses together, and I thought that would be the final scene. Only because I was seeing it. It did not become the final scene. And, as Luke was helping his daughter conceal the crime, I discovered something: in his first thirteen pages of talking he had said, that, in love, feeling should be subordinate to action. Yet here he was, acting only because of his feelings—love for his daughter—and paying no heed to his belief in good action, no matter what one feels.

The story's action ends; Luke's daughter drives home to Florida. He talks again. On my last day of longhand work, the sunlit day after the blizzard, I left my desk to make another cup of tea and said to my wife, "He's talking again. Now he's talking to *God*." I took the tea to my desk, picked up the pen Luke was holding anyway, and held on, while he talked to God. God talked too; Luke gave Him his lines. Then he stopped and, with gratitude and joy, I placed at the end of the story its final period.

Polishing

Polishing for publication is the last step the writer takes before revealing the "Pot" he or she's glazed for the world to see—and judge!

Polishing means exactly what we'd think it would—putting the spit-shine on a short story before sending it out in an envelope to be considered for publication. Polishing includes close attention to spelling, grammar, and punctuation—attention which, as I've insisted, must go beyond the spelling and grammar checks of even the best word processing programs. In this capacity, a single trusted reader or a close-knit workshop group of writers is invaluable. Recognition of standard manuscript format is also a good idea. Remember, when you finally feel ready to begin submitting your work for consideration of publication, you are in competition with hundreds, and per-haps, depending on where you choose to send your story, thousands, of other manuscripts. You want to make your short story as easily accessible as pos-sible—at least on the surface! I once received a short story that had been typed, single-spaced in the available blank space on the back of old *Reader's Digest* covers! At the time I was reading upwards of fifty or so manuscripts a day every day on top of my other responsibilities as a teacher and a writer. Needless, to say, I plopped the story in the return envelope unread. I don't mean to sound heartless—I've had my struggles as a writer, too—but I feel strongly that the writer must meet the editor half-way.

A good essay to read on "Publishers and Publishing" is by C. Michael Curtis, Senior Editor of *The Atlantic Monthly,* where for the past twenty or so years he been largely responsible for almost of the fiction the magazine has published. The essay was originally written for *On Writing Short Sto-ries,* but was also published under the title "How to Read a Rejection Slip" in *Poets and Writers.* Curtis considers all aspects of polishing toward pub-lication, from "How to Read a Rejection Slip" to "Cover Letters," "Quar-terlies versus Slicks," "Simultaneous Submissions," "General Cautions," and a word on "Editors."

Another aspect of polishing is the fact of revision after a story has been accepted for publication. When my short story "Snow Dreams" was slated for publication in the Winter 98–99 issue of *DoubleTake,* Alexa Dilworth, who was then an associate editor, helped me ready the galleys of the story to go to press.

Alexa made it clear from the start that any changes to be made were entirely up to me. They would, she said, publish the story exactly as I'd polished and sent it. She did, though, she wrote, have a few "suggestions." She Fed-Exed a copy of the galley that she had carefully edited, marking her suggestions in pencil. Fortunately, Alexa was not suggesting any major revisions. I'd done that sort of ground-breaking work in the year and half it took me to come to terms with how to tell the story. All but one of her suggestions hinged on the use of a word, a clarification, or a possible deletion. I considered each of her suggestions, talked them over with my wife Sarah, and then phoned Alexa. We spent the next hour or so going over each of her notations and talking through the reasons. Some suggestions I agreed with immediately. Others I didn't agree with. Overall, her comments helped me see my polished story as "new again" and allowed me to tighten and clarify it again. Below I've offered a copy the galleys we worked on as well as the final story as it appeared in *DoubleTake* and, later, *The Pushcart Prize Stories 2000.* Afterward I've offered comments on the changes I made, or chose not to make, and some explanation as to why.

15.gg.walbert/bailey (fiction) 9/6/98 2:27 PM Page 7

*Comes in Corrections 9/11/98.
*Can pick by wednesday with end changes.

FICTION

tion, fingering those initials he had stitched in red. It was clear to me even then that he had worked on the letter like a boy who wants to be a writer. Certain words broke his true voice, were tried on, tested for fit. They were a hat too big for him–the Randall I knew interrupted again and again by the Randall Randall might have become. The *Hell*, as I have mentioned. A line from some dead poet–*I would think of a thousand things, lovely and durable, and taste them slowly*–I had heard him recite in his room a hundred times, and other words I recognized as words still left to learn. It seemed he wanted to cram everything in.

Still, it is a beautiful letter. I have saved it for years. It finds its way into my hands at the oddest times, and when it does I always hold it for a while, rereading the envelope. Teddy

shouts *Carry on!*, and I curse him. All of them. Then I pull out the paper, one folded sheath, and unfold it as slowly as I would a gift I'd never opened. My fear is that somehow in my absence, his words have come undone, been shaken loose, rearranged, so that what I will find is no more than a page of randomness, letters shuffled into forms with no meaning, indecipherable, foreign.

But there! My name in salutation, the sweetness of the attendant *Dear*. I'm again as I was, as he may have pictured me–writing at that desk beneath the window, the metal newly polished, the air fresh, eucalyptus-scented, the sea lions barking–when he signed *Love, Randall*, and underlined it with a flourish as elegant as a bow. ■

Changes in house 9/16/98

Snow Dreams

BY TOM BAILEY

I

THE SIDE DOOR cracks open. I expect my eldest–dark, curly-headed Gary David–but it's my eighteen-year-old, blond Kevin, who slides in from outside, red-eyed and sheepish. I look him up and down as I hold the bowl and beat the batter. He's standing, hands pocketed, casting around the kitchen, glancing at the sink, the clock, the floor, the beamed ceiling, the smoking Upland. I've tried to raise my boys like I've managed to train every dog I've ever owned–with a biscuit in my left hand and a switch in my right–and I'm burning now to smack this son of mine with the accusation of what he knows is right, because I brought up both of them to know better than to drink and ever handle a gun. I wait for Kevin's eyes to finally meet mine and then, using a firm gaze, I give him a spank-hard look. He glances away, ashamed, I think, and I go back to pouring out our pancakes, reach for the boiling coffee.

There's a low scuff-kick at the door and Kevin has to unstick his hands from his Carhartts to open it for Gary David loaded up past his chin with split wood. To see my two grown sons standing side by side, I imagine folks could get the idea my Susan's made a practice of visiting long, lazy afternoons with the postman–summer day to winter night different as these two boys are. Kevin's more simply the spitting

image of who I used to be before I suddenly, at the age of nineteen, while serving my time in Nam, split out of my issue with a last thirty-seven pound, three-and-a-quarter inch growing spurt, before I rolled over forty-five and my own bright blue eyes dimmed, and I got fixed with these squarish, silver-rimmed bifocals, when I still had all of my own straw-blond, thick, and wavy hair. Standing next to him, Gary David–both in looks and in his shyness and care–mirrors his granddaddy, Susan's black-headed part Onondaga daddy, as if he'd sat up in the grave and lurched back out into the world for one more tall, stiff try at things.

Another, bigger, difference between them is that my youngest, Kevin, is the first of us Hazens to go on to school past the *ninth grade*, taking classes now down by the local junior college in Canton. Next year, though, he wants to transfer full-time to Cortland State. He wants to live over three hours away and have us pay for him to earn himself a *real* degree. The first two times he mentioned this I felt the pressured dollar sign of it ticking bomb-big behind my left eye. The third time I exploded, yelling out before Susan could grab my knee and squeeze, *You just want to be on the parental dole your whole goddamn life! You don't want to have to ever work for a living!* Gary David, who's more sensible about these things, is going to be a carpenter after me. He'll find himself a nice girl like that Anne Burke whose

or ✓   CHANGE ¹

Pick up wednesday

Galleys for "Snow Dreams" by Tom Bailey

15.gg.walbert/bailey (fiction)   9/6/98 2:27 PM   Page 8

FICTION

family's lived outside Sebattis near long as we Hazens have. He'll marry and name his first boy Gary. But what I find most curious in their natures is that while Gary David was born with the heart and desire, born with the *belief* in the building, his brother Kevin has the better hands, a sharper eye for the truths of wood grains and the absolute honesty of plumb lines. Though perhaps even more strange still is that these two boys—these two *men*—aged a good five years apart and night and day opposite as they are can be such good friends.

Gary David's sniffing strong over Kevin. "You leave any at the brewery?" he asks. "Who was it over, not that Jeanie Prescott again?" By not answering Kevin convicts himself. "Aw, Kev . . .," Gary David starts and gently sets down the wood like you wouldn't expect a boy to—even while he's talking to Kevin being considerate of his mother sleeping upstairs. Kevin simply stands with his hands in his pockets, blinking, red-eyed. He's brought this girl around once or twice, and I guess she's green-eyed cute enough for dating. But she's from *New York City* of all places, just going to school up here in our North Country so she can ski seven months of the year, and she's not one of us or even remotely of our kind.

Two weeks ago Kevin asked me if he could skip his buck this season, and when I asked and eyed him why he confessed it was because this Jeanie didn't *like* it. She didn't want him to go because she didn't think hunting was *right.* "No," I said to him, "no, you can't *skip* it," and stood up and left him standing there, more abrupt with him than I'd meant to be I guess, but too full of the voice-shaking responsibility of it right then to speak reasonably. This responsibility which was my father's responsibility before mine and his father's responsibility before him: the necessity of fulfilling our tags toward stocking three freezers to get us through one of these no-fooling winters again. If we want to eat that is.

For us, deer season's not a matter of plaqueing a staring head nor congratulating ourselves over a rack of horns. For us, hunting's as crucial as surrounding every inch of spare space under our extra-wide porch and eaves with carefully cut, dried, and split wood—never imagining, not even able to imagine nor capable of comprehending in the blistering chainsaw heat of summer, that we could ever in twelve straight hard winters use all we've stacked, and then and again stumped equally as incredulous every May when we have to scramble up the last left skinny sticks and shavings of bark to heat the freezing kitchen, first 5:00 A.M. This one single and unforgiving truth, out of which the responsibility I'm speaking was born: that it's already time to start the dragging and sawing and splitting again that very same afternoon if we're going to be ready for the first freeze come September. It's all about living up here—*surviving*—and so far as I'm concerned there *is* no difference between the two, but

it's the huge *difference* between us Hazens and a lot of other folk who don't know or have any idea at all about the cold.

I cut my eyes at the clock. It's already three minutes past our 2:50 A.M. time to have left and be gone. I get up with my plate, rinse it off in the sink. My boys follow behind me doing the same, and then we grab our gear, ease out the door, and crunch across the crust of snow to the truck.

* * *

It's a thirty-minute drive in to our spot, winding back through the preserve and up and across Big Cloud Mountain, onto a half oval of road bordered to the east by an icy brook. Having wound and humped to be here by 5:00, we sit silently in the truck and stare through the glare of our headlights. A teal-colored Chevy and a brown Impala squat in our space. A neon-pink bumper sticker on the truck shouts: THIS BUCK HUNTS! We pop the doors and climb out into the shadow dark, and it doesn't take a flashlight to show us by the heavy frosted glass that these fellows must've come in last night, before gun season started.

I'm quick to anger, but only a few things make me mad. If these men have broken one rule to get their deer, they won't hesitate to break another or another after that. They're the kind of men who, I know, *will do what it takes.* I knew their kind in Nam, and I could tell some stories of things they're capable of that would make your hair go straight. I've known their kind here at home, too, watched them do carpentry, say, on a government job like HUD. You'd tear out that already straightened hair to see the work these men do, screwing everyone but themselves. When I hear nightmares of evil in this world, it always comes to me in this man-shape of sloppiness and a too easy, unearned return. And it's this evil that I'm constantly on guard against—my mission I guess—what in the passing on of an honest way of living this life I hope to give the strength of to my two sons, a strength which they'll have to call upon to fight against it long after I'm gone.

Gary David breaks off the cold snap of silence. "What do you think, Dad?"

I try to put the best face on it I can. I tell myself: *There are 20,000 acres in front of us.* We'll turn our backs on their tracks and head the other way.

"Get the rifles, Gary David," I say.

The moon's up, spotlight bright. I lead and Gary David and Kevin follow. We walk down a gentle slope and then we begin the climb. The hill goes steep, mountains suddenly steeper. With all the clothes and the silly shell bag I've got slung over my shoulder I feel heavy and robotic, old. Gary David and Kevin pitched in and bought the bag for me last Christmas, and though to me it seems worse than useless with rifles on a one-day hunt, the least I can do to avoid the waste is to put it to work and carry it for them. It's unscuffed, though off-colored by dust, too stiff and strangely new and—

15.gg.walbert/bailey (fiction)   9/6/98 2:27 PM   Page 9

FICTION

for my comfort anyway—a little too close to the size and shape of a woman's purse. My own thirty-aught shells I still keep safe in looped elastic over my breast pocket the way my father did, the same way my grandfather carried his. My boys stay right behind me the whole while, young, walking easily, their breath lightly silvering.

Shots ring out into the moonlight at 3:55 A.M. They slap, *bang bang bang bang bang bang,* and then echo booming between the rows of hills. Then there're two guns, three. The first one's reloaded and starts in again, *bang bang bang bang bang bang.* All of them rage away. There are a few distinct cracks. A *ppp.* Then there's silence, a harder and stiller silence as if it seemed like having been disturbed so violently. Waiting crouched in the aftermath of the ambush, my body's tensed tight, reminded of war. It's against the law to shoot until first light, but from our right, from the east, we hear a thin but distinct, "Ya-*hooooo!*" Weekend blasters, sons-of-a-goddamn-bitches, crazy men. We angle even more sharply southwest away from them, push on, marching faster, in deeper, and then on faster and further and in deeper still.

On the down side of a saddle-humped mountain, in a circled clearing, we stop for a coffee break, eat the sugared pancakes we pocketed along, the close winter sky graining a hint of light. Sitting in the dark, under a brightening sky, the cold surrounding us hard and crisp and clear as a shield, warm deep down inside our Carhartts, I think how it's times like these, moments like this pure still moment, that make me glad of who I am and that I've got two sons to remind me of it, to line the path and keep me on it, sons who'll carry on this life and the respect for it long after I'm gone. And it's in this simple flash of living that I can see the war and the killing I did clearly, the good it did for me, perhaps the only good it did for any of us: it helped me to recognize moments like this one, to note and appreciate them in a way and feel them with a white-flared intensity I wouldn't never've known if I hadn't ever cared and feared so for life, and not just my own.

I take a sip of the hot coffee and glance at my sons. In this sudden second I nearly manage to tell them I love them—both of them—different as they are and always will be for me, and that I'm glad they're here with me now, but even thinking to blurt out *I love you* shrinks my throat tight to strangling, I think, *This is what it means to be out here more than anything, deeper even than the professed and hammered-home responsibility.* And I suddenly realize the obvious untold reason I snapped at Kevin for not wanting to come hunting with us this season. The truth I know deep down's I couldn't live without either one of them. I cast back the dregs of my coffee and snuff my sleeve, manage to croak a harsh, "We'll never get a goddamn deer if you girls keep lollygag-

ging." They shuffle to their feet and then we start again on our mission march.

* * *

The country we now find ourselves in has changed from fat oak and maple. Now it's rock-rugged, spruce-filled and shale-scaled. A tremendous valley opens out to our left and in the speck bottom of it there's an iced-blue mountain lake sparkling silver with the first rayed flashings of sunshine. We'll never hound down a buck like this, and ready or not it's time for me to plan a strategy and split us up. I pick the first suitable tree for Kevin, a curiously forked spruce with a wide view of this expanse, the natural path ridge line coming up and the new day. We leave him there, looking sleepy-headed, but safe in the knowledge that the hard march's sweated the last of the alcohol out of him, and then Gary David and I push on and up and over the long slope. I place him at the top of the next piney ridge. Then I push on up and down and around along the same ridge for another half mile.

The single beech I find has a great sky-reaching spread of limbs, and I squirm out a comfortable way to wedge myself in, sweeping the open V-sights of my Remington .30-06 over the maze of thickets and snow below. It's winter's dawn and we're ready and waiting, the opening daylit hour of the first day of hunting season each year when the most bucks are shot, before they've been alerted to the fact they're in season again, and we're far enough out in these woods that I don't think we'll have any trouble with idiots and their carelessness. I think how I would've driven myself and my boys another five miles simply to escape them and the threat of some stupid accident.

Then I hear the shaking of the brush, a racked buck stumbling toward me through the thick-tangling scrub. *Impossible,* I think, but know, too, from faith—all the stories I've ever heard or even told, the statistics I can quote, that it's exactly this unexpected moment which I should expect and for which I should be ever vigilant. I finger a cartridge out from the elastic above my chest pocket, feed it in and gently lock home the bolt, flick off my safety and snug my cheek, seat the sights, pointing the aimed V up wind. The buck's sixty yards off. He stops and I cock—shoots a warning, and I feel the hard berry in my chest, the levered, but then he starts crashing carelessly forward toward me again—the new morning's icy light catching the flash of his huge brush-like rack.

There's an impact thump like kicking a plump pumpkin, the shot echoing crisply cracked and then a rush as the buck tumbles bagged heavy into a white-stat=ced silence. And I'm breathing hard, raspily recovering from a full dose of buck fever as I shimmy fast down the beech. My rifle seared empty, the bolt thrown open, I jump from five feet up, climb

15.gg.walbert/bailey (fiction)   9/6/98 2:27 PM   Page 10

FICTION

to my feet, dust the snow quickly off, and then I chamber another round.

The buck's fallen just behind a tall drift and inside one of the dense thickets. Just last year my sons and I sat around the kitchen table shaking our heads over the unbelievable newspaper story of an experienced hunter who'd been gored nearly to death by a big buck he'd wounded crazy, how he'd had to crawl himself out of the woods holding onto his own spilled entrails. From where I am I can see the flecked red shining brilliantly. There's a flailed path back where he sprinted then fell.

I tiptoe in, safety off again, finger on the trigger, use the barrel to press aside the buck-colored brush, and peek carefully in.

II

The first shot slapped Kevin straight up out of an uneasy sleep where he'd been dreaming Jeanie had him pinched by the nose and was fussing and fussing at him like a crow. He staggered, grabbed the branch in front of his face, feeling the uncomfortable ache of having wedged himself by the crotch into the crotch of the odd, hairy tree, and touched the cold hurt of his exposed nose, ran the drip of it onto his sleeve.

He heard Jeanie's cawing again and then he looked straight up to see the crow alone on the top branch, laughing at him. He pointed his levered .30.30 up at it and watched it flap slowly up and wheel away within easy reach of his sights. Rings of sound continued to bind them ripple by him, smoothing out and out until the snow cushioned the woods silent and peaceful again. Kevin wondered who had taken the shot, his father or Gary David? If either of them had taken a shot, he knew neither had missed. He himself hadn't even bothered to load his rifle. Then he heard a second flat slap. It shocked sharply past, the echoed ripples touching lightly by him again. *Good,* he thought, *because if they get two we can leave. We'd have to leave,* he thought, *or we wouldn't be able to carry out all the meat.* Though if he knew his father, Mr. Gary Hazen, they *would* carry out every single slab and scrap of venison and usable hoof and horn, regardless if they *could* carry it out or not. His father made a special carpenter's glue from the hooves, rigged gunracks with the wired foreleg. He even took the incredible time necessary to hand-buff indestructible knife handles from the horns. So, Kevin sat cramped and cold in the tree, hoping hard they had gotten two, but hoping too and just as hard they wouldn't get three.

The thing was, leaving Jeanie's dorm room the night before, he had promised—in fact he had *sworn* to her—that he would tell his father that morning. He had just found out himself that Friday night, but he had promised he would have it out *before* they went hunting. But, of course, he had-

n't. He *had* meant to. On the way home he had stopped in at the Lantern and had eight beers to pump himself up for it and, sitting at the bar glowing gold, he had felt cocksure, strong, thinking how maybe he'd just kick his goddamn father's ass, tell him to fuck the hell off and mind his own business—and not just about this either, but about transferring down to State when Jeanie did to earn a four-year degree, hunting, cutting and splitting all that ridiculous firewood year in and year out, about becoming a carpenter, the whole bullshit dump truck load full of it—but when he'd climbed out of his beaten Dodge in front of the house at 2:00 A.M., he'd felt the cold. He'd felt suddenly too tired to hash or duke it out. Somehow he'd scratched at the door and had stepped into the warm kitchen without saying anything. Then they were in the truck and then, head down, paying for the beers and no sleep with every uphill step, he'd hiked way the hell out here, and now he was in this tree and now, hoping his father and his brother both had gotten their precious bucks so he could go the hell home and get some sleep.

Kevin glanced at his watch. Nearly two and a half hours had passed since his father and brother had left him. The morning sunshine flashed, glittering gold. It was amazingly cold for that time of year, but after three winters of hardly any snow or any serious North Country cold, the old men at the diner had predicted last week's November blizzard far back in the strangest wet, chilly August any of them had ever seen or even heard tell about. Kevin himself had to admit he liked the snow. There was something blanket-comfortable about it. And in the snow he didn't mind the cold so much. Jeanie was from the city, from Queens actually, and she didn't like the cold. She did like to ski, though, and so the snow had grown up as a bond between them.

Snow.

Kevin closed his eyes against the four-walled whiteness, but felt her setting up on an elbow again, watching him for his reaction. She was touching up a single hair on his chest, slowly curling it around her perfect red fingernail, queuing up the question mark of it. He'd wondered then if she wanted him to yell at her or just scream or maybe whoop for some sort of joy. But the news had knocked him out. TKO'd, his dream-self stood up out of his floored body and walked out the door and down the hall and down and around the steps, out onto the perfect, snow-covered campus lawn. Then, as if he were a kid again, he was angeled out in the snow, on his back waving his arms—his wings—his legs, the sweep of his robe, and the snow was falling softly down, down and down, blanketing him, his whole body down to his tingling toes, his chest icing ice solid, blueing his lips, sticking white to his eyelashes, softly white, padding white, and the growing weight of it white-pressing his eyelids past zigzagging reds into a deep, dark-sliding blackness: avalanched alive. That's

15.gg.walbert/bailey (fiction) 9/6/98 2:27 PM Page 11

FICTION

when he'd opened his eyes to find Jeanie still staring down at him. In this snow dream his planned life died, school and a degree froze and then melted that easily away and he saw himself getting up out of the bed of some house which his smiling father and his happy goddamned brother would help him build, getting up every single morning at 5 A.M. to go work off the loan he was meeting every month on some new stupid shiny red, big-tired truck, working every available odd overtime job just as his father had always done, frugal with every spare second of his whole life, just to keep the baby (then babies) in diapers, in bonnets, in pureed pears. He saw a gray lunch-boxed lunch, his own coffee thermos (bought on sale), then back to sawdust in his boots, the always aching shoulders, earning his father's calluses, wearing his father's chosen life as if it were his own.

Then though, too, he'd felt Jeanie's lips burn straight down to kiss his naked chest, reawakening him, his desire rising through the cold to hard-aching reality again. He'd rolled up from underneath it all slowly then, and their lips had met and he'd tasted her tears, arched up to her as she gripped him, and they'd made love again and then again before he went to face him, his promise, their bond, sealing it, sealed: their future lives.

"Just goddamnit," Kevin said to himself. He scraped away from the tree and peeled back his sleeve to check his watch. It had been nearly three hours now since they'd split up. There hadn't been any more shots, but neither had his father sent Gary David back to fetch him so that he could help them clean and strip red, the carcasses. He glanced around his assigned clearing. His eyes stung, felt sandpapered bald from lack of sleep. He circled them wet and then, the unloaded rifle slung over his shoulder, he worked himself loose from his stand, and started down the tree. He'd use the shots as an excuse to go see.

*　*　*

The two sets of boots tracked an easy path through the snow, his father's footsteps bigger, pressed deeper, and then Gary David's smaller and lighter, pressed just inside the trail breaking bigger tracks, his older brother trying unsuccessfully—or so it seemed to Kevin, it had always seemed this way to Kevin—to fill them. And as he trudged on after them, purposefully stepping just off their beaten path, making himself do the harder work of breaking new snow, he couldn't help but think to himself that as much as he loved his big brother, when it came to their father he also thought of him as a bit of a strung puppet, a dummy for the things their father wanted him to think and say.

Inside a stand of wind-strafed pine, Kevin stopped where he could see his father had set Gary David to give him a view of the entire valley. He saw where the tracks stopped to go up, but Gary David wasn't there. He circled the tree. On the other side, his father's bigger boots trudged off, and then he saw where Gary David had jumped down into them, sinking into his tracks again. Kevin's first panged thought was that his father had come back for his brother but not for him. Then he noticed both sets of tracks headed out. Neither set pointed back. And then standing under the pine puzzling down, Kevin grinned, and then standing up under the tree in the snow patting over his pockets to confirm it, he laughed outloud: his *father* had been carrying the shell bag!

In their marched hurry, and because it was not the way the Hazens had *always* done things—not the way *his father's father* had done it and *his father's father's father* before him—not a fixture, in the way his dad had orchestrated, ordered, and directed every hunt for the past eight years that Gary David and he had been traipsing through these woods after him—he'd simply and ridiculously forgotten to dole out their ammo to them.

Kevin saw his own caught dilemma: obvious as it could be that for the past three hours he hadn't even tried to load his rifle. He'd been sitting in his stand, sound asleep, dreaming. *Unforgivable.* And his father wouldn't forgive or let him forget about it either—not ever. Kevin could hear the told story of it over and over again during their clinking breakfasts at the diner, the head shaking and chuckles it would always get.

Gary David must have realized the mistake as soon as he'd gotten himself good and safely situated and, of course, it had been his older brother who had climbed all the way back down and who had fallen in behind their father and who was probably trudging back toward Kevin right now, sacrificing his own precious hunting time for his younger brother who hadn't even tried to load his rifle and who didn't even give a damn. Kevin felt pretty shitty about that. But he still couldn't help but smile—no matter what the consequences. The whole forgetful episode reminded him of a mistake he himself might easily have made any hour of any day of any week, but it delighted him to no end his father had done such a typical, stupid thing. He *is* human, Kevin thought, pleased and amazed. It was a good feeling, and he stored the warmth of it away, thinking how he might very well need it sometime later that day.

He started off after them, feeling almost happy, feeling better, at least, than he had felt all day. He followed the two sets of tracks for a long while, uphill and through the snow. The first thing Kevin caught sight of was a caution-road-sign flag of safety orange. He stopped, seeing, but in the harsh glare unable to imagine or make out at all what it was exactly he saw. It looked to him as if he'd caught his father scraping and groveling. He was on his knees, bowing low, inchwormed up as if he were praying in the snow, the brand new shell bag. Then, from ten yards, Kevin saw his brother Gary David sprawled flat, the

15.gg.walbert/bailey [fiction]   9/6/98 2:27 PM   Page 12

FICTION

snow red-mapped telltale around him. He heard his own howl. Shocked still, he saw the rifle barrel choked-off in his father's mouth.

III

It was late afternoon: twelve hours since they'd stepped out of the truck in the clearing beside the frozen stream at 5:00 A.M. The temperature had risen in the earlier, full, clear sunshine, but now, with the long winter's night around them, the cold was closing in. Kevin stoked the fire and the flames jumped wild, hissing. His father lay close beside the fire covered as warmly as Kevin could imagine to make him. When Kevin had first recognized what had happened, he'd felt his world physically tilt, heave, then slither from beneath his feet. He'd landed, clutching snow, felt his stomach lurch and roll—he couldn't help this and it wouldn't stop—then, still stringing spit, he'd crawled quickly forward toward them, patting blindly over the crusted and blinding snow. Kevin had let go of his brother's pipe-cold arm and had reached out and touched his father's wrist to feel a thin pulse hiding just below the skin. With the realization that his father was still alive, he'd forced himself to shove his brother's death aside and had pulled himself up through the horror of it with one single-minded, numbed-stupid, but saving thought: *fire.*

After he had kindled the wet sticks and built the flames hot enough to support the frozen limbs and had scavenged and carried back armload after armload of wood from beneath snow drifts to keep the flames going strong, Kevin had taken the careful time necessary to wrap his father's sticky head, torn cheek and blown jaw in his own t-shirt before realizing he too was starting to chill, to chatter dangerously himself.

Of course, Kevin had no idea just how seriously cold it would get that night. If his father had ever allowed them to pack along a radio, he would have heard the flurried broadcast of warnings, and if he had he might have pushed on through the dark toward the heater in the truck without waiting for his mother to get worried enough to send the Rangers out after them, knowing that if there was no chance of making it there was also very little choice but to try. The coming cold, sweeping into the snow left by the blizzard in the mountains that night was expected to break every record for November, but then the actual temperature of 17 below would exceed even those record-breaking expectations. What Kevin could sense, though, even without a weather advisory on the radio, was the increasingly still and silent razor edge of the air. Even the fire seemed to be having more and more trouble breathing, the flames going thickish and slow, glowing blue, low and close over the orange coals. Kevin looked to his father then, but his father's eyes were rolling uncontrolled, between snapping

suddenly open to out cold closed. Kevin felt a sudden flaring. No matter what happened to them then, he wanted his father to know that what had happened to Gary David that morning hadn't been his fault. It had obviously been an *accident,* and accidents happened no matter how carefully you planned or dreamed or wished for something else. *Didn't he know something about that?* He wished then he had told his father that he was going to marry Jeanie, about the baby they were going to have. He'd planned to stand up and say to him: *I will live my own life, make decisions as my own man, but I will respect you and the way you raised me always.* And that's when he heard himself say out loud: "I love you, too, Dad." Kevin felt rushed through blue space. He trailed his father back to find himself seated beside him before the fire again, overwhelmed by the aftershot, shocked understanding of what, all along, his father had really been trying to teach Gary David and him about surviving in the cold. Then, without his having to think further about it or even plan, Kevin laid down in the snow on top of his father, pulling over him the stored warmth of his own arms and legs. He closed his eyes and dreamt the Rangers stumbled upon them just before dawn. ∎

12 DOUBLETAKE WINTER 1999

TOM BAILEY

Snow Dreams

I

THE SIDE DOOR CRACKS OPEN. I EXPECT MY ELDEST—DARK, CURLY-HEADED Gary David—but it's my eighteen-year-old, blond Kevin, who slides in from outside, red-eyed and sheepish. I look him up and down as I hold the bowl and beat the batter. He's standing, hands pocketed, casting around the kitchen, glancing at the sink, the clock, the floor, the beamed ceiling, the smoking Upland. I've tried to raise my boys like I've managed to train every dog I've ever owned—with a biscuit in my left hand and a switch in my right—and I'm burning now to smack this son of mine with the accusation of what he knows is right, because I brought up both of them to know better than to drink and ever handle a gun. I wait for Kevin's eyes to finally meet mine and then, using a firm gaze, I give him a spank-hard look. He glances away, ashamed, I think, and I go back to pouring out our pancakes, reach for the boiling coffee.

There's a low scuff-kick at the door and Kevin has to unstick his hands from his Carhartts to open it for Gary David loaded up past his chin with split wood. To see my two grown sons standing side by side, I imagine folks could get the idea my Susan's made a practice of visiting long, lazy afternoons with the postman—summer day to winter night different as these two boys are. Kevin's more simply the spitting image of who I used to be before I suddenly, at the age of nineteen, while serving my time in Nam, split out of my issue with a last thirty-seven pound, three-and-a-quarter inch growing spurt, before I rolled over forty-five and my own bright blue eyes dimmed, and I got fixed with these squarish, silver-rimmed bifocals, when I still had all of my own straw-blond, thick, and wavy hair. Standing next to him, Gary David—both in looks and in his shyness and care—mirrors his granddaddy, Susan's black-headed, part Onondaga daddy, as if he'd sat up in the grave and lurched back out into the world for one more tall, stiff try at things.

Another, bigger, difference between them is that my youngest, Kevin, is the first of us Hazens to go on to school past the twelfth grade, taking classes now down at the local junior college in Canton. Next year, though, he wants to transfer full time to Cortland State. He wants to live over three hours away and have us pay for him to earn himself a real degree. The first two times he mentioned this I felt the pressured dollar sign of it ticking bomb-big behind my left eye. The third time I exploded, yelling out before Susan could grab my knee and squeeze, *You just want to be on the parental dole your whole goddamn life! You don't want to have to ever work for a living!* Gary David, who's more sensible about these things, is going to be a carpenter after me. He'll find himself a nice girl like that Anne Burke whose family's lived outside Sebattis near long as we Hazens have. He'll marry and name his first boy Gary. But what I find most curious in their natures is that while Gary David was born with the heart and desire, born with the *belief* in the building, his brother Kevin has the better hands, a sharper eye for the truths of wood grains and the absolute honesty of plumb lines. Though perhaps even more strange still is that these two boys—these two *men*—aged a good five years apart and night and day opposite as they are, can be such good friends.

Gary David's sniffing strong over Kevin. "You leave any at the brewery?" he asks. "Who was it over, not that Jeanie Prescott again?" By not answering Kevin convicts himself. "Aw, Kev . . . ," Gary David starts and gently sets down the wood like you wouldn't expect a boy to—even while he's talking to Kevin—being considerate of his mother sleeping up-stairs. Kevin simply stands with his hands in his pockets, blinking, red-eyed. He's brought this girl around once or twice, and I guess she's green-eyed cute enough for dating. But she's from *New York City* of all places, just going to school up here in our North Country so she can ski seven months of the year, and she's not one of us or even remotely of our kind.

Two weeks ago Kevin asked me if he could skip his buck this season, and when I asked and eyed him why, he confessed it was because this Jeanie didn't *like* it. She didn't want him to go because she didn't think hunting was right. "No," I said to him, "no, you can't *skip* it," and stood up and left him standing there, more abrupt with him than I'd meant to be I guess, but too full of the voice-shaking responsibility of it right then to speak reasonably. This responsibility which was my father's responsibility before mine and his father's responsibility before him: the necessity of fulfilling our tags toward stocking three freezers to get us through one of these no-fooling winters again. If we want to eat that is.

For us, deer season's not a matter of plaqueing a staring head or congratulating ourselves over a rack of horns. For us, hunting's as crucial as surrounding every inch of spare space under our extra-wide porch and eaves with carefully cut, dried, and split wood—never imagining, not even able to imagine nor capable of comprehending in the blistering chainsaw heat of summer, that we could ever in twelve straight hard winters use all we've stacked, and then and again stumped equally as incredulous every May when we have to scramble up the last skinny sticks and shavings of bark to heat the freezing kitchen at 5 A.M. This one single and unforgiving truth, out of which the responsibility I'm speaking was born: that it's already time to start the dragging and sawing and splitting again that very same afternoon if we're going to be ready for the first freeze come September. It's all about living up here—*surviving*—and so far as I'm concerned there is no difference between the two, but it's the huge *difference* between us Hazens and a lot of other folk who don't know or have any idea at all about the cold.

I cut my eyes at the clock. It's already three minutes past our 2:30 A.M. time to have left and be gone. I get up with my plate, rinse it off in the sink. My boys follow behind me doing the same, and then we grab our gear, case out the door, and crunch across the crust of snow to the truck.

• • •

It's a thirty-minute drive in to our spot, winding back through the preserve and up and across Big Cloud Mountain, onto a half oval of road bordered to the east by an icy brook. Having wound and humped to be here by three, we sit silently in the truck and stare through the glare of our head-lights. A teal-colored Chevy and a brown Impala squat in our space. A neon-pink bumper sticker on the truck shouts: THIS BUCK HUNTS! We pop the doors and climb out into the shadow dark, and it doesn't take a flashlight to show us by the heavy frosted glass that these fellows must've come in last night, before gun season started.

I'm quick to anger, but only a few things make me mad. If these men have broken one rule to get their deer, they won't hesitate to break another or another after that. They're the kind of men who, I know, *will do what it takes.* I knew their kind in Nam, and I could tell some stories of things they're capable of that would make your hair go straight. I've known their kind here at home, too, watched them do carpentry, say, on a government job like HUD. You'd tear out that already straightened hair to see the work these men do, screwing everyone but themselves. When I have nightmares of evil in this world, it always comes to me in this man-shape of sloppiness and a too-easy, unearned return. And it's this evil that I'm constantly on guard against—my mission I guess—what in the passing on of an honest way of living this life I hope to give the strength of to my two sons, a strength which they'll have to call upon to fight against it long after I'm gone.

Gary David breaks off the cold snap of silence. "What do you think, Dad?"

I try to put the best face on it I can. I tell myself: *There are 20,000 acres in front of us.* We'll turn our backs on their tracks and head the other way.

Write a Short Story! 155

"Get the rifles, Gary David," I say.

The moon's up, spotlight bright. I lead and Gary David and Kevin follow. We walk down a gentle slope and then we begin the climb. The hill goes steep, mountains suddenly steeper. With all the clothes and the silly shell bag I've got slung over my shoulder I feel heavy and robotic, old. Gary David and Kevin pitched in and bought the bag for me last Christmas, and though to me it seems worse than useless with rifles on a one-day hunt, the least I can do to avoid the waste is to put it to work and carry it for them. It's unscuffed, though off-colored by dust, too stiff and strangely new and—for my comfort anyway—a little too close to the size and shape of a woman's purse. My own .30 shells I still keep safe in looped elastic over my breast pocket the way my father did, the same way my grandfather carried his. My boys stay right behind me the whole while, young, walking easily, their breath lightly silvering.

Shots ring out into the moonlight at 3:53 A.M. They slap, *bang bang bang bang bang bang,* and then echo booming between the rows of hills. Then there're two guns, three. The first one's reloaded and starts in again, *bang bang bang bang bang bang bang.* All of them rage away. There are a few distinct cracks. A pop. Then there's silence, a harder and stiller silence now it seems for having been disturbed so violently. Waiting crouched in the aftermath of the ambush, my body's tensed tight, reminded of war. It's against the law to shoot until first light, but from our right, from the east, we hear a thin but distinct, "Ya-*hooooo!*" Weekend blasters, sons-of-a-goddamn-bitches, crazy men. We angle even more sharply southwest away from them, push on, marching faster, in deeper, and then on faster and farther and in deeper still.

On the down side of a saddle-humped mountain, in a circled clearing, we stop for a coffee break, eat the sugared pancakes we pocketed along, the close winter sky graining a hint of light. Sitting in the dark, under a brightening sky, the cold surrounding us hard and crisp and clear as a shield, warm deep down inside our Carhartts, I think how it's times like these, moments like this pure still moment, that make me glad of who I am and that I've got two sons to remind me of it, to line the path and keep me on it, sons who'll carry on this life and the respect for it long after I'm gone. And it's in this simple flash of living that I can see the war and the killing I did clearly, the good it did for me, perhaps the only good it did for any of us: it helped me to recognize moments like this one, to note and appreciate them in a way and feel them with a white-flared intensity I would never've known if I hadn't ever cared and feared so for life, and not just my own.

I take a sip of the hot coffee and glance at my sons. In this sudden second I nearly manage to tell them I love them—both of them—different as they are and always will be for me, and that I'm glad they're here with me now, but even thinking to blurt out *I love you* shrinks my throat tight to strangling. I think, *This is what it means to be out here more than anything, deeper even than the professed and hammered-home responsibility.* And I suddenly realize the obvious untold reason I snapped at Kevin for not wanting to come hunting with us this season. The truth I know deep down's I couldn't live without either one of them. I cast back the dregs of my coffee and snuff my sleeve, manage to croak a harsh, "We'll never get a goddamn deer if you girls keep lollygagging." They shuffle to their feet and then we start again on our mission march.

● ● ●

The country we now find ourselves in has changed from fat oak and maple. Now it's rock-rugged, spruce-filled, and shale-scaled. A tremendous valley opens out to our left and in the speck bottom of it there's an iced-blue mountain lake sparkling silver with the first rayed flashings of sunshine. We'll never hound down a buck like this, and ready or not it's time for me to plan a strategy and split us up. I pick the first suitable tree for Kevin, a curiously forked spruce with a wide view of this expanse, the natural path ridgeline coming up and the new day. We leave him there, looking sleepy-headed, but safe in the knowledge that the hard march has sweated the last of the alcohol out of him, and then Gary David and I push on and up and over the long slope. I place him at the top of the next piney ridge. Then I push on up and down and around along the same ridge for another half mile.

The single beech I find has a great sky-reaching spread of limbs, and I squirm out a comfortable way to wedge myself in, sweeping the open V-sights of my Remington .30-.06 over the maze of thickets and snow below. It's winter's dawn and we're ready and waiting, the opening daylit hour of the first day of hunting season each year when the most bucks are shot, before they've been alerted to the fact they're in season again, and we're far enough out in these woods that I don't think we'll have any trouble with idiots and their carelessness. I think how I would've driven myself and my boys another five miles simply to escape them and the threat of some stupid accident.

Then I hear the shaking of the brush, a racked buck stumbling toward me through the thick-tangling scrub. *Impossible,* I think, but know, too, from all the stories I've ever heard or even told, the statistics I can quote, that it's exactly this unexpected moment which I should expect and for which I should be ever-vigilant. I finger a cartridge out from the elastic above my chest pocket, feed it in and gently lock home the bolt, flick off my safety and snug my cheek, seat the sights, pointing the aimed V upwind. The buck's sixty yards off. He stops and sneeze-snorts a warning, and I feel the hollow hurry in my chest, the fevered, hot-to-cold itching sweat that he's somehow caught my scent or simply *sensed* me in this tree, but then he starts crashing carelessly forward toward me again—the new morning's icy light catching the flash of his huge brushlike rack.

There's an impact thump like kicking a plump pumpkin, the shot echoing crisply, and then a rush as the buck tumbles bagged heavy into a white-staticed silence. And I'm breathing hard, raspily recovering from a full dose of buck fever as I shimmy fast down the beech. My rifle seared empty, the bolt thrown open, I jump from five feet up, climb to my feet, dust the snow quickly off, and then I chamber another round.

The buck's fallen just behind a tall drift, inside a mess of thickets. Just last year my sons and I sat around the kitchen table shaking our heads over the unbelievable newspaper story of an experienced hunter who'd been gored nearly to death by a big buck he'd wounded crazy, how he'd had to crawl himself out of the woods holding onto his own spilled entrails. From where I am I can see the flecked red shining brilliantly. There's a flailed path back where he sprinted then fell.

I tiptoe in, safety off again, finger on the trigger, use the barrel to press aside the buck-colored brush, and peek carefully in.

II

The first shot slapped Kevin straight up out of an uneasy sleep where he'd been dreaming Jeanie had him pinched by the nose and was fussing and fussing at him like a crow. He staggered, grabbed the branch in front of his face, feeling the uncomfortable ache of having wedged himself by the crotch into the crotch of the odd, hairy tree, and touched the cold hurt of his exposed nose, ran the drip of it onto his sleeve.

He heard Jeanie's cawing again and then he looked straight up to see the crow alone on the top branch, laughing at him. He pointed his levered .30-.30 up at it and watched it flap slowly up and wheel away within easy reach of his sights. Rings of sound continued to bind then ripple by him, smoothing out and out until the snow cushioned the woods silent and peaceful again. Kevin wondered who had taken the shot, his father or Gary David? If either of them had taken a shot, he knew neither had missed. He himself hadn't even bothered to load his rifle. Then he heard a second flat slap. It shocked sharply past, the echoed ripples touching lightly by him again. *Good,* he thought, *because if they get two we can leave. We'd have to leave,* he thought, *or we wouldn't be able to carry out all the meat.* Though if he knew his father, *Mr. Gary Hazen,* they *would* carry out every single slab and scrap of venison and usable hoof and horn, regardless if they *could* carry it out or not. His father made a special carpenter's glue from the hooves, rigged gunracks with the wired forelegs. He even took the incredible time necessary to hand-buff indestructible knife handles from the horns. So Kevin sat cramped and cold in the tree, hoping they had gotten two, but hoping just as hard they wouldn't get three.

The thing was, leaving Jeanie's dorm room the night before, he had promised—in fact he had *sworn* to her—that he would tell his father that morning. He had just found out himself that Friday night, but he had promised he would have it out *before* they went hunting. But, of course, he hadn't. He *had* meant to. On the way home he had stopped in at The Lantern and had eight beers to pump himself up for it and, sitting at the bar glowing gold, he had felt cocksure, strong, thinking how maybe he'd just kick his goddamned father's ass, tell him to fuck the hell off and mind his own business—and not just about this either, but about transferring down to State when Jeanie did to earn a four-year degree, about hunting, cutting and splitting all that ridiculous firewood year in and year out, about becoming a carpenter, the whole bullshit dump truck load full of it—but when he'd climbed out of his beaten Dodge in front of the house at 2 A.M., he'd felt the cold. He'd felt suddenly too tired to hash or duke it out. Somehow he'd scratched at the door and had stepped into the warm kitchen without saying anything. Then they were in the truck and then, head down, paying for the beers and no sleep with every uphill step, he'd hiked way the hell out here, and now he was in this tree and now he was hoping his father and his brother both had gotten their precious bucks so he could go the hell home and get some sleep.

Kevin glanced at his watch. Nearly two and a half hours had passed since his father and brother had left him. The morning sunshine flashed, glittering gold. It was amazingly cold for that time of year, but after three winters of hardly any snow or any serious North Country cold, the old men at the diner had predicted last week's November blizzard far back in the strangest wet, chilly August any of them had ever seen or even heard tell about. Kevin himself had to admit he liked the snow. There was something blanket-comfortable about it. And in the snow he didn't mind the cold so much. Jeanie was from the city, from Queens actually, and she didn't like the cold. She did like to ski, though, and so the snow had grown up as a bond between them.

Snow.

Kevin closed his eyes against the four-walled whiteness, but felt her setting up on an elbow again, watching him for his reaction. She was touching up a single hair on his chest, slowly curling it around her perfect red fingernail, queuing up the question mark of it. He'd wondered then if she wanted him to yell at her or just scream or maybe whoop for some sort of joy. But the news had knocked him out. TKO'd, his dream-self stood up out of his floored body and walked out the door and down the hall and down and around the steps, out onto the perfect, snow-covered campus lawn. Then, as if he were a kid again, he was angled out in the snow, on his back waving his arms—his wings—his legs, the sweep of his robe, and the snow was falling softly down, down and down, blanketing him, his whole body down to his tingling toes, his chest icing ice-solid, blueing his lips, sticking white to his eyelashes, softly white, padding white, and the growing weight of it white-pressing his eyelids past zigzagging reds into a deep, dark-sliding blackness: avalanched alive. That's when he'd opened his eyes to find Jeanie still staring down at him. In this snow dream his planned life died, school and a degree froze and then melted that easily away and he saw himself getting up out of the bed of some house which his smiling father and his happy goddamned brother would help him build, getting up every single morning at 5 A.M. to go work off the loan he was meeting every month on some new stupid shiny red, big-tired truck, working every available odd overtime job just as his father had always done, frugal with every spare second of his whole life, just to keep the baby (then babies) in diapers, in bonnets, in pureed pears. He saw a gray lunch-boxed lunch, his own coffee thermos (bought on sale), then back to sawdust in his boots, the always aching shoulders, earning his father's calluses, wearing his father's chosen life as if it were his own.

Then, though, he'd felt Jeanie's lips burn straight down to kiss his naked chest, reawakening him, his desire rising through the cold to hardaching reality again. He'd rolled up from underneath it all slowly then, and their lips had met and he'd tasted her tears, arched up to her as she gripped him, and they'd made love again and then again before he went to face him, his promise, their bond, sealing it, sealed: their future lives.

"Just goddamnit," Kevin said to himself. He scraped away from the tree and peeled back his sleeve to check his watch. It had been nearly three hours now since they'd split up. There hadn't been any more shots, but neither had his father sent Gary David back to fetch him so that he could help them clean and strip the carcasses. He glanced around his assigned clearing. His eyes stung, felt sandpapered bald from lack of sleep. He circled them wet and then, the unloaded rifle slung over his shoulder, he worked himself loose from his set stand, and started down the tree. He'd use the shots as an excuse to go see.

· · ·

The two sets of boots tracked an easy path through the snow, his father's footsteps bigger, pressed deeper, and then Gary David's smaller and lighter, pressed just inside the trail breaking bigger tracks, his older brother trying unsuccessfully—or so it seemed to Kevin, it had always seemed this way to Kevin—to fill them. And as he trudged on after them, purposefully stepping just off their beaten path, making himself do the harder work of breaking new snow, he couldn't help but think to himself that as much as he loved his big brother, when it came to their father he also thought of him as a bit of a strung puppet, a dummy for the things their father wanted him to think and say.

Inside a stand of wind-strafed pine, Kevin stopped where he could see his father had set Gary David to give him a view of the entire valley. He saw where the tracks stopped to go up, but Gary David wasn't there. He circled the tree. On the other side, his father's bigger boots trudged off, and then he saw where Gary David had jumped down into them, sinking into his tracks again. Kevin's first panged thought was that his father had come back for his brother but not for him. Then he noticed both sets of tracks headed out. Neither set pointed back. And then standing under the pine puzzling down, Kevin grinned, and then standing under the tree in the snow patting over his pockets to confirm it, he laughed out loud: his *father* had been carrying the shell bag!

In their marched hurry, and because it was not the way the Hazens had *always done things*—not the way *his father's father* had done it and *his father's father's father* before him—not a fixture, in the way his dad had orchestrated, ordered, and directed every hunt for the past eight years that Gary David and he had been traipsing through these woods after him—he'd simply and ridiculously forgotten to dole out their ammo to them.

But Kevin saw his own caught dilemma, too: it was as obvious as it could be that for the past three hours he hadn't even tried to load his rifle. He'd been sitting in his stand, sound asleep, dreaming. *Unforgivable.* And his father wouldn't forgive or let him forget about it either—not ever. Kevin could hear the told story of it over and over again during their clinking breakfasts at the diner, the head shaking and chuckles it would always get.

Gary David must have realized the mistake as soon as he'd gotten himself good and safely situated and, of course, it had been his older brother who had climbed all the way back down and who had fallen in behind their father and who was probably trudging back toward Kevin right now, sacrificing his own precious hunting time for his younger brother who hadn't even tried to load his rifle and who didn't even give a damn. Kevin felt pretty shitty about that. But he still couldn't help but smile—no matter what the consequences. The whole forgetful episode reminded him of a mistake he himself might easily have made any hour of any day of any week, but it delighted him to no end his father had done such a typical, stupid thing. He *is* human, Kevin thought, pleased and amazed. It was a good feeling, and he stored the warmth of it away, thinking how he might very well need it sometime later that day.

He started off after them, feeling almost happy, feeling better, at least, than he had felt all day. He followed the two sets of tracks for a long while, uphill and through the snow. The first thing Kevin caught sight of was a caution road-sign flag of safety orange. He stopped, seeing, but in the harsh glare unable to imagine or make out at all what it was exactly he saw. It looked to him as if he'd caught his father scraping and groveling. He was on his knees, bowing low, inchwormed up as if he were praying in the snow, the brand-new shell bag strapped on his back. Then, from ten yards, Kevin saw his brother Gary David sprawled flat, the snow red-mapped tell-tale around him. He heard his own howl. Shocked still, he saw the rifle barrel chocked-off in his father's mouth.

III

It was late afternoon: twelve hours since they'd stepped out of the truck in the clearing beside the frozen stream at 3 A.M. The temperature had risen in the earlier, full, clear sunshine, but now, with the long winter's night around them, the cold was closing in. Kevin stoked the fire and the flames jumped wild, hissing. His father lay close beside the fire covered as warmly as Kevin could imagine to make him. When Kevin had first recognized what had happened, he'd felt his world physically tilt, heave, then slither from beneath his feet. He'd landed, clutching snow, felt his stomach lurch and roll—he couldn't help this and it wouldn't stop—then, still stringing spit, he'd crawled quickly forward toward them, patting blindly over the crushed and blinding snow. Kevin had let go of his brother's pipe-cold arm and had reached out and touched his father's wrist to feel a thin pulse hiding just below the skin. With the realization that his father was still alive, he'd forced himself to shove his brother's death aside and had pulled himself up through the horror of it with one single-minded, numbed-stupid but saving thought: *fire.*

After he had kindled the wet sticks and built the flames hot enough to support the frozen limbs and had scavenged and carried back armload after armload of wood from beneath snow drifts to keep the flames going strong, Kevin had taken the careful time necessary to wrap his father's sticky head, torn cheek, and blown jaw in his own T-shirt before realizing he, too, was starting to chill, to chatter dangerously himself.

Of course, Kevin had no idea just how seriously cold it would get that night. If his father had ever allowed them to pack along a radio, he would have heard the flurried broadcast of warnings, and if he had he might have pushed on through the dark toward the heater in the truck without waiting for his mother to get worried enough to send the Rangers out after them, knowing that if there was no chance of making it there was also very little choice but to try. The coming cold, sweeping into the snow left by the blizzard in the mountains that night was expected to break every record for November, but then the actual temperature of 17 below would exceed even those record-breaking expectations. What Kevin could sense, though, even without a weather advisory on the radio, was the increasingly still and silent razor-edge of the air. Even the fire seemed to be having more and more trouble breathing, the flames going thickish and slow, glowing blue, low and close over the orange coals. Kevin looked to his father then, but his father's eyes were rolling uncontrolled, between snapping suddenly open to out-cold closed. Kevin felt a sudden futile flaring. No matter what happened to them then, he wanted his father to know that what had happened to Gary David that morning hadn't been his fault. It had obviously been an *accident,* and accidents happened no matter how carefully you planned or dreamed or wished for something else. *Didn't he know something about that?* He wished then he had told his father that he was going to marry Jeanie, about the baby they were going to have. He'd planned to stand up and say to him: *I will live my own life, make decisions as my own man, but I will respect you and the way you raised me always.* And that's when he heard himself say out loud: "I love you, too, Dad." Kevin felt rushed through blue space. He trailed his father back to find himself seated beside him before the fire again, overwhelmed by the aftershot, shocked understanding of what, all along, his father had really been trying to teach Gary David and him about surviving in the cold. Then, without his having to think further about it or even plan, Kevin angeled his stored warmth down over his father. He closed his eyes and dreamt the Rangers stumbled upon them just before dawn.

In thinking through Alexa's concerns I had to keep in my mind my own strong intentions in the story, and the hardwon understanding of it I'd come to in the time it took me to write it. I also had to keep in mind my own ideas about my "voice" as a writer, without becoming mulish to suggestions. Much of the way I hear my "voice" is based on strong Anglo Saxon language, assonance and alliteration. I find that my prose is often controlled by these rhythms, which are in turn created by the emotion of a scene. Like a poem with a certain rhyme scheme the words I choose are often *there* for me in the sound of the sentence or building of sentences. An example of this is in the paragraph where Gary and his sons first hear the "shots ring out into the moonlight at 3:53 A.M." In the original version my sentences sounded like this:

> Shots ring out into the moonlight at 3:53 A.M. They slap, *bang bang bang bang bang bang,* and then echo booming between the rows of hills. Then there're two guns, three. The first one's reloaded and starts in again, *bang bang bang bang bang bang.* All of them rage away. There are a few distinct cracks. A pop. Then there's silence, a harder and stiller silence now, it seems, for having been disturbed so sudden and violently.

The first cut Alexa suggested was simply a copyediting consideration of getting rid of the commas, which were unnecessary. The second cut had more to do with the sound of the sentence. You can see I've already taken some poetic license with language, "a harder and stiller silence," and the short fragments "A pop." to try to capture the isolated feelings of the sounds of the gun shots: all that banging! These things seemed to work. But the second repetition of "sudden and violently," though it rolls rhythmically along with the first part of the sentence seems unnecessarily repetitive. "Violently" is the word that stands out here and punctuates the sentence most powerfully. I agreed with Alexa that the sentence should read:

> Then there's silence, a harder and stiller silence now it seems for having been disturbed so violently.

Another sentence where I considered cut for similar reasons is in the paragraph that begins "Then I hear the shaking of the brush. . . ." The passage begins "The buck's sixty yards off." And the particular sentence originally read:

> He sneeze-snorts a warning, and I feel the hollow-hurry in my chest, the fevered, hot-to-cold itching sweat that he's somehow caught my scent or simply sensed me in this tree, but then he starts crashing carelessly forward toward me again— the new morning's icy light catching the flash of his huge brush-like rack.

Alexa questioned my use of "sneeze-snorts." She suggested I simply use "snorts," which is very-like the sound a buck makes. But I needed to make another connection here; I needed to companion the buck's snort with a human noise, which in retrospect the reader would understand, even if at the moment they believed along with Gary that it was the snort of a buck, and so I declined her suggestion. In the next paragraph, however, I took her advice and revised the "crisply cracked" to read simply "echoing crisply."

Another good suggestion Alexa made was to call into question a language-tangled image of a thicket. In the next to last paragraph of Gary's section I'd originally written:

> The buck's fallen just behind a tall drift and inside one of the dense wall-thick thickets.

Talk about too much of a good thing! You'll see that I've written in the margin "THINK ABOUT IT." I took her suggestions and changed the sentence to read:

> The buck's fallen just behind a tall drift, inside a mess of thickets.

Such considerations constituted the bulk of changes I ended up making in the galleys, though you can see that in III I went so far as to edit out substantial parts of two entire sentences. But the point we ended up discussing at length was the final image of the story, where Kevin covers his father with his own body. In the original I'd written:

> Then, without having to think further about it or even plan, Kevin laid down in the snow on top of his father, angeling over him with the stored warmth of his own arms and legs.

The image was (of course) perfectly clear to me, but Alexa simply couldn't see the final act I had in mind. You'll see I've written "WORK ON THIS" in the margins, and you can bet I did. A few of my scribblings adorn the bottom of the page, but I carried this image around with me for days. I'd work my vision of it one way and then another. Finally I came up with this much simplified image:

> Then, without his having to think further about it or even plan, Kevin angeled his stored warmth down over his father.

Having the help of an editor as good as Alexa was a big help in polishing the story. Together we "finished" "Snow Dreams."

A LAST COMPANIONABLE WORD

Remember our fictional student Jack? Well, he's back. He's sitting in my office hanging his head over the manuscript of yet another "failed" story. And then he pops the question: "I know you've been writing this book and all. But do you *really* believe anyone can be taught to write fiction? I mean give it to me straight. I can take it."

"Yes, Jack," I nod, "I do."

And I really do! The art of fiction begins with an attention to craft—the craft of writing as well as the craft of reading—and craft can be taught. We can learn to understand how significant details help to make the "lie" of any story truly believable, and we can certainly learn to become more sensitive and aware of the complexities of developing character or be taught to think about how meaning operates in a short story. Of course, the answers we come up with at end our own affair. Remember, no rules!

But can we really teach someone to be a great writer or even a very good writer? This isn't a question that would-be writers like Jack or the rest of us need to ask. To paraphrase Faulkner again, the beginning writer is too busy learning to wait to be taught. But a good teacher can offer guidance, give direction—there are terms to consider that can help us talk about what it is we do when we write or read a short story that *works*. But as I've stressed again and again, at The End, it is only the judgment of the individual writer in application of the craft of stories, striving to make his or her own short story new again in his or her own particular way, that will leave the signature that others may still be reading a hundred years from today.

Works Consulted

Abbey, Edward. *The Monkey Wrench Gang.* Philadelphia: Lippincott, 1975.

Agee, James, and Walker Evans. *Let Us Now Praise Famous Men.* Boston: Houghton Mifflin, 1941.

Allen, Jerry. "Introduction." *Great Short Works of Joseph Conrad.* New York: Harper and Row, 1967.

Atwood, Margaret. "Introduction: Reading Blind." *The Best American Short Stories 1989.* Ed. Margaret Atwood. Boston: Houghton Mifflin, 1989.

Babel, Isaac. "My First Goose." *The Collected Stories of Isaac Babel.* Trans. Walter Morison. New York: Meridian, 1960.

Bach, Gerhard, and Blaine Hall, eds. *Conversations with Grace Paley.* Jackson: University Press of Mississippi, 1997.

Bailey, Tom, ed. *On Writing Short Stories.* New York: Oxford University Press, 2000.

———. "Snow Dreams." *DoubleTake Magazine.* Winter 1998–99.

Baldwin, James. "Sonny's Blues." *Going to Meet the Man.* New York: Dial, 1965.

Bambara, Toni Cade. "The Lesson." *Gorilla, My Love.* New York: Random House, 1972.

Barth, John. *Lost in the Funhouse: Fiction for Print, Tape, Live Voice.* New York: Anchor Books, 1988.

Barzun, Jacques. *On Writing, Editing, and Publishing.* Chicago: University of Chicago Press, 1986.

Bausch, Richard. *The Fireman's Wife and Other Stories.* New York: Linden Press, 1990.

———. "Letter to the Lady of the House." *The Selected Stories of Richard Bausch.* New York: Modern Library, 1996.

Baxter, Charles. *Burning Down the House: Essays on Fiction.* St. Paul, Minn.: Graywolf Press, 1997.

———. *Through the Safety Net: Stories.* New York: Vintage Books, 1998.

Beattie, Ann. "The Burning House." *The Burning House: Short Stories.* New York: Random House, 1982.

Beer, Thomas. *The Mauve Decade: American Life at the End of the Nineteenth Century.* New York: Knopf, 1937.

Bell, Madison Smartt. *Narrative Design: A Writer's Guide to Structure.* New York: Norton, 1997.

Bernays, Anne, and Pamela Painter. *What If? Writing Exercises for Fiction Writers.* New York: HarperCollins, 1995.

Berriault, Gina. *Women in Their Beds: New and Selected Stories.* Washington, D.C.: Counterpoint, 1996.

Blake, William. "Tiger, Tiger, Burning Bright." *Songs of Innocence and of Experience.* Ed. Andrew Lincoln. Princeton, N.J.: Princeton University Press, 1991.

Borges, Jorge Luis. "The Garden of Forking Paths." *Labyrinths: Selected Stories and Other Writings.* New York: New Directions, 1964.

Boswell, Robert. "The Darkness of Love." *Dancing in the Movies.* Iowa City: University of Iowa Press, 1986.

Brodkey, Harold. "Verona: A Young Woman Speaks." *Stories in an Almost Classical Mode.* New York: Alfred A. Knopf, 1985.

Burroughs, Franklin. "Compression Wood." *The Best American Essays 1999.* Ed. Edward Hoagland. New York: Houghton Mifflin, 1999.

Burroway, Janet, ed. *Writing Fiction: A Guide to Narrative Craft.* 4th ed. New York: HarperCollins College Publishers, 1996.

Carver, Raymond. "Cathedral." *Cathedral.* New York: Alfred A. Knopf, 1985.

———. *Fires: Essays, Poems, Stories.* New York: Vintage Books, 1989.

Casey, John. *Spartina.* New York: Vintage Books, 1998.

Cassill, R.V. *Writing Fiction.* 2nd ed. Englewood Cliffs, N.J.: Prentice Hall, 1975.

Charters, Ann. *The Story and Its Writer: An Introduction to Short Fiction.* 4th ed. Boston: Bedford Books, 1995.

———. *The Story and Its Writer: An Introduction to Short Fiction.* 5th ed. Boston: Bedford/St. Martin's, 1999.

Chaucer, Geoffrey. "The Knight's Tale." *The Canterbury Tales.* Trans. Nevill Goghill. London: Penguin, 1977.

Chavkin, Allan, ed. *Conversations with John Gardner.* Jackson: University Press of Mississippi, 1990.

Chavkin, Allan, and Nancy Feyl Chavkin, eds. *Conversations with Louise Erdrich & Michael Dorris.* Jackson: University Press of Mississippi, 1994.

Chekhov, Anton. "The Lady with the Pet Dog." *The Portable Chekhov.* Trans. Avrahm Yarmolinsky. New York: The Viking Press, 1987.

Cisneros, Sandra. "Never Marry a Mexican." *Woman Hollering Creek and Other Stories.* New York: Vintage Books, 1992.

Conrad, Joseph. *Almayer's Folly: A Story of an Eastern River.* Garden City: Doubleday, Page, 1923.

———. "Preface to 'The Nigger of the Narcissus.'" *Great Short Works of Joseph Conrad.* New York: Harper & Row, 1967.

Conroy, Frank. "The Writer's Workshop." *On Writing Short Stories.* Ed. Tom Bailey. New York: Oxford University Press, 2000.

Cowley, Malcolm, ed. *Writers at Work: The Paris Review Interviews.* 1st series. New York: The Viking Press, 1958.

Cronin, Gloria L., and Ben Siegel, eds. *Conversations with Saul Bellows.* Jackson: University Press of Mississippi, 1994.

Curtis, C. Michael. "Publishers and Publishing." *On Writing Short Stories.* Ed. Tom Bailey. New York: Oxford University Press, 2000.

Davis, Lydia. "A House Besieged." *Break It Down.* New York: High Risk Books, 1996.

de Maupassant, Guy. *Pierre and Jean.* Trans. Leonard W. Tancock. New York: Viking Penguin, 1979.

———. "The String." Trans. E. Boyd. *The Collected Novels and Stories of Guy de Maupassant.* New York: Alfred A. Knopf, 1951.

———. "The Writer's Goal." *The Story and Its Writer: An Introduction to Short Fiction.* Ed. Ann Charters. 5th ed. Boston: Bedford/St. Martin's, 1999.

Dexter, Pete. *Paris Trout.* New York: Penguin, 1989.

Didion, Joan. "Last Words." *The Best American Essays 1999.* Ed. Edward Hoagland. New York: Houghton Mifflin, 1999.

Dillard, Annie. *The Writing Life.* New York: HarperCollins, 1989.

Dubus, Andre. *Selected Stories.* New York: Vintage Books, 1996.

———. "The Habit of Writing." *On Writing Short Stories.* Ed. Tom Bailey. New York: Oxford University Press, 2000.

Dybek, Stuart. "Wild Orchids." *DoubleTake Magazine.* Winter 1998–99.

Elbow, Peter. *Writing without Teachers.* New York: Oxford University Press, 1973.

Elkin, Stanley. "A Poetics for Bullies." *Criers and Kibitzers, Kibitzers and Criers.* New York: Random House, 1966.

Erdrich, Louise. "Saint Marie." *Love Medicine.* New York: HarperPerennial, 1983.

Faulker, William. "A Rose for Emily." *Collected Stories of William Faulkner.* New York: Vintage Books, 1977.

———. "Introduction." *The Granta Book of the American Short Story.* Ed. Richard Ford. London: Granta Books, 1998.

———. "Nobel Prize Acceptance Speech." *Essays, Speeches, and Public Letters.* Ed. James B. Meriwether. New York: Random House, 1966.

———. "Two Soldiers." *Collected Stories of William Faulkner.* New York: Vintage Books, 1977.

Ford, Richard. "Rock Springs." *Rock Springs: Stories.* New York: Vintage Books, 1988.

Forster, E. M. *Aspects of the Novel.* New York: Harcourt Brace Jovanovich, 1955.

———. *A Passage to India.* New York: Harcourt, Brace and Company, Inc., 1924.

Frazier, Charles. *Cold Mountain.* New York: Vintage Books, 1998.

Gardner, John. *On Becoming a Novelist.* New York: HarperCollins, 1985.

———. *On Moral Fiction.* New York: Basic Books, 1978.

———. *The Art of Fiction.* New York: Random House, 1985.

Gass, William. *Fiction and the Figures of Life*. Boston: David R. Godine, 1979.

——. "In the Heart of the Heart of the Country." *In the Heart of the Heart of the Country, and Other Stories*. New York: Harper & Row, 1968.

——. "The Pederson Kid." *In the Heart of the Heart of the Country, and Other Stories*. New York: Harper & Row, 1968.

Gilman, Charlotte Perkins. *The Yellow Wallpaper and Other Writings*. New York: Bantam Books, 1989.

Gwynn, Frederick L., and Joseph L. Blotner, eds. *Faulkner in the University: Class Conferences at the University of Virginia 1957–1958*. Charlottesville: University Press of Virginia, 1977.

Halliwell, Stephen. *The Poetics of Aristotle: Translation and Commentary*. Chapel Hill, N.C.: The University of North Carolina Press, 1987.

Hannah, Barry. "Testimony of Pilot." *Airships*. New York: Grove Press, 1994.

Hansen, Ron. *Desperadoes*. New York: HarperPerennial, 1997.

Harvey, Gordon. *Elements of the Academic Essay*. Handout. Cambridge, Mass.: Harvard University Expository Writing Program, 1997.

——. *Writing with Sources: A Guide for Students*. Indianapolis: Hackett Publishing, 1998.

Heffron, Jack, ed. *The Best Writing on Writing*. Cincinnati: Story Press, 1994.

——. *The Best Writing on Writing*. vol. 2. Cincinnati: Story Press, 1995.

Hemingway, Ernest. "Chapter XII." *In Our Time*. New York: Scribner, 1958.

——. "Hills Like White Elephants." *Men Without Women*. New York: Scribner, 1955.

——. *True at First Light*. New York: Scribner, 1999.

Hemley, Robin. *Turning Life into Fiction*. Cincinnati: Story Press, 1994.

Hills, Rust. *Writing in General and the Short Story in Particular*. Boston: Houghton Mifflin, 1987.

Hoagland, Edward. "Introduction: Writers Afoot." *The Best American Essays 1999*. Ed. Edward Hoagland. New York: Houghton Mifflin, 1999.

Homer. *The Odyssey*. Trans. Robert Fagles. New York: Penguin, 1997.

Hopkins, Gerard Manley. "Pied Beauty." *Poems of Gerard Manley Hopkins*. Ed. Norman H. MacKenzie. 4th ed. New York: Oxford University Press, 1976.

Huddle, David. *The Writing Habit: Essays*. Layton, Utah: Peregrine Smith Books, 1991.

Hurston, Zora Neale. "Spunk." *Spunk: The Selected Stories of Zora Neale Hurston*. Berkeley, Calif.: Turtle Island Foundation, 1985.

James, Henry. *Daisy Miller*. New York: Tor Books, 1991.

Janouch, Gustav. *Conversations with Kafka*. Trans. Goronwy Rees. 2nd ed. New York: New Directions, 1971.

Jewett, Sarah Orne. *The Country of the Pointed Firs*. Mineola, N.Y.: Dover Publications, 1994.

Johnson, Denis. "Car Crash While Hitchhiking." *Jesus' Son: Stories*. New York: Farrar, Straus, Giroux, 1992.

Jones, Thom. "The Pugilist at Rest." *The Pugilist at Rest: Stories.* Boston: Little, Brown, 1993.

Joyce, James. "Araby." *Dubliners.* New York: Dover Publications, 1991.

Jussawalla, Feroza, ed. *Conversations with V.S. Naipaul.* Jackson: University Press of Mississippi, 1997.

Kafka, Franz. "The Metamorphosis." *The Penal Colony, and Other Stories.* Trans. Willa and Edwin Muir. New York: Schocken Books, 1995.

Kaplan, David Michael. *Revision: A Creative Approach to Writing and Rewriting Fiction.* Cincinnati: Story Press, 1997.

Kenner, Hugh. *A Homemade World: The American Modernist Writers.* London: Marion Boyers, 1977.

Kercheval, Jesse Lee. *Building Fiction: How to Develop Plot and Structure.* Cincinnati: Story Press, 1997.

Kermode, Frank, ed. *Selected Prose of T.S. Eliot.* New York: Harcourt Brace Jovanovich, 1975.

Kincaid, Jamaica. "Girl." *At the Bottom of the River.* New York: Farrar, Straus, Giroux, 1983.

Krementz, Jill. *The Writer's Desk.* New York: Random House, 1996.

Krutch, Joseph Wood. "Introduction." *Walden and Other Writings by Henry David Thoreau.* Ed. Joseph Wood Krutch. New York: Bantam Books, 1962.

Kundera, Milan. "The Hitchhiking Game." *Laughable Loves.* Trans. Suzanne Rappaport. New York: Alfred A. Knopf, 1974.

Lawson, Lewis A., and Victor A. Kramer, eds. *Conversations with Walker Percy.* Jackson: University Press of Mississippi, 1985.

Leavitt, David. "Braids." *The Story and Its Writer: An Introduction to Short Fiction.* Ed. Ann Charters. 4th ed. Boston: Bedford Books, 1995.

Le Guin, Ursula. "The Ones Who Walk Away from Omelas." *The Wind's Twelve Quarters: Short Stories.* New York: Harper and Row, 1975.

Lodge, David. *The Art of Fiction.* London: Penguin, 1992.

Madden, David. *Revising Fiction: A Handbook for Fiction Writers.* New York: New American Library, 1995.

Magee, Rosemary M., ed. *Conversations with Flannery O'Connor.* Jackson: University Press of Mississippi, 1987.

Marius, Richard. *A Writer's Companion.* New York: Alfred A. Knopf, 1985.

———. *A Writer's Companion.* Second Edition. New York: McGraw-Hill, Inc. 1991.

———. *A Writer's Companion.* Fourth Edition. Boston: McGraw-Hill College, 1999.

Marquez, Gabriel Garcia. "A Very Old Man with Enormous Wings." *Leaf Storm and Other Stories.* Trans. Gregory Rabassa. Boston: Harper Collins Publishers, Inc. 1971.

McAlexander, Hubert H., ed. *Conversations with Peter Taylor.* Jackson: University Press of Mississippi, 1987.

McCarthy, Cormac. *Blood Meridian, Or, The Evening Redness in the West.* New York: Vintage Books, 1992.

McKnight, Reginald. *White Boys: Stories.* New York: Henry Holt, 1998.

McPherson, James Alan. "Elbow Room." *Elbow Room: Stories.* Boston: Little, Brown, 1977.

————. *Hue and Cry: Short Stories.* Boston: Little, Brown, 1969.

Miller, James E. Jr, ed. *Theory of Fiction: Henry James.* Lincoln: University of Nebraska Press, 1972.

Minot, Susan. "Lust." *Lust and Other Stories.* Boston: Houghton Mifflin, 1989.

Moody, Rick. *The Ring of Brightest Angels Around Heaven: A Novella and Stories.* Boston: Little, Brown, 1995.

Moore, Lorrie. "Four Calling Birds, Three French Hens." *Birds of America.* New York: Alfred A. Knopf, 1998.

Mukherjee, Bharati. "The Management of Grief." *The Middleman and Other Stories.* New York: Grove Press, 1988.

Munro, Alice. "Boys and Girls." *Discovering Fiction.* Ed. Hans P. Guth and Gabriele L. Rico. Englewood Cliffs, N.J.: Prentice Hall, 1993.

Myers, D.G. *The Elephants Teach: Creative Writing Since 1880.* Englewood Cliffs, N.J.: Prentice Hall, 1996.

Oates, Joyce Carol. "Heat." *Heat and Other Stories.* New York: Dutton, 1991.

————. "Reading as a Writer: The Artist as Craftsman." *On Writing Short Stories.* Ed. Tom Bailey. New York: Oxford University Press, 2000.

O'Brien, Tim. *The Things They Carried.* Boston: Houghton Mifflin, 1990.

O'Connor, Flannery. "A Good Man is Hard to Find." *A Good Man is Hard to Find and Other Stories.* New York: Harcourt Brace, 1955.

————. "The Element of Suspense in A Good Man Is Hard To Find." *The Story and Its Writer,* 4th ed. Ed. Ann Charters. Boston: Bedford Books, 1995. Pp. 1549–1552.

————. "Everything That Rises Must Converge." *Everything That Rises Must Converge.* New York: Farrar, Straus, Giroux, 1965.

————. "On Her Own Work." *Mystery and Manners: Occasional Prose.* Ed. Sally Fitzgerald. New York: Farrar, Straus, Giroux, 1969.

————. "Writing Short Stories." *Mystery and Manners: Occasional Prose.* Ed. Sally Fitzgerald. New York: Farrar, Straus, Giroux, 1969.

O'Connor, Frank. *Collects Stories.* New York: Vintage Books, 1982.

————. *The Lonely Voice: A Study of the Short Story.* Cleveland: World Publishing Co., 1963.

————. Interview. In *Writers at Work: The Paris Review Interviews.* Ed. Malcolm Cowley. New York: The Viking Press, 1957.

Olsen, Tillie. "I Stand Here Ironing." *Tell Me a Riddle.* New York: Dell, 1961.

————. *Silences.* New York: Delacorte Press, 1978.

Ozick, Cynthia. *Metaphor and Memory: Essays.* New York: Alfred A. Knopf, 1989.

————. "The Shawl." *The Shawl.* New York: Vintage Books, 1990.

Paley, Grace. "Goodbye and Goodluck." *The Little Disturbances of Man.* New York: Penguin Books, 1985.

Perrotta, Tom. *Bad Haircut: Stories of the Seventies.* New York: Berkley Publishing Group, 1997.

———. *Election.* New York: Berkley Publishing Group, 1998.

———. *Joe College.* New York: St. Martin's Press, 2000.

———. *The Wishbones.* New York: Berkley Publishing Group, 1998.

Phillips, Jayne Anne. *Black Tickets.* New York: Delacorte Press, 1979.

———. *Sweethearts.* Oakland, Calif.: Bookpeople, 1982.

Plimpton, George, ed. *Writers at Work: The Paris Review Interviews.* 2nd series. New York: The Viking Press, 1963.

———. *Writers at Work: The Paris Review Interviews.* 3rd series. New York: The Viking Press, 1967.

———. *Writers at Work: The Paris Review Interviews.* 4th series. New York: The Viking Press, 1976.

———. *Writers at Work: The Paris Review Interviews.* 5th series. New York: The Viking Press, 1981.

———. *Writers at Work: The Paris Review Interviews.* 6th series. New York: Viking Penguin, 1984.

———. *Writers at Work: The Paris Review Interviews.* 7th series. New York: Viking Penguin, 1986.

———. *Writers at Work: The Paris Review Interviews.* 8th series. New York: Viking Penguin, 1988.

Poague, Leonard. *Conversations with Susan Sontag.* Jackson: University Press of Mississippi, 1995.

Poe, Edgar Allan. "The Importance of the Single Effect in a Prose Tale." *The Story and Its Writer: An Introduction to Short Fiction.* Ed. Ann Charters. 4th ed. Boston: Bedford Books, 1995.

Pynchon, Thomas. *V.* New York: Perennial Library, 1986.

Searles, George J. *Conversations with Philip Roth.* Jackson: University Press of Mississippi, 1992.

Silko, Leslie Marmon. "Yellow Woman." *Storyteller.* New York: Arcade Books, 1989.

Singer, Isaac Bashevis. "The Little Shoemakers." Trans. Isaac Rosenberg. *The Riverside Anthology of Short Fiction: Convention and Innovation.* Ed. Dean R. Baldwin. Boston: Houghton Mifflin, 1997.

Smiley, Jane. *A Thousand Acres.* New York: Random House, 1991.

Standley, Fred L., and Louis H. Pratt, eds. *Conversations with James Baldwin.* Jackson: University Press of Mississippi, 1989.

Stegner, Wallace. *On the Teaching of Creative Writing: Responses to a Series of Questions.* Ed. Edward Connery Lathem. Hanover, NH: Montgomery Endowment, Dartmouth College: University Press of New England, 1988.

Stein, Gertrude. *How to Write.* New York: Dover Publications, 1975.

Steinbeck, John. "The Chrysanthemums." *The Long Valley.* New York: The Viking Press, 1938.

Stone, Robert. *Bear and His Daughter.* Boston: Houghton Mifflin, 1997.

Strunk, William Jr., and E.B. White. *The Elements of Style.* 3rd ed. New York: Macmillan, 1979.

Styron, William. *The Confessions of Nat Turner.* New York: Vintage Books, 1993.

———. *Darkness Visible: A Memoir of Madness.* New York: Vintage Books, 1992.

———. *Sophie's Choice.* New York: Vintage Books, 1992.

Tan, Amy. "Two Kinds." *The Joy Luck Club.* New York: Putnam, 1989.

Taylor-Guthrie, Danille, ed. *Conversations with Toni Morrison.* Jackson: University Press of Mississippi, 1994.

Taylor, Peter. "The Old Forest." *The Old Forest and Other Stories.* Garden City, N.Y.: Dial Press, 1985.

Thoreau, Henry David. *Walden and Other Writings.* New York: Bantam Books, 1982.

Toomer, Jean. *Cane.* New York: Modern Library, 1994.

Tolstoy, Leo. *Talks with Tolstoy.* Ed. A. B. Goldenweizer. Trans. S. S. Koteliansky and Virginia Woolf. New York: Horizon Press, 1969.

Twain, Mark. "Baker Bluejay's Yarn." *The Portable Mark Twain.* New York: The Viking Press, 1959.

Tyler, Anne. *The Accidental Tourist.* New York: Berkley Books, 1986.

Ueland, Barbara. *If You Want to Write.* St. Paul, Minn.: Graywolf Press, 1987.

Updike, John. "A & P." *Pigeon Feathers and Other Stories.* New York: Alfred A. Knopf, 1962.

———, ed. *The Best American Short Stories of the Century.* Boston: Houghton Mifflin, 1999.

———. "The Literary Life." *Civilization* (Dec/Jan 1996–97): 56–59.

Vaughn, Stephanie. "Able, Baker, Charlie, Dog." *Sweet Talk.* New York: Random House, 1990.

Volkov, Solomon. *Conversations with Joseph Brodsky: A Poet's Journey Through the Twentieth Century.* Trans. Marian Schwartz. New York: The Free Press, 1998.

Walker, Alice. *The Color Purple.* New York: Harcourt Brace Jovanovich, 1982.

Wallace, David Foster. "Girl with Curious Hair." *Girl with Curious Hair.* New York: W.W. Norton, 1989.

———. *Infinite Jest.* Boston: Little, Brown, 1996.

Warren, Robert Penn. "Blackberry Winter." *The Circus in the Attic and Other Stories.* New York: Harcourt Brace, 1948.

Welty, Eudora. *One Writer's Beginnings.* Cambridge, Mass.: Harvard Press, 1984.

———. *The Eye of the Story: Selected Essays and Reviews.* London: Virago Press, 1987.

West, James L.W. III, ed. *Conversations with William Styron.* Jackson: University Press of Mississippi, 1985.

Woiwode, Larry. *Beyond the Bedroom Wall: A Family Album.* St. Paul, Minn.: Gray-wolf Press, 1997.

————. *The Neumiller Stories.* New York: Farrar, Straus, Giroux, 1989.

Wolff, Tobias. "Bullet in the Brain." *The Night in Question: Stories.* New York: Vintage Contemporaries, 1997.

————. *In the Garden of the North American Martyr: A Collection of Short Stories.* New York: Ecco Press, 1981.

————, ed. *Matters of Life and Death: New American Stories.* Green Harbor, Mass.: Wampeter Press, 1983.

————. *The Barrack's Thief.* New York: Ecco Press, 1984.

Woodruff, Jay, ed. *A Piece of Work: Five Writers Discuss Their Revisions.* Iowa City: University of Iowa Press, 1993.

Ziegler, Alan. *The Writing Workshop.* vol. 1. New York: Teachers and Writers Collaborative, 1981.

————. *The Writing Workshop.* vol. 2. New York: Teachers and Writers Collaborative, 1984.

Zinsser, William, ed. *Inventing the Truth: The Art and Craft of Memoir.* Boston: Houghton Mifflin, 1988.

Index